NEGLECTED & FORGOTTEN

Fauquier County, Virginia, French & Indian War, Revolutionary War, & War of 1812 Veterans

Muster Rolls, Pension Lists, Declarations & Certificates, Land Warrants, Heirs at Law, Court Martials

From the Military Record Series of the
Fauquier County, Virginia, Clerks Loose Papers

1759-1825

Compiled by
Joan W. Peters, C.G.R.S.

HERITAGE BOOKS
2008

HERITAGE BOOKS
AN IMPRINT OF HERITAGE BOOKS, INC.

Books, CDs, and more—Worldwide

For our listing of thousands of titles see our website
at
www.HeritageBooks.com

Published 2008 by
HERITAGE BOOKS, INC.
Publishing Division
100 Railroad Ave. #104
Westminster, Maryland 21157

Copyright © 2004 Joan W. Peters

Other books by the author:

Abstracts of Fauquier County, Virginia Birth Records, 1853-1896

Being of Sound Mind: An Index to the Probate Records in Fauquier County Virginia's Clerks Loose Papers and Superior and Circuit Court Papers, 1759-1919

Fauquier County, Virginia's Clerk's Loose Papers: A Guide to the Records, 1759-1919

Military Records, Certificates of Service, Discharge, Heirs, and Pensions Declarations and Schedules from the Fauquier County, Virginia Court Minute Books, 1784-1840

Military Records, Patriotic Service, and Public Service Claims from the Fauquier County, Virginia Court Minute Books, 1759-1784

Military Records, Pension Applications, Heirs at Law and Civil War Military Records from the Fauquier County, Virginia Court Minute Books, 1840-1904

Prince William County, Virginia General Index to Wills, 1734-1951

The Tax Man Cometh—Land and Property in Colonial Fauquier County, Virginia: Tax List from the Fauquier County Court Clerk's Loose Papers, 1759-1782

All rights reserved. No part of this book may be reproduced or transmitted in any form or by any means, electronic or mechanical, including photocopying, recording or by any information storage and retrieval system without written permission from the author, except for the inclusion of brief quotations in a review.

International Standard Book Numbers
Paperbound: 978-1-58549-923-6
Clothbound: 978-0-7884-7654-9

*Dedicated to the memory of the families and soldiers
who fought to defend their beliefs and rights as a free people.*

ACKNOWLEDGEMENTS

The military records in this book were found among the Clerk's Loose Papers in the vault of the Fauquier County Court House. Fauquier County received a grant from the Virginia State Library in the fall of 1993 to arrange, preserve, and store the early County records dating from 1759-1832 and make them accessible to the research public.

Mr. William D. Harris, the former Clerk of the Court and Mrs. Gail Barb, the present Clerk were instrumental in the County's receipt of grant preservation funds for the preservation of these early records.

David Martin, Karen Hughes White and Joan Peters were responsible for the processing and preservation of the Clerk's Loose Papers. Kate Neckerman provided discerning and perceptive editorial comments regarding the introduction to these records. Christine Rose's outstanding book on Military Pension law provided a lucid and clear translation of the Pension law "legalese" to make it readily comprehensible to a family historian with a potential war veteran in their family's past.

The Military Records found here are all from the Clerk's Loose Papers and are presented here for the first time; they comprise records from the first Box in the Military Records Series and date from 1759-1825. Among the records re-discovered during this grant were Revolutionary War Pension Declarations and Warrants along with officer oaths and two nineteenth century court-martials.

COVER ILLUSTRATION:

The image on the front cover is a scanned reproduction of a 1789 Revolutionary War Invalid Pension for Judah Levi, age 28, late a private in a detachment of the Virginia Line under the command of Colonel Buford.

BACK COVER ILLUSTRATION:

The image on the back cover is a scanned reproduction of an 1802 List of Revolutionary Pensioners for Virginia.

Introduction

1. Why Neglected and Forgotten?

Most of the veterans whose records appear here fought in the American Revolution either as part of the Continental Establishment, as part of a State regiment, as part of an independent command, or as part of the county's militia. Most were young. Many were poor, from families who held leases from wealthy landowners such as Thomas Lord Fairfax, or the Lees – Richard Henry and Thomas. Others were yeoman farmers -- small landowners working small farms.

Some fought to free themselves from taxes and regulation of their lives. Taxes touched all walks of their life. The government could (and did) tax any legal document. This included deeds and wills, along with licenses for marriages or for keeping an ordinary or tavern. Even playing cards had to be printed on distinctive embossed paper. Newspapers could only be printed on expensive government paper. Advertisers had to pay a tax to print a forthcoming sale of property, a reward for a runaway servant or an announcement about a new patent medicine. These taxes angered the wealthy and fostered a simmering resentment among the farmers, tradesmen and merchants in towns along Virginia's rivers.

To many of these soldiers, the war was a life-changing event. Fauquier soldiers fought in New York, New Jersey, Delaware and Pennsylvania in the north. They survived Valley Forge. Others headed south only to be captured when the British seized Charleston. Those who were not captured fought at Cowpens and at Guilford Courthouse. Still others made it to Yorktown where they celebrated the final victory over Cornwallis.

They returned home heroes. As a result of their wartime experiences, many were not willing to return to eking out an existence on a leasehold rented from a wealthy land owner. Some of these men settled in the hollows and back woods of the county, determined to resist any payment of taxes or rent. Some headed west with a land warrant, delivered to them as part of their recruitment. Wounded veterans supplemented their subsistence, living on a disability pension or on the bounty of neighbors. As Virginia worked to stabilize its economy and to rework its infrastructure in a post war setting, these veterans began to drop from the scene and from the memories of both state and federal governments.

Since many of the papers in the Clerks Loose Papers between 1759-1825 are pension declarations, I have given a brief synopsis of the pension law as found in Christine Rose's *Military Pension Laws 1776-1858* (San Jose, CA: The Rose Family Association, 2001). This may aid in understanding the reasons for the filing of the various declarations found in this book.

2. Military Pension Enactments during the Revolutionary War: Disability and Invalid Pensions

During the revolutionary war, the Continental Congress passed five resolutions that dealt with pensions to those disabled, maimed or otherwise wounded in the service of their country.[1]

In general, the resolutions to invalids and disabled soldiers followed the terms in the 1776 act known as the National Pension Act and provided for half their monthly pay for life or for as long as the disability continued. Every commissioned or non-commissioned officer and private soldier or seaman in the United States Army or Navy who lost a limb or was disabled during the war against the British was eligible. Congress set conditions for eligibility: soldiers had to be able to perform guard or garrison duty and serve in an invalid corps. Those men eligible for naval benefits had to be capable of doing any duty on board and were liable for such employment there.[2]

The 1778 enactment provided specific conditions for the disabled or invalid soldier to collect his pension. He had to be found capable of doing guard or garrison duty and had to serve in the invalid corps if required. If he refused, his name was to be struck off the pensioner list. If he refused because he had a family, then the Governor of the state in which he resided could grant the disabled soldier in question an exemption from such service. The soldier then produced this certificate to obtain his pension.[3]

If the soldier received his disability when he was a prisoner or was unable to produce the required certificate due to the death of his officers or physicians or surgeons, then he could apply to the Governor of the state in which he lived for his disability pension. Upon showing satisfactory proof that he was disabled or maimed either in the service of his country or as a prisoner and producing the requisite certificate from the Governor, he could receive his pension.[4]

- **1809-007 Judah Levi's Pension Warrant**

The scanned image on the front cover of this book illustrates such a certificate from Governor Randolph of Virginia. It was found in the county basement vault, in the drawer of the Clerks Loose Papers for 1809.

> I do with the advice of the Council hereby certified that Judah Levi age about 28 years late a private in a detachment of the Virginia line under the command of Col° Buford & whose pay was at the rate of L24 per annum, Was disabled in the Service of the United States by Several wounds on the head and face and a wound by a bayonet through the left thigh;
>
> And that he is continued on the Pension List, with an allowance of Fifteen pounds per annum from the first day of January One thousand Seven hundred and Eighty Six~
>
> Given under my hand as Governor of the Commonwealth of Virginia at Richmond, this 30th day of January 1789~
>   T. Meriwether   (Signed) Beverley Randolph [5]

Pensions certificates like this example may be found through out the military records in the Clerks Loose Papers.[6]

In April 1782, Congress resolved that sick and wounded soldiers who were stipulated to be unfit for duty either in the field or garrison and who applied for a discharge rather than serve in the invalid corps could be discharged and entitled to a pension at $5.00 per month in lieu of other payments. Congress further recommended the state in which the soldier lived as the agency to pay out the monies for these pensions.[7]

In 1785, the Continental Congress defined more precisely the conditions for receiving benefits for disabilities. Congress required from each state a list of all disabled officers, soldiers and seamen who had served in the state militia or the United States army or navy. The disability incurred had to render them incapable of military duty or of finding work.

Congress required the States' lists to identify these soldiers by name, regiment, and rate of pay, age, and disability. The list was to be sent to the Secretary of War within a year of the State legislature passing legislation for this purpose. Another list of invalids with the same information was to be made and also sent to the Secretary of War.

Congress also stipulated that an invalid soldier, officer or seaman had to produce a certificate from the commanding officer or surgeon of the regiment, ship, corps or company in which he served or from a physician or surgeon of a military hospital. Congress would accept other "good and sufficient testimony, setting forth the disability and that he was then disabled" while serving his country.[8]

3. Military Pension Enactments during the Revolutionary War: Commissioned Officers and Supernumeraries

There were eight resolutions passed by the Continental Congress relating to pensions for commissioned officers and supernumeraries. Basically these acts stipulated half pay for commissioned officers for seven years[8]. In August 1780, Congress extended the same benefits to commissioned officers who served until the end of the war and to widows (until they died or intermarried) and orphans of deceased soldiers.[9] In November 1780, Congress extended these benefits to major and brigadier generals who stayed in the service until the end of the war.[10]

Finally, in 1783, Congress passed the Commutation Act for officers who remained in service until the end of the war. They were to be entitled to five years' full pay, or to securities at six percent a year, instead of the earlier half pay for life. This act was also extended to state militia not belonging to the State lines. Officers could not individually accept or refuse these payments; they had to do so collectively at the option of the lines of the respective states within six months of the date of the resolution.[11]

Supernumerary officers, on the other hand, in November 1778, were entitled first to one year's pay;[12] two years later, to half pay for seven years.[13]

4. Military Pensions Law after the Revolutionary War: Selected Acts

The United States Congress continued to be concerned about its officers, its wounded and disabled pensioners and the widows and orphans of deceased army and naval officers. Indeed the bulk of legislation passed by Congress served to tighten the existing law to prevent pension fraud and abuse.[14]

- **(Stat.) 376 [& 378-378] Ninth Congress. Session I. 1806**

In 1806, the ninth Congress consolidated the disability and invalid pension act to include any commissioned or non-commissioned officer, musician, soldier, marine or seaman or member of a state militia unit. This pension act served as the basis for all subsequent acts.

He must
1) Have been in the service of the United States or in the line of his duty
2) Have received known wounds in the revolutionary war
3) Not have deserted
4) Have either resigned his commission or taken a discharge due to disability
5) Have received a disability when taken captive by the enemy and remained a prisoner or on parole until the end of the war
6) And had, in consequence of the wounds he received, become so disabled as to render him unable to obtain subsistence by manual labor.

On substantiating his claim, he would then be placed on the pension list of the United States, during his life or the continuance of the disability and would be entitled to a just and proper sum of money.

Congress also dealt with the measure of proof for the veteran's claim:
1) The veteran needed an affidavit concerning his disability to be issued by his commanding officer or two other credible witnesses.
2) He had to prove, by at least one credible witness that he continued in service unless discharged. If an officer, he had to prove he resigned his commission in consequence of his disability or as a result of having been a prisoner or having given his parole.
3) He had to state that he was not on the pension list of any state.[15]

Unfortunately, the same cannot be said for Congress' addressing the needs of veterans who could no longer support themselves or their families because of their reduced circumstances. It was not until 1816, some thirty-three years after the end of the revolutionary war, that Congress addressed the needs of the poor and indigent veterans, in such reduced circumstances that they could no longer support themselves.

- **(Stat.) 285 [& 286]. Fourteenth Congress. Session I. 1816.**

The 1816 Act extended pension benefits to eligible officers or private soldiers of the militia, or to any non-commissioned officer, musician or private, who enlisted for a year or eighteen months. Benefits were also extended to any eligible commissioned officer of the regular army who had died while in service during the revolutionary war or died after the war as a result of wounds suffered during the war. It applied to those veterans with a surviving widow and/or children under the age of sixteen.

The widow or children were entitled to receive half the monthly pay for five years that the deceased soldier or officer was entitled at his death. If the widow died or remarried, then the benefits would go to the child or children.

If a non-commissioned officer, musician or private soldier of the regular army had died in battle or of wounds or disease while in the revolutionary war and left a child or children under sixteen years of age, then their guardian had until 1817 to relinquish the bounty land claim of the deceased veteran to the United States War department and receive, instead, half the monthly pay of the deceased for a term of five years.[16]

- **(Stat.) 410 [& 411] Fifteenth Congress. Session I. 1818.**

Another act passed by the fifteenth Congress in 1818 took up the matter of veterans in need of assistance who had served in the revolutionary army and navy. This act applied to veterans who

1) Served for the duration of the war or for a term of nine or more months at any period of the war on the continental establishment or in the naval service of the United States.
2) Were resident citizens of the United States
3) Were in such reduced circumstances in life, that they are in need of assistance from his county for support
4) Had substantiated their claim to a pension.

If the veteran were an officer, he would receive $20.00 per month during his lifetime. If a non-commissioned officer, musician, mariner, marine or private soldier, he would receive $8.00 a month during his life. The veteran must have relinquished his claim to every previous pension allowed him before he can receive this assistance.

In order to receive a pension under this act, the veteran must make a declaration, under the oath of affirmation, before the district judge of the United States or before any judge or court of record of the county and state in which he resides. He must give the following information in this declaration:
1) His unit, company, regiment and line
2) When he entered the service
3) When he left the service
4) If in the navy, the name of the vessel, his rank, and time, and manner for leaving the service.

Once the judge of the Court of record was satisfied that the declaration was correct and true, he was to certify and send the testimony and proceedings to the Department of theSecretary of the War. The Secretary then looked at the application. If he was satisfied that the applicant met the criteria in the pension legislation, the applicant's name would be placed on the pension list.[17]

There are at least eight 1818-1819 pension applications to the Fauquier County Court, to be found in these pages, by veterans who were entitled to pensions under the 1818 act.[18] A summary of three representative declarations appear below:

- ○ **1818-003 Thomas Groves' Pension Declaration**

Thomas Groves applied for a pension in March 1818. The particular details of where he served, his units and length of service were all found in his application. He was upwards of 50 years of age with a wife (unnamed) and children (also unnamed) He stated that he was in very reduced circumstances and in need of assistance from his country. Captain Daniel Marr attested to Thomas Grove's service in an affidavit filed with this pension declaration. The Court certified that they were satisfied that the information contained in the declaration was true and sent it to the Secretary of the War Department for processing.[19]

- ○ **1818-004 David Ball's Pension Declaration**

David Ball applied for a pension in June 1818 stating that he served in Captain John Blackwell's company, attached to the 3rd Virginia Regiment. He fought at Monmouth and was discharged in February 1779 in Middlebrook New Jersey. Colonel Joseph Blackwell's affidavit confirming this service was filed with the pension application.[20]

- ○ **1819-001 John Bell's Pension Declaration**

John Bell was another veteran in need of assistance. He filed his pension application in November 1819. At the time he was 58 years old. He enlisted in Prince William County as a waggoner in January 1782 and received a discharge (since lost) in 1783. Affidavits of Nathaniel Grigsby and Baylis Grigsby attested to his need due to age and infirmity. Bell had a family as well and found himself in such reduced circumstances as to stand in need of his country for support.

Charles Atwell's affidavit attested to John Bell's revolutionary war service. Atwell was a Captain of artillery, and stated that John Bell enlisted for a year in 1782 as a soldier under Captain Henry Margaram of the artillery. Bell served in transporting ammunition and artillery from York, Virginia to Boston, Massachusetts.[21]

- **(Stat.) 502. Fifteenth Congress. Session II. 1819.**

In 1819, Congress extended half pay pensions for an additional five years to widows and children of officers, seamen and marines who were killed in battle or died of wounds received in battle or who died in the naval service of the United States during the revolutionary war.

- **(Stat.) 569 [& 570]. Sixteenth Congress. Session I. 1820.**

Pensioners who received benefits according to the 1818 act and had received the payments due March 4, 1820, would now have to exhibit to a court of record in the county, city or borough in which he resided, a schedule subscribed by the applicant, of his whole estate and income in order to continue to collect their pensions.

Applicants must subscribe and take a written oath or affirmation that he
1) Was a resident citizen of the United States on 18 March 1818.
2) Had not disposed of any part of his property by sale or gift or any other way with intent to diminish in order to be eligible for this pension.
3) Had no property in trust; nor has any person property, securities, contracts or debts in trust for himself.
4) Had only the income contained in a schedule annexed to his application.

Then the Clerk of Court was to certify the schedule along with the opinion of the court regarding the value of the property and send the papers to the Secretary of War… The original schedule and oath or affirmation was to be filed in the clerk's office of the court…

On receipt of the copy of the schedule and oath or affirmation, the Secretary of War could strike from the pension list the names of anyone who, in his opinion, was not in such indigent circumstances as to be unable to support himself without the assistance of his country.

Every person placed on the pension list because of a disability from known wounds in the revolutionary war who had relinquished a disability pension in order to avail themselves of the 1818 act and this amendment, if stricken from this list, was to be restored to his old disability pension.[22]

There are some two dozen pension applications, including several re-applications, which relate to this law, filed between 1820-1821, in these pages.[23] A synopsis of three of these applications appear below:

- **John Horrell's 1820 Pension Declaration for relief**

John Horrell applied for a pension initially in March 1820, when he was than 60 years old. He had served in the 1st Maryland Line under Col. Peter Adams, commander of the Regiment. He had enlisted in 1778 under Capt. William Bruce for the duration of the war. He had been discharged in 1783 in Charles County, Maryland at the house of General Smallwood.. He had received his pension up to March 4, 1820 – Pension number 15.301.

His oath or affirmation and schedule of property included 3 horses, 13 old sheep, 7 lambs, 7 cattle, 22 hogs, 4 pair of gears, one lot of tools, one lot of ploughs and a wagon, 6 chains, a table and chest, 2 wheels, 2 bee stands and kitchen furniture. He had outstanding debts of $80.00.

Horrell gave his occupation as that of a farmer; he cultivated rented land. He was disabled in his shoulder and nearly blind. He had nine children, four of whom lived with him: John, Peter, Nancy and Isaac. Only two were able to help him around the farm.

Charles Chinn's sworn affidavit stated that he had known John Horrell for several years and that he was indeed needy and indigent and could not support himself without public or private charity.

John Horrell's schedule of property, valued by appraisers appointed by the Fauquier County Court was also included with the application. His entire estate came to $165.50, and took into consideration his outstanding debt of $88.00.[24]

John Horrell (or Herald, as his name was sometimes spelled) reapplied in April 1821, giving the same information about his unit, service and schedule. He added some more information about his children. His eldest son James was between twenty-nine and thirty years of age, married and lived to himself. His son Will, was about twenty-seven, unmarried and lived to himself. His son John was about twenty-five. He worked for himself and aided his father "but little". His son Peter, twenty-two, worked for himself, helping his father only a little.

His daughter Nancy, age twenty, lived with her father doing weaving and spinning at her father's house. She received most of the profits of her labor. His son Isaac, about eighteen, lived at home and helped his father. Son Matthew, age fifteen, lived at home and helped his father as well. Son Hugh, age twelve, was able to do just a little work. His youngest child, daughter Patsy, was about nine years old and too young to help. John's wife was old and infirm (and unnamed), racked with pain and "a dead expense to him".

William Urton filed his sworn affidavit with this second application, stating that John Horrell is needy and in indigent circumstances and could not "support himself without public or privat [sic] charity."[25]

- ### Spencer Anderson Sr's 1820 Pension Declaration for relief

Spencer Anderson Sr was another veteran who filed his pension application for benefits under the 1818 and 1820 act. He was 70 years old. He had enlisted in 1776 for two years under Captain Philip Lee of the 3rd Virginia, commanded first by Colonel Thomas Marshall and later by Colonel William Heath. He had received an honorable discharge at the expiration of his term, which he had lost during a Militia tour in 1778. He had seen service at Brandywine and Germantown; he had received a wound over his eye at Princeton.

He had made his original declaration "as well as I can recollect" in the spring of 1819. His pension certificate number was 12.459. His declaration also contained his oath or affirmation and details about his occupation and family. "I am", he says, "a coarse carpenter… [F]rom my age, failure of my eyesight and pains, I am unable to do half the work of an able bodied man… and what I do, is not done in a workman-like manner…"

His wife, Susan was 76. Spencer Anderson and his wife lived with their son, on whose hospitality they were entirely dependent. His schedule showed that he had a set of coarse carpenter tools, a square black walnut table and a garden hoe, all worth a total of $7.00.[26]

- ### James Lyon's 1820 Pension Declaration for relief

James Lyon, another indigent veteran, filed his pension declaration in August 1820. He was fifty-six years old at the time of his application. Lyons had enlisted as a soldier for two years under Captain Gustavus Brown Wallace of the 3rd Virginia Regiment on the Continental line, commanded by Colonel Mercer and Lt. Colonel George Weedon. Lyon had served under Captain Wallace for 22 months and under Captain Lowe for two months. He had fought in the battles of Harlem Heights and the White Plains. Captain Lowe had discharged him at Philadelphia. He lost his discharge.

His original declaration was made in the Fauquier County Court in June 1818. His pension certificate was number 5259 and he had received his pension up to March 4, 1820. His oath followed along with his schedule whose items included a shop board, a goose… a set of tea cups and saucers, six tea spoons, a looking glass, shaving box and razor and an earthen bowl.

By profession, James Lyon had been a tailor. He had no wife at the time of the declaration although he did have three children: John, age 40; James, age 37; and Nancy, aged 33. None of his children lived with him. He obtained no assistance from any of them. James stated that he had been afflicted with rheumatism and had become too infirm and unable to support himself by his trade due to a defect in his sight. He boarded with a private family. He drew his sole support from his pension.[27]

These three veteran's applications reveal the amount of military, family, economic and occupational information to be found in these pension declarations. In each case, the Court adhered to the guidelines posted in the 1818 and 1820 pension law.

5. Contents found in the Military Records from the Clerks Loose Papers 1759-1825

The papers in this first box of Military Records in the Clerks Loose Papers encompass a history of Fauquier's colonial and post revolutionary war military establishment. There are even a few records dating to the French and Indian War as well as several revolutionary war muster rolls. There are a variety of revolutionary war records: copies of records for Heirs at Law, Certificates of Service for deceased soldiers, discharge papers, 1799 and 1800 pension lists, and of course a variety of pension declarations from widows of deceased soldiers and from veterans themselves. There are one or two 1812 pension declarations and several pension declarations for an increase in a pension. All of the pension material is worth close examination.

In addition, Militia recommendations, commissions and oaths for military officers between 1785-1823 add further insight into Fauquier's militia set up. Court martial bounds are set up for the militia companies and fines are assigned for non-attendance to militia gatherings.

One of the most interesting cases in these papers involves the court martial of Major Townshend Dade in November 1807.[28] There is yet another fascinating court martial, that of Colonel John Kemper.[29] The court martial moved into County Court as a slander suit instituted by Colonel Kemper against Owen Thomas and others.[30]

Finally there is a folder of historic signature folders.[31] These include various Militia Commissions signed by well-known local military figures, like Robert Randolph and pension warrants and certificates signed by Virginia governors. The military records for this 1759-1825 period end with a resolution passed by the County Court, members of the Fauquier bar and officers of the Fauquier Militia to commemorate the death of Colonel Robert Randolph.

6. Conclusions

I have been asked how these military records in the Clerks Loose Papers differ from the military records in the County Court Minute Books. The records in the Clerks Loose Papers **are** the *original* records. Many of the military records in the Clerks Loose Papers were not copied into the County Court Minute and Order Books.

These papers are of great genealogical and historical value. The pension declarations and material having to do with the French and Indian War, Revolutionary War and War of 1812 are especially important as they provide brief glimpses of how a nineteenth century veteran lived. In many instances, these men, who came home heroes, were forced to show everyone how really poor they were. They were forced to live through adversity and humiliation, and to ask neighbors and friends to testify to their poverty.

In 1818, so many indigent veterans applied for pension benefits that the 1820 law forced other restrictions on them. Schedules of their property must be valued. Neighbors must testify to their reduced circumstances. These were proud men whose service to their country had been neglected and forgotten. The pension declarations tell their story poignantly and eloquently.

Each of these records has a story to tell that helps us to understand a time long gone by. Whether a court martial, a pension list, a slander suit, a military commission, or a certificate of heir ship, these documents lend an articulate and expressive credibility to the men represented in these papers.

End Notes

1. Rose, Christine. *Military Pension Laws, 1776-1858* (San Jose, CA: Rose Family Association, 2004), pp.1-4.

2. *Ibid.*, p. 1.

3. *Ibid.*,, pp. 1-2.

4. *Ibid.*,, p. 2.

5. *1809-007 Pension Certificate of Judah Levi*, on p. 110 of this book.

6. Other examples include *1793-002 Pension Certificate of Benjamin Taylor* and the *1709-003 Pension Certificate of John Wheeler*, both on p. 10 of this book.

7. Rose, p. 3.

8. *Ibid.*,, p. 4.

9. *Ibid.*,, p. 2-3.

10. *Ibid.*

11. Ibid., p. 4.

12. *Ibid.*,, p. 2.

13. *Ibid.*,, p. 3.

14. *Ibid.*,, p. 5 ff.

15. *Ibid.*,, p. 12.

16. *Ibid.*,, p. 16-17.

17. *Ibid.*,, p. 18.

End Notes (Cont.)

18. See these 1818 Pension Declarations: *1818-003, Thomas Groves; 1818-004, David Ball; 1818-005, John Ball; 1818-005, John Powell; 1818-006, William Thayer*, pp. 37-40; *1819-001, John Bell;, 1819-002, Certification of Service for David Ball*, pp. 41-42 of this book.

19. *1818-003 Thomas Groves Pension Declaration*, on p. 37 of this book.

20. *1818-004 David Ball's Pension Declaration*, on p. 38 of this book.

21. *1819-001 John Bell's Pension Declaration*, on pp. 41-42 of this book.

22. Rose, pp. 19-20.

23. See these 1820 Pension Declarations: *1820-001, John Horrell* on pp 43-44; *1820-002, Spencer Anderson* on pp. 44-45; *1820-003, David Ball* on p. 45; *1820-004, James Arrow Smith* on pp. 46-47; *1820-005, William Drone* on pp. 47-48; *1820-006, William Stribling* on p. 49; *1820-007, Philip Lynor* on p. 50; *1820-008, John Laws* on pp. 51-53; *1820-009, James Lyons* on pp. 53-54; *1820-010, Thomas Groves* on pp. 55-56; *1820-011, Rust Hudson* on pp. 56-57; *1820-012, Benjamin McKnight* on pp. 57-58; *1820-013, John Smith* on pp. 58-59; *1820-014, John Roach* on pp. 59-60; *1820-015, John Bell* on p. 61; *1820-016, William Hughlett* on p. 62; *1820-017, Gideon Johnston* on pp. 62-64; *1820-018 William Thayer* on pp. 65-66; *1820-019 Joseph Blackwell* on pp. 66-67; *1820-020 John Franklin* on pp. 67-68; *1820-021 Andrew Green* on pp. 68-69; *1821-002 Daniel Boyd* on pp. 69-71; *1821-003, John Horrell* on pp. 71-72; *1821-004, Joseph Anderson* on pp. 73-74.

24. *1820-001, John Horrell's Pension Declaration*, pp. 43-44 of this book.

25. *1821-003, John Horrell's Pension Declaration*, pp. 71-72 of this book.

26. *1820-002, Spencer Anderson's Pension Declaration* on pp. 44-45 of this book.

27. *1820-009, James Lyon's Pension Declaration* on pp. 53-54 of this book.

28. *1807-001, Major Townshend Dade's Court Martial Papers* on pp. 20-200 of this book.

29. *1824-001 Colonel John Kemper's Court Martial* on pp. 79-93 of this book.

30. *1824-002 John Kemper v. Owen Thomas and others. Slander* suit filed with *1824-001 Court Martial*. Slander suit is found on pp. 94-109 of this book.

31. The Historic Signatures Folders encompasses folders *1793-002 to 1821-006* on pp. 111-113 of this book.

Abbreviations

Acc^d	Accused
Adj^t. Genl	Adjutant General
Appear'd	appeared
Armis^d	Armistead
Aug^t	August or Augustine
Cap/Capt	Captain
Ch^s	Charles
Chs/Chas.	Charles
Comd^t	Commandant
Com^n	Commission
Ct^l	Continental
C^{ty}/Ct^y	County
Deced/dec^d	Deceased
Deft/Defend^t	Defendant
D^y Clk	Deputy Clerk
Edm:	Edmund/Edmond
Esqr	Esquire
Et altera	Latin for "and others"
Et als.	Latin for "and others"
F. C./ Fauq^r	Fauquier County
F. C. C.	Fauquier County Court
Genl	General
Geo:	George
Hab^s Corp^s	Latin for "Habeus Corpus", literally "have his body"
Inf^{ty}	Infantry
Int.	Interest
J. P. F. C.	Justice of the Peace, Fauquier County
Ja^s	James
Jno/ Jno.	John
J^o / Jo^s	Joseph
J^r	Junior
L^t / Lt.	Lieutenant
Maj^r	Major
M^o Ob^t	Most Obedient
Nathl	Nathaniel
Nove^{br}	November
Pltf/ Pltff(s)	Plaintiff(s)
p^r	per
Pres^t	President
Pro^s / Prosc^r	Prosecutor
rec^d	received
Robt	Robert
Robt/ Rob:	Robert

Abbreviations (Cont.)

Saml / Samll.	Samuel
Spe^c	Specification
S^r / Sr.	Senior
Steph:	Stephen
&c/ tc	etc
^ text ^	^ text interlined in record ^
Super^y	Supernumerary
Th. / Th^s	Thomas
Thos/ Tho.	Thomas
Va. / V^a	Virginia
Vide	Latin for "See"
Vol.	Volume or Volunteer. Use in context.
W^m	William

Military Records from Fauquier County Virginia Clerk's Loose Papers, Military Record Series 1759-1825

[AUTHOR'S NOTE: The contents of these transcribed records from Fauquier's military records relate to French and Indian War service, Revolutionary War Service, the War of 1812 and military matters like pension warrants, military commissions, court martials and memorials by county officials concerning the death of public officials with military experience.]

1761-001   1760 Treasury of Virginia Account for duty of Joseph May's slave Mary Rockingham
from *Champe & Co. v. Mays, Joseph*
    Debt on 1760 account for L5
    1760 Joseph Mays of Stafford
        to Treasury Virginia for Duty of 1 slave Mary Rockingham   L5
        E. E. p. John Champe & Co.

1764-001 Militia Claim of Thomas Ward
From *Sinclair, John Jr. v. Ward, Thomas*
    1764 Thomas Ward
        To your Militia claim assigned me + which after war you sold to another   L5

1764-002 Rental Promissory Note of James Wheatley of Fauquier Militia to Jacob Ramey
James Wheatley of Fauquier Militia (under command of Captain Thomas Marshall) to Jacob Ramey
    Know all men by these presents that I James Wheatley belonging to the fauquire [sic] Milicia [sic] under the command of Capt Thomas Marshal Do promise to pay or cause to Be paid rent to Jacob Ramey the just and full Sum of four pound cur^t money of Virginia on or Before the tenth Day of December Next Ensuing In Wittness [sic] my hand this 7 Day of October 1764. WQ
                      (Signed) James Wheatley

1775-001   A List of Arms in the Company of Militia under Hezk. Turner's Command

Name	Arm	Condition
John Atiheson	Rifle	in good order
George Ash	ditto	ditto
John Austin	ditto	ditto
Nathaniel Moss	ditto	ditto
James Davis	ditto	ditto
Sam^{ll} Atiheson	ditto	ditto
Nathaniel Wilson	smooth bore	ditto
Simon Williams	ditto	ditto
James Allensworth	ditto	ditto
Wharton Ransdell	ditto	ditto
Edward Ransdell	ditto	ditto
George Homes	ditto	ditto - very sorry
Thos Adams	ditto	ditto ditto
John Suttle	ditto	Unfit for use till Repaired
Kimble Hicks	ditto	ditto

            (Signed)   Hez^k Turner

Military Records from Fauquier County Virginia Clerk's Loose Papers, Military Record Series 1759-1825

1781-001 A Letter from Brigadier General Weedon to Colonel of Fauquier County Militia

Fredericksburg 21 Feby 1781

Dear Sir

    You have no doubt rec^d the Governor's Orders to draw out one fourth of your Militia + march them to this place. His Excellency assured me the ¼ of your County would amount 270 Men in that Case you will please order the following proportion of Officers, Viz one Col. one Major 5 Captains + 11 Subalterns (one of which will do the duty of Adjutant + 5 Serg^{ts} to each Company of 50 Men. [A]ny further arrangement will be made here; I must request you my dear Col. to send us as many Arms as you possibly can + would also recommend it to them to bring each Man a Blanket of their own. Much depends on expedition on this matter + must therefore press your utmost exertion. I am Sir

                              Your most Ob^t Servt

Commanding Officer of Fauquier County

                                  G Weedon BG

[front of envelope]

                              [torn] llie Service

    The Officer Commanding the
        Militia

Express   Fauquier County
G Weedon BG

                        1   400   400
                        1   55   55
                        1   35   35
                        1   40   40
                        4   7   28
                        1   15   15
                        1   20   20
                                    ―――――
                                     583
                                       3
                                   ―――――
                                 174.18
                                    42
                                 ―――――
                                 21618

                        4) 107,4) 270
                                  8
                                ―――
                                27

1782-001 Revolutionary War Soldiers, Miscellaneous Lists, Fauquier County Militia (original) Req. C 7106

[Note: This is a photostat copy of the List. On the reverse side of this list, it says "Virginia State Library Dec. 1, 1958"]

List # 1

Names	Rank	Month	Day	Remarks
George Armstrong	Private	2	10	
Fielding Scantling	ditto	2	10	
Charles Kemper	ditto	2	10	
Philip Spiller	ditto	2	10	
James Noriss	ditto	2	10	
Elijah Anderson	ditto	2	10	
William Withers	ditto	2	10	
William Lynn	ditto	2	10	
James Kemper	ditto	2	10	
David Allason	ditto	2	10	
William Bishop	ditto	2	10	
Nimrod Taylor	ditto		22	discharg^d Augt 13th 81
Ozias Cooke	ditto		22	discharg^d Same time
John Williams	ditto		22	discharg^d Augt 12th 81
John Lutrell	ditto		39	discharg^d Augt 29th 81
Joseph Burdett	ditto		29	discharg^d Augt 19th 81
Joshua Lutrell	ditto		29	discharg^d Same time
Richd Northent	ditto		29	Died Augt the 19th 81
John Brown	ditto	2	10	
William St[e]ward	ditto	2	2	Continued in service
John Withers	ditto	2	10	

Cap. Ball   October 26 1782
Fauq^r
This day Came before me Capt. John Ball and Made oath that the within Payroll is just and True. Given under my hand.
    (Signed) William Pickett
  Examined
  (Signed) E. [F?] Edmonds Col^o

[Page torn] Company was ten days on their March
[Page torn]   n^d the Army.   John Ball Captn

1782-001 Revolutionary War Soldiers, Miscellaneous Lists, Fauquier County Militia (original) Req. C 7106

[Note: This is a photostat copy. On the reverse side of this list it says "Virginia State Library Dec. 1, 1958]

List # 2

Names	Rank	Month	Days	Remarks
John Ball L5	Capt.		62	
James Hathaway	Lieut.		62	Promoted 9 Augt to Capt.}
ditto ditto [lined through]	Capt.	[lined through]	14	discharg^d 23rd Augt 81 }
Joseph Nelson	Ensign	[month illegible]		discharg^d 27th Sept 81
William Metcalf	Serg^t		27	Promoted to Ensign 19th Sept
ditto ditto	Ensign	[illegible]	19	
William Mcbride	Serg^t	2	10	
John Kemper	ditto	2	10	
Toaneis Suddoth	ditto	2	10	
William Mulliken	Corp^l		21	
ditto ditto	Serg^t	1	19	Made a Serg^t of Augt 11th 81
James Elliss	Corp^l	2	10	
Tilman Kemper	Corp^l	2	10	
William Scoggin	Private	1	11	
ditto ditto	Serg^t		29	Made a Serg^t of Augt 24th 81
David McClanaham	Private	2	10	
John Suddoth	ditto	2	10	
George Riley	ditto	2	10	
Benjamin Corder	ditto	2	10	
Nimrod Haddux	ditto	2	10	
Richard King	ditto	2	10	
Samuell Burk	ditto	2	10	
James Shackelford	ditto	2	10	
James Gafney	ditto	2	10	
Nathan Ellis	ditto	2	10	
Joseph Darnall	ditto	2	10	
William Crosby	ditto	2	10	
James Sharp	ditto	2	10	
George James	ditto	2	10	
Marshall Johnson	ditto	2	10	
James Fletcher	ditto	2	10	
Anthony Jett	ditto	2	10	
Robert Luttrell	ditto	2	10	
Richard Corum	ditto	2	10	
Henry Bosne	ditto	2	10	
Marmaduke Brown	ditto	2	10	
George Dixon	ditto	2	10	
Henry Horton	ditto	2	10	
Martin Parker	ditto	2	10	
John Gibson	ditto	2	10	
Benjamin Barby	ditto	2	10	
John Anderson	ditto	2	10	
George Singer	ditto	2	10	

1782-001 Revolutionary War Soldiers, Miscellaneous Lists, Fauquier County Militia (original)   Req. C 7106

[Note: This is a photostat copy of the List. On the reverse side of this list, it says "Cap Wm. Triplett, Fauquire [sic] (Cavalry) wants swearing to atta. certificate from the Executive." Paybook]

List # 3 Pay Roll of Capt William Triplett Company of Militia Cavalry from Fauquier County for Two Months Commencing the 20th [the rest of the page is torn and words are illegible]

No.	Names	Rank	Commt.	Time of Service Mth	Pay Days	Casualties
1.	William Triplett	Capt.		2	13	
2.	Permeanis Bullett	Lieut.		2	15	
3.	John Obannion	Corp^l		2		Resigned 6th Augt 81
4.	Thomas Gibson	Corp^l			15	Appointed 6th Augt 81
5.	Joseph Doniphan	QMS		2		
6.	William Jones	Serg^t		2		
7.	Enoch Smith	ditto		2		
8.	Taliaferro Grigsby	Privt		2		
9.	Lewis C[illegible]	ditto				
10.	George Conway	Do.				
11.	George Austin	Do.				
12.	Edward Suttle	Do.				
13.	Reuben Bramblett	Do.				
14.	Elijah Barton	Do.				
15.	Stephen Childs	Do.				
16.	Nimrod Stone	Do.				
17.	John Elliott	Do.				
18.	John Murphey	Do.				
19.	Ruben Jones	Do.				
20.	Jonathan Green	Do.				
21.	Carr Bailey	Do.				
22.	John Stamps	Do.				
23.	John W. Jones	Do.				
24.	George Cardam	Do.				
25.	Joseph Russell	Do.				
26.	Wright Baily	Do				
27.	Reuben Rogers	Do.				
28.	Thomas [illegible]	Do. [Name on a fold]				
29.	Charles Wickleff	Do.				
24.	George Peak	Do.				
25.	Price Keys	Do.				
26.	Edward Freeman	Do.				
27.	Lency Edwards	Do.				
28.	Elisha Barton	Do.				
29.	Martin Brown	Do.				

[Note: There is no name or number for 21. In the above list. There are also two lines of writing on the bottom of this list that are illegible. It appears that the paper may have gotten wet and the writing has faded in consequence.]

1783-001 Certificate of Service for John Morgan, Sgt. Continental Line

I do certify that John Morgan Enlist^d into the Continenttel Service for three years to Serve as Sergeant and died in Service.

Given under my hand Ap^l 28th, 1783.

(Signed) James Wright, Capt. C^{tl} Line

1783-002 Petition for Tax Relief for Charles Garner, a soldier in the Revolution

To the right Honoreble [sic] Cort [sic] of Folkquier [sic] the Petision [sic] of **Charles Garner** that he hath Been a solder in the 3 years servis [sic] and did get lame so that he is scarce Able to get his liven and he Begs that your worships Wold pleas to exempt him from Paying the nesery [sic] tacksses [sic] as his Property is But Small. May the 22 1783

    (signed) Charles Garner

[On the reverse side of the petition, it reads: "to the right Honorble Cort at Festry"[sic]]

1783-003 Certificate of Service for Thomas Green, killed at Battle of Brandywine

This is to Certify that **Thomas Green** Inlisted [sic] with me January the twenty seventh 1777 for the term of three years. I do further Certify that he was kill'd at the Battle of Brandy Wine, Given Under my hand this 3rd Day May 1783.

    (Signed)   Tho Blackwell Capt C OR

1784-001 Public Service Claim of Wm. Woodside

Wm. Woodsides Certificates for five Waggons + Teams

one bought in Oct^o 1780 @ L7.800. + the other in Nov 1780 at L10,000 signed by Richd Young ADQM + also by James Hunter bought for the use of the Southern Army allowed L241.19.1

1784-002 Abstracts from the Minute Books 1773-1784

[Note: These lists are handwritten abstracts from the Court Minute Books 1773-1784. See the Court Minute Books for those years or Peters, Joan W. *Military Records, Patriotic Service & Public Service Claims from the Fauquier County Virginia Court Minute Books Volume 1 1759-1784* (Westminster, MD: Willow Bend Books, 1999). I have not copied these lists here.]

1786-001 Request by Judah Levy to send his pension allowance for 1786

Sir:

    I shou'd be humbly thankful to you to send my pension or Allowance by the bearer Due for the year 1775 and this Shall be your Recp^t for the Same, and much Ob^t Sr^t

        Your Able Serv't
            his
       (Signed) Judah (X) levy
           mark

To

    The Publick Treasuror [sic]
    Test John Mauzy

1786-002 Certificate of Service of Joshua Jenkins, a Soldier in Captain John Ashby's Company in 3rd Virginia Continental Regiment

This is to Certify that **Josiah Jinkins** a Soldier in Capt John Ashbys Company in the 3^d Virginia Continantal [sic] regiment Inlisted [sic] in February 1776 for Two Years and Died in Philadelphia in December the same year given under my hand the 6th day of Octr 1786.

        (Signed) Nathl Ashby, Lieut. 3^d V.R.
          John Ashby Capt. 3^d V.R.

1786-003 Petition of Elizabeth Cunningham, widow of a soldier killed in the service of his country

The **Petition of Elizabeth Cunninhame** [sic] Humbly sheweth The Worshipfull Court of Fauquier Now Siting That her Husband entered into the service of the Country as a Soldier leaving a Number of Children with her, (who dyed in the Service) That she has laboured hard to support them without either land or any other property to support [lined through and "assist" inserted] them ~~on~~ but her own labour which afford them + herself exceeding [word illegible] fair, Your Petitioner prays Your Worshipfull Court to make some allowance in aid of their Support which bears so heard on her + Shall ever pray +c +c

Unsigned by petitioner

1787-001 Pension Declaration of Anne Jenkins, widow of Private Josiah Jenkins, who died in the service.

Anne Jenkins produced a Warrant in these words to wit "I do with the advice of the Council I hereby certify that Ann Jenkins Widow of Josiah Jenkins who was a Private in the [space blank] and died in the service of the United States is entitled to the sum of eight pounds yearly: which allowance is to commence from the first day of January 1787. Given under my hand as Governor of the Common Wealth of Virginia at Richmond this 1st day of October 1787. Edm: Randolph." And the said Ann Jenkins having made oath according to law. It is ordered that the Sheriff pay her the said Eight pounds.

1788-001 Militia Lists for Upper and Lower Battalion

Officers recommend^d 1788 Feb^y [word illegible]

Upper Battalion
- Captains
  - Robert Layton
  - Joseph Obanion
- Lieutenants
  - Benjn Glascock
  - Armistead Morehead
  - William Young
  - Saml Obannion
  - Robert Sinclair
- Ensigns
  - Charles West
  - William Dearmont
  - John Norris
  - William Singleton
  - John Oreer
  - John Morehead Junr
- Infantry
  - Captain John Peyton Harrison
  - Lt. Saml Turner
  - Ensign John Edmund

Lower Battalion
- Capt^s
  - John James
  - Wm. Eustace Junr
  - Thomas Gibson
  - Gust^a Jennings
- Lieut^s
  - Peter Conway
  - John Hogan
- Ensigns
  - Hancock Eustace
  - John Young
- Light Infantry
  - Capt Lin Stark [scratched out]
  - Capt Wm Foote
  - Lt. William Lowry
  - Ensign Travis Crump

1789-001 from Payne, Wm. v. Hitt, Harmon, Debt on an Account

From the papers of Suit (Suit was dismissed in June with costs)
To the worshipfull court of Fauquier County William Payne Senr
Humbly sheweth that Harmon Hitt stand Indebted to him five pounds by an account And refuseth Payment
wherefore your Petitioner Prays Judgment against him for the same with Costs. And shall Pray +c.
Mr Harman Hitt D^r in account with Wm. Payne Senr
1781 April 3rd To 35 days service in the Melicia [sic] at 80 dollars per day agreeable to the scale of depreciation it comes to 4/8Z, 4 Specie per pay

The amount is 8 pounds eight shilling	L	8. 8. 0	
		3. 0. 0	
Ballance due William Payne	L	5. 8. 0	
By 8/. Deducted		8. 0	
	due L	5. 0. 0	

Contra C^r
By Cash received of Mr Harmon Hitt three hundred pounds settled by the scale it comes to three pounds specie.

1793-001 Letter and Militia Lists for Fauquier County, September 1793

Letter to the Honorable Henry Lee, Governor from F. Brooke, Clerk of Court
On Reverse side of Letter:
   Militia Return of County [of] Fauq^r

On "Letter" side:
   Sir:
      Immediately on the receipt of your letter enclosing an act of the last session of assembly respecting the appointment of Militia Officers, we convened ourselves for the purpose of carrying the law into execution. But we immediately discovered (from the last returns of the Militia (a copy of which is herewith transmitted to you) that as the County of Fauquier composed only one regiment and a regiment consisted only of 640 men. We could not possibly execute the law, in the manner prescribed. We therefore considered it (circumstances as we are with almost three times the number of Militia that constitutes a regiment) most prudent to defer acting under the law, till the [word illegible] session of the legislature. We are therefore now to request you, to lay before the assembly, a statement of the number of Militia in the County of Fauquier that they may make, such alterations, in the law, as will enable us to carry it into execution. By order of the Court of Fauquier county. [Month obscured by ink blot] 1793. F. Brooke C.C.

1793-001 A General Return of the Militia of the County of Fauq^r, September 1793

Companies	Col^o	Lt. Col^o	Majr	Capt^s	Lt^s	Ensigns	Sergt^s	Rank + File
	2	1	2					
Capt. Balls Comp^y	--	--	--	1	1	1	3	56
Capt. Rixey				1	1	1	3	91
Capt. Rogers				1	1	1	3	64
Capt. Timberlake				1	1	1	2	103
Captn Smith				1	1	1	1	52
Captn Weaver				1	1	1	2	64
Capt. Barbee				1	1	1	3	65
Capt. Jennings				1	1	1	3	74
Capt. Obannon				1	1	1	1	97
Capt. Dearing				1	1	1	3	92
Capt. Withers				1	1	1	3	71
Capt. Flowrie				1	1	1	3	54
Capt. Wm Jennings				1	1	1		72
Capt. Layton				1	1	1	~	102
Capt. Thomas Gibson				1	1	1	3	81
Capt. Eustace				1	1	1	3	86
Capt. Winn				1	1	1	3	67
Capt. Pearle				1	1	1	~	80
Capt. Glascock				1	1	1	~	55
Capt. Thos Smith				1	1	1	3	67
Capt. James				1	1	1	~	64
Capt. Doniphan				~	1	1	~	66
	2	1	2	20	22	22	42	1623

1793-001 A List of the Guard summoned by John Bronaugh, DS 28 January 1793

William Ball commander
William Oden
Richard Churchwell
Reubin Kemper
William Fousher
Francis Suddith
Nat Foster
Ned Digges
John Rennoe
John Chilton
John Nellson
John Morrison
William Day
~~Richard Fisher~~ John Coffee
George Kemper
Joseph Jackman
Charles Christie

1793-001 A List of the Guard summoned by John Bronaugh, DS 28 January 1793 (Cont.)
~~James~~ Stephen Kemper
Jacob Richards
James Kibble

A List of the Guard Summond by John Bronaugh, D.S. 28th January 1793

1793-002 Pension Warrant of Benjamin Taylor, Private Illinois Regiment and wounded in 1781 in engagement with Indians

I do with the advice of Council hereby certify, that Benjamin Taylor late a private in the Illinois Regiment and disabled in an Engagement with the Indians in the year 1781, is put on the list of Pensioners with an allowance of fifteen pounds yearly commencing the first day of January One thousand seventeen hundred and ninety three, pursuant to an Act of Assembly passed at the last Session for 'allowing Pensions to certain persons.'
               Given under my hand as Governor of the Commonwealth of Virginia at Richmond this 26th day of March 1793.
 Sam Coleman
           Henry Lee
At a Court held for Fauquier County the 22d day of April 1793.
This pension warrant was presented to the Court and ordered to be recorded.
   Teste
     F Brooke CC

1793-003 Pension Warrant of John Wheeler, a soldier in the Virginia Line, wounded in Revolutionary War

I do with the advice of Council hereby certify that pursuant to an Act of Assembly passed the 30th of November 1791, John Wheeler who served as a Soldier in the Virginia Line during the late War and in the course thereof received several Wounds, is put on the list of Pensioners with an allowance of eight pounds yearly commencing the first day of January One thousand seven hundred and ninety two.
   Given under my hand as Governor of the Commonwealth of Virginia at Richmond this 11th day of October 1793.
Sam Coleman   Henry Lee

1795-001 Service and Discharge papers of John Ville, alias John Wills, a Private in the Fusiliers of the First Partisan Legion
from *Tarte, Alexander v. Ville, John Court Papers,* a suit for debt. (March 1795, Agreed)
- From Narratio of Alexander Tarte

Fauquier County to wit
 Alexander Tarte complains John Ville alias Wills of a plea of Trespass on the case for this to wit the said Defendant having served as a private soldier in the fusillers commanded by [space left blank] in the late war between Great Britain and America was entitled to pay and depreciation when the Army was disbanded to wit to the sum of 230 75/90 dollars, and afterwards to wit on the [space blank] day of [space blank] in the year of our Lord 17 [space blank] at the Parish of [space blank] of County aforesaid, for and in consideration of the sum of [space blank] current money of Virginia to him paid by the Plff, sold all his right and title to his pay as a Soldier as aforesaid to the said Plff, by means of which sale so made as aforesaid the Plff became entitled to have and receive the said sum of 230 75/90 dollars the pay and depreciation of the said Defendant while a Soldier in the Army of the United States.

1795-001 Service and Discharge papers of John Ville, alias John Wills, a Private in the Fusillers of the First Partisan Legion from *Tarte v. Ville Court Papers*, a suit for debt. (Cont.)

Nevertheless the said Defendant regardless of the sale which he had made to the plff and how to injure oppress + defraud the Plff in this behalf afterwards to wit on the [space blank] day of [space blank] at the Parish + County afors^d received all the pay + Depreciation wch he was entitled to and refuses to deliver the same to the Plff, whereby the Plff saith he has Sustained damage to the value of [space blank] + therefore he brings suit tc.

                                 Marshall for Plff

Pledges of Prosecution   J^{no} Doe + Richd Roe

- **Discharge Papers of John Ville with Deposition of Johnston Smith of Alexandria:**

This is to certify that John Ville a Private in the fusillers in the *First Partisan Legion*, under my Command has served faithfully + Bravely, to this Day, is hereby discharged from the Service of the *United States*, in Pursuance of Orders received from the commander in chief, bearing Date the third instant.

I farther certify that John Ville a Private in the fusillers having been Enlisted in the State of Virginia is intitled [sic] by the Resolution of Congress of the 13th February 1779, to the Benefits that have been, or hereafter shall be, granted by the said State to the Noncommissioned Officers and Soldiers of the said Line.

     (Seal)   Given under my Hand and Seal at *York Town*, this fifteenth Day of November, 1783
        Ex^d Lt. Colo. Bonais Brigadier General
        The Books of the Legion
        Attest [first name covered by seal and on a fold] Swartz
        Adjutant of the Legion
27 September 1781

Pay Office Decem^r 15, 1791, it appears by the receipt produced by Capt De Bell, Agent for [blank] demands Legion. That John Ville has recovered Certificate for his pay amounting to 230 75/90 dollars, which was all [word illegible] him. (signed) Joseph Flower, Adj. Brg.

1795-002 Request by John Wheeler for his Pension allowance to be sent to Pickett & Blackwell
Gent
     Please Give my Pension due for the year one thousand Seven hundred + Ninety five to Pickett & Blackwell when due + Oblige yours

To the Court of Fauquier County   **Jno Wheeler**
Test   26th March 1795
Jno. [line through]   Edwd Digges Jr.

1796-001 1784 Bond from Thomas Blackwell to Wm. Bryan for Blackwell's yearly pay as a Revolutionary Officer as part of the purchase price for land bought from Bryan

Know all men by these presents that We Thomas Blackwell, Armistead Churchill + William Grant of the County of Fauquier are held and firmly bound unto Wm. Bryan of the said County in the Sum of Two hundred and Eighty eight pounds to which payment well + truly to be made to the said Wm Bryan his heirs Exors Adm^{rs} or afsigns we bind ourselves our heirs Exor^s + adm^{rs} Jointly and severally firmly by these presents Sealed with our Seals De'led this 6th day of March 1784.
     [The words on this line are on a fold and not legible]

1796-001 1784 Bond from Thomas Blackwell to Wm. Bryan for Blackwell's yearly pay as a Revolutionary Officer as part of the purchase price for land bought from Bryan. (Cont.)

Bound Thos Blackwell + the s^d William Bryan relative to [paper torn. Word not legible] purchase of a Tract of land where the s^d Blackwell now lives. The s^d Blackwell in part payment for the said land has agreed to assign over to the said Bryan all his right and title to a Years pay given formerly by Congress to Such Officers as were sent home as Supernumeraries, and also agrees to endeavour to obtain a Certificate for the same [the next several words are blotted out and look as if they were lined through]

And if such Certificate, or other assurance cannot be obtained That then + in that case the said Thomas Blackwell Obliges himself to furnish the said Wm Bryan with another Cont^l Certificate of the same amount—Now the Condition of the above Obligation is such that if the above bound Thos Blackwell shall well + truly stand to + comply with the above agreement then the above Obligation Void Else in force + Virtue.

Sealed + Delev^d in presence of }   A. Churchill, Wm. Grant   (Signed) Tho Blackwell

It is agreed before Signing that if the s^d Blackwell does not within the space of Six months obtain the first mentioned Certificate or other assurance as [word illegible] per numary then the s^d Blackwell to furnish s^d Bryan with another Continental Certificate to the amount of the above ment^d being One hundred + forty four pounds.
    [?] Brooke
    Wm Bronaugh

[Reverse Side of Bond]
This is to Certify that I acknowlidg [sic] to pay the [word illegible] trust of this within Debt to the Sd. Wm. Bryan before [lined through] from the time it Became due til it is fulley paid.
September the 12th 1786.
Test   Tho Blackwell
Robt Layton
Wily Roy

March the 7th 1788
Recv^d of C^{ol} Thomas Blackwell, L141-19-11s of the within Certificate.

This 4th day June Setled [sic] the within Bond and find a ballance of [word blotted and appears to be lined through] fourteen pounds four Shillings + Six pence Specie to bear Interest till paid.
       (Signed) Thos Blackwell
[Note: The Settlement above mentioned was made in June 1796 by which time Wm. Bryan had returned from Kentucky.]

1796-002 County Militia List of 85th Regiment for 1796
A List of Officers to be recommended to fill up Vacancies in the 85th Reg^t

---

James White recommended as Lieut. In Capt Bradfords Company in the 1st Battalion 85 Reg^t Vice **Joe Heale** resigned.
Stephen Robinson as Ensign Vice James Vice **James White** promoted

Edwin Porter recommended as Ensign in Capt Chiltons Company in the 1st Battalion 85 Reg^t Vice **Wiley Roy** removed.

William Dulin recommended as Ensign in Capt Buckners company 1st Battalion 85 Reg^t Vice **George Kemper** promoted

Sanders Morris recommended as Lieut. In Capt Fallis's Company 2^d Battalion 85 Reg^t Vice **Hancock Eustace** resigned.
Thos Brookes as Ensign in the same Vice **John Conwey** removed.

Ben Fallis recommended as Ensign [crossed out] Lieut. In Capt Esthams Company of the 2^d Battalion 85 Reg^t vice **Joe George** [next word illegible] **Taliafero Shoemate** Ensign vice **Ben Fallis** promoted.

Jonathan Gibson [next 3 words illegible] for Ensign in Capt Gibsons Company 2^d Battalion 85 Regt.

1796-003 1796 List of Officers of County Militia to whom Oath of Office was administered [Papers include letter and list of officers, both signed by Robert Randolph] [MISSING FROM BOX]

1797-001 A 1797 List of Militia Officers [Post Revolutionary War Militia List]
On reverse side of List:
    Jno Edmonds   Nathl Ashby

                              Militia Officers

John Edmonds   Nathl Grigsby
Wiley Roy   Wm Clarkson
Thos Chilton   Minor Winn
Wm Clarkson
Minor Winn
Wm Edmonds
Wm Stuart

George Edmonds   Nimrod Ashby

Wiley Roy   Wiley Roy
Thos Chilton   Thos Chilton
Wm Edmonds   Wm. Clarkson
                            Minor Winn
                            Wm Edmonds

1798-001   Commission of Enoch Smith, Lieutenant, 1st Battalion, 85th Regiment, 5th Brigade, 2nd Division of Militia, signed by Governor James Wood 6/30/1798.

No.
The Commonwealth *of* Virginia

To **Enoch Smith** Gentleman:
KNOW you, that from the special trust and confidence reposed in your fidelity, courage, activity and good conduct, and upon the recommendation of the court of the county of **Fauquier**   our Governor, in pursuance of the act for regulating the militia of this Commonwealth, doth appoint you the said **first** Lieutenant in the **fifth** Battalion of the **Second** Regiment, the   Brigade and **Second**   Division of the said militia, to take rank as such agreeably to the number and date hereof.
IN TESTIMONY WHEREOF,   These our letters are sealed with the seal of the Commonwealth and made patent.

WITNESS **James Wood** , Esquire, our said Governor, at Richmond, this **30**th day of **June**   1798.
  (REGISTERED.)
   Sam Coleman

(Seal)   **James Wood**

1799-001   Thomas Hunton, Captain of Troop of Cavalry, 2nd Regiment, 2nd Division of Virginia Militia - commission and oath administered 9/23/1799.
  Fauquier Sc^t
    Thomas Hunton a Captain of a Troop of cavalry in the Second Regiment and Second division of the Militia of Virginia – produced his Commission to me and took the oath prescribed by Law. Given under my hand this 23^d day of September 1799.
       (Signed) Wm Edmonds J^r

1799-002 Military Warrant No. 167 for 2,000 acres of Land in Kentucky of Thomas Ransdell, Officer in US Army in Revolutionary War
from Chancery *Obannon, John v. Ransdell, Thomas's Admr.*

Land Office Military Warrant N° 167
    To the principal Surveyor of the Lands set apart for the Officers and Soldiers of the Commonwealth of Virginia. (Seal)   This shall be your Warrant to survey and lay off in one or more Surveys for Thomas Ransdall his Heirs or Afsigns, the Quantity of four Thousand Acres of land, due unto the said Thomas Ransdall In consideration of his services for three years as a Capt. Of the Virginia line agreeable to a Certificate from the Governor and Council received into the Land Office. Given under my hand and the Seal of the said Office, the 9th day of March in the Year one Thousand Seven Hundred and 83.
         (Signed)   John Harvie Re, L Off.
I do certify that the above is a copy of Thomas Ransdalls land Warrant now in my pofsefsion, a part thereof yet unsatisfied. Given under my hand and Seal of Office this 7th Day of September 1797.
         (signed) Richard Anderson

  [Note: On 5/11/1793 Thomas Ransdell conveyed all his right, title, and Interest in and to an Entry for 2,000 acres of land for a Military claim for services performed in the Army of the United States, to Wm. Bryan. The land was located between the Scioti River + the mouth of the Little Miami in the North West Side of the Ohio River, numbered agreeable to a lottery #1027. This conveyance was signed and sealed by Thomas Ransdell and witnessed by Charles Marshall and Francis Brooke.]

1799-002 Military Warrant No. 167 for 2,000 acres of Land in Kentucky of Thomas Ransdell, Officer in US Army in Revolutionary War (Cont.)

Survey No. 1027 for 1,000 acres, part of **Military Warrant No. 167** was **assigned** by Chilton Ransdell, brother of Thomas who is deceased in 1799, **to John Obannon of Woodford County, Ky**. along with the assignment of the right and interest of Maria and John Chilton Ransdell, Thomas's infant children.
[Note: Survey and conveyance above are found in Chancery 1799-031 Obannon v. Ransdell's Admr.]

1800-001 List of Revolutionary War Pensioners for 1799

- List #1 List of Pensioners continued by the Honourable [sic] the Executive, for the Year 1799, to be paid out of the revenue for that year.

PENSIONERS	ALLOWANCE		
	L	s	d
Booker, Sarah	8		
Carr, Elizabeth	8		
Camron, Catharine	10		
Collins, Charles	12		
Cunningham, Elizabeth	12		
Davis, Ann	10		
Dobson, Mary	8		
Edmunds, Sarah	8		
Gregory, Hannah	24		
Hillion, Selby	8		
Hargrove, Ann	6		
Howell, Jemima	10		
Highland, Furguson	10		
Lewis, Edward	15		
Lyon, Mary	18		
Leman, John	5		

PENSIONERS	ALLOWANCE		
	L	s	d
McClintich, Alice	12		
Marshall, John	15		
Rose, Patty	8		
Riddle, Richard	5		
Southall, Elizabeth	12		
Shepherd, Ann	18		
Scurry, John	8		
Toomey, Elizabeth	12		
Tucker, William	12		
Windham, Mary	5		
Wright, John	12		

Samuel Shepard, Auditor, Auditor's Office, 7th January 1800

1800-001 List of Revolutionary War Pensioners for 1799 (Cont.)
- **List #2 List of Pensioners for 1800**

LIST OF PENSIONERS *Continued by the Honorable the Executive, for the year **1800**, to be paid out of the Revenue for that year.*

NAMES	ALLOWANCE	
	L	s
Mary Boush	74	
Mary Bedolph	5	
Comfort Bloxom	10	
Mary Brooks	8	
Jane Burn	6	
Elizabeth Burke	12	
John Cullins	12	
William Courtney	12	
Judith Carter	8	
Eve Clark	12	
Mary Dillard	12	
Mary Dolton	6	
Mary Edwards	6	
Sarah Edmunds	8	
Robert Ferguson	12	
Frederick Fisher	75	
Thomas Fenn	12	
William T. Goulding	12	
Margaret Grotin	12	
Andrew Green	8	
Margaret Gamble	22	
Albion Gordon	15	
John Groom	72	
Benjamin Hoomes	8	
Ann Hogshire	3	
Samuel Kirkpatrick	12	
Robert Leonard	8	
Elizabeth Lovell	12	
Elizabeth Mann	15	
James McAmith	18	
William Musgrove	9	
Joseph Mayes	9	
Mary McCarty	60	
William McGuire	15	
John McKenny	15	
John Marshall	10	
Alexander McFarlane	12	
Eleanor McGovern	8	
Leander Overstreet	30	
Mary Ramsay	8	
Lewis Ranse	10	
James Robinson	10	

1800-001 List of Revolutionary War Pensioners for 1799 (Cont.)
- List #2 List of Pensioners for 1800

LIST OF PENSIONERS *Continued by the Honorable the Executive, for the year 1800, to be paid out of the Revenue for that year.*

NAMES	ALLOWANCE	
	L	s
Susannah Rawlings	8	
Susannah Rowland	15	
Mary Roebuck	10	
Lucy Robertson	12	
Betsy Rigg	10	
Jesse Ruble	12	
William Smith	10	
Elizabeth Snale	15	
Sarah Stacey	15	
William Shepherd	7	10
Richard Taylor	120	
John Thompson	15	
Hanna Thatcher	8	
Mary Whitt	12	
Robert White	48	
Sarah Wilkerson	6	

SAMUEL SHEPARD, AUDITOR

Richmond, January 9, 1801

1801-001 Commonwealth Account with Robert Randolph for Regimental Accounts
[Post Revolutionary War Regimental Accounts]

1802-001 Regimental Account of 44th Regiment, Thomas Chilton, Colº Commandant

The Commonwealth of Virginia [word illegible] Thomas Chilton, Colº Commandant of the 44 Regiment of Virginia [word illegible]

To My Order on Sheriff of Fauqr in favour of Peter Glascock – on a/c of Wm Metcalfe Clerk of court Martial	$43.~
To ditto in favour of **Capt John Edmonds** for Cash to buy a Drum	$8.~
To ditto in favour of **Capt Saml Ashby** for Cash to buy a Drum	$8.
To my orders in favour of Captains **Joham Obannon, Welford Johnson, Henry Peyton, + William Barker** for Cash to buy Drums, tc.	$32.
	$91.

(Signed) **Thomas Chilton**
Colº Comd 44th Regmt of Virga, June 26th 1802

1802-002 1802 List of Militia Recommendations

George Martin   Ensign 2 bat   85 Regt   in the room of George Bowmer removed

William Gunnion   Ensign 2 bat   85 Regt in the room of Jnº Marlow [?] who refuses to accept

1802-002 1802 List of Militia Recommendations (Cont.)

Tho James swore to his Com: as Ensig[n] first bat 85 Reg[t] before

R Randolph Gen [?] [Number scratched out] Oct[r] 1802

1803-001 1803 List of Militia Recommendations 1803-002

Daniel Marr   Capt. 2d b 85 Reg[t] in the room of A. Jennings
George Martin Sen[r] in room of D. Mar[r]
George Duff Ensign in the room of Martin

1803-002 List of Revolutionary Pensioners

A List of PENSIONERS, continued by the Honorable Executive, for the year 1802 – to be paid out of the Revenue for that year.

NAMES		ALLOWANCE PER ANN.		
Bradston	Wm.	L	12	
Booker	Sarah		8	
Cullins	Jno.		12	
Clements	Charles		12	
Cornhill	Mary		12	
Courtney	Wm.		12	
Cunningham	Elis[abet]h.		12	
Cook	Mary		12	
Dillard	Mary		12	
Davis	Ann		12	
Furgusson	Robert		12	
Foster	Frederick		12	
Goulding	Wm.		12	
Gordion	Albion		12	
Hodges	Jos.		12	
Hyland	Ferguson		10	
Howell	Jemima		10	
Hargrove	Ann		6	
Leonard	Robert		12	
M[c]Clintick	Alice		12	
Mayes	James		8	
M[c]Carty	Mary		9	
Shepherd	Jno.		12	
Scrurry	Jno.		8	
Stuart	Alexander		8	
Shepherd	Wm.		7	10 [s]
Shepherd	Ann		18	
Tucker	Wm.		12	
Tanner	Dorothy		8	
Thatcher	Hanna		8	
Toomey	Elis[abet]h.		12	
Willson	Willis		40	
Windham	Mary		5	

S SHEPARD, Auditor

Auditor's Office, 27[th] January, 1803.

1804-001 Robert Randolph's Regimental Account with the Commonwealth

The Common Wealth of Virginia in Account with Robert Randolph

1804

Nov 15	To Chilton Ransdell as Clerk to the court Marshall for one year ending this day	9-0-0
	To Fielding S^{t}Clair as adjutant for one year ending this day	9-0-0
	To Thomas Groves for six days attending as Drummer at 12/~ per day	3-12-0
	To James Smith as provost Marshall for one year ending this day	4-10-0
[Nov] 26	To Joseph Jones for two days attending as Fife Major at Battalion + Regimental Muster at 12/: per day	1-4-0
		27-6-0

1804 Contra

Nov 15	By my certificate to the sheriff in favor of Chilton Ransdell	9-0-0
	By my certificate in favor of F. Sinclair	9-0-0
	By my certificate in favor of Tho Groves	3-12-0
	By my certificate to the sheriff in favor of James Smith	4-10-0
[Nov] 26	By my certificate in favor of Joseph Jones for two days service as fifer	1-4-0
		27-6-0

E.

(Signed)   **Robt. Randolph Lieut. Col^o Comn^d 85 Reg^t**

Reverse side of Account reads
A/C R Randolph with Com Wealth 1804

1805-001 Oaths of Lieutenant James Neale and Ensign Francis Hathaway, Militia Officers, 85th Regiment

Fauquier Sc^t

This day James Neale, and Francis Hathaway personally appear^d before me one of the Justices of the Peace for the County aforesaid and took the Oath proscribed by Law to be taken by Militia Officers, the said Neale as Lieut. In the first Batt^n + Eighty fifth Reg^t of the Virginia Militia and the s^d Hathaway as Ensign in the same Batt^n + Reg^t. Given under my hand this 24th day of June 1805.

(Signed) Thornton Buckner

1805-002 Regimental Order for Court-martial boundary line between 1st and 2nd Battalion of 85th Regiment.

Agreeable to an **Order of Court Martial** held at German town the 30th Novr 1805 we whose names are under written having met at Fayetts Ville 13th of Decr 1805 in presence of Major Gibson have proceeded **to lay off and ascertain a boundery [sic] line between the first and Second Battalion of the 85 Reg^t as follows** Viz: Beginning at Beverlys Mill (formerly Lawsons and running with the Road which divides the plantations of C^{ollo} Blackwell + Major Bronaughs till it intersects the Sandy ford road and with the last mentioned road through Fayetts to the first left hand Road below the plantation of the late Robert Hensons and with the Said left hand Road to the Marsh Road a little below Mrs Moxley and with the Marsh road to the cross road leading from Capt Balls Mill to the elk Run road + with the Elk Run road to the crab tree branch at Willow green and thence with the crab tree branch to Turkey Run and from thence with the Said turkey Run to its junction with Cedar Run at Woodstock and So with Cedar Run to Prince William. Witness Our hand the day above written.

(Signed)   Enoch Withers, John Bronaugh
              Augt Jennings, Yellis Johnson

1806-001 Sale by Philip Mallory to Joseph Chilton of 4,000 acres of Military Lands

Memorandum of an agreement between Philip Mallory + Joseph Chilton. I the s^d Mallory doth bargain + Sell to the s^d Chilton… 4000 acres of Military land clear of all incumbrance to the present date + doth agree to give a general warrantee for so much land With suffitient Sureties to make so much land good and the said Chilton [word illegible] may examine [examine is lined through] have until the [words are blotted out and appeared to be lined through] to recant the bargain if they think proper + the money Said Mallory is indebted to s^d Chilton's [word illegible] Jo^s Chilton [word illegible] shall draw bearing Int[erest] [inserted: from this date] provided the bargain stands good [inserted: otherwise to remain in force], the am^t of purchase four thousand dollars to be paid in following manner.

A lot formerly owned by Saml Boucher under Lease with the mill all the appurtenances the timbers for saw Mill so far as has been got by Jno Riley J^r to pay the debt due J S Chilton … allso the Debt due Thos [next two words are illegible] Chilton and to pay the remainder in three annual payments (Equal) so as to make up the ballance.

1806-002 Wm. R. Smith's oath as Captain of Troop of Cavalry, 2nd Regiment, 2nd Division

This is to certify that William R. Smith came before me a Justice of the Peace of the County of Fauq^r and made oath to his Commission as Capt. Of a Troop of Calvary Situated in the Second Reg^t and Division   this 20th of Sep^t 1806

        (Signed) Th: Hunton

1806-003 Thomas Hunton's oath as Major of 2nd Battalion, 2nd Regiment of Cavalry

Fauquier County   to wit

This day Thomas Hunton came before me a Justice of the peace for S^d County and made oath to his Commission as Maj^r to the Second batallion of the Second Regiment of Cavalry given under my hand this 2^d day of may 1806.

        (Signed)   Richd Rixey J^r

1807-001 Court-martial Papers of Major Townsend Dade of 2nd Battalion + 36th Regiment

- Summons:

[Greetings are illegible]

You are hereby commanded to summon John Wills, John Williams, Enoch Aram, Luke Cannoy, Levi Scott, Joseph Smith, Walter Ashmore, and John McRae – to appear at Fauquier Courthouse on the third Monday in November and before the Court Martial, then and there to be convened of which Brigadier General Thomson Mason is President – to testify and the truth to say on behalf of the Common Wealth of Virginia in a certain controversy between the Commonwealth and Major Townshend Dade—And this you shall in no wise Omit: and have then there this Writ === Given under my hand this 30th October 1807.

        (Signed) James Williams MG 2nd D.V.M.

Collen Campbell, ~~Joseph Lynn~~, George Carney, Richard Cole, Beverley W Booner, Seth Botts, John Hays, George Wedon, Joseph Brady, ~~John Lyton~~

Reverse of Summons:

    Prince William to wit

This Day personally appeard before me William Grant a Justice of the peace for s^d County ^ George Renoe ^ and made Oath that he had served Each of the above Named persons with the within Subpoena given under my hand this 13 Day of Novemb^r 1807…

        (Signed) W Grant

1807-001 Court-martial Papers of Major Townsend Dade of 2nd Battalion + 36th Regiment

- Proceedings

At a Division court Martial held at Fauquier Court house on Monday the 16th day of November 1807 by the orders of Major General James Williams for the trial of Major Townshend Dade of the ^ 2nd Battallion + 36 Regiment ^ arrested upon the following charges to wit

1st For disobeying orders
2nd For ungentlemanly conduct
3rd For being intoxicated when on duty
4th For breaking open letters which were addressed to the Commandant of the 36th Regiment

Present. Genl Thompson Mason   President
        Col° William Tyler
        Col° Thornton Buckner
        Col° Thomas Broadus
        Col° Hugh Douglas
        Major Owen Sullivan
        Major Thomas Spindle
        Major Josiah White [scratched out]
        Capt. Thomas Brooke
        Capt. John Obannon
        Capt. Stanton Slaughter
        Capt. Thomas White
        Hugh R. Campbell   Judge advocate
        Benjamin V. Lakin   Provost Martial

1807-001 Court-martial Papers of Major Townsend Dade of 2nd Battalion + 36th Regiment

[Page 2]

Ordered that the court Martial be adjourned untill tomorrow ten o'clock a sufficient member of officers not having appeared.

        (signed) Thomson Mason, B. Genl + Mus^t C.M.

At a Division court Martial Continued/held at Fauq^r Court house on Tuesday the 17th Novr 1807. By the orders of Major General James Williams for the trial of Major Townshend Dade of the 2nd Bat^l + 36th Regim^t.
[next two lines are scratched out and illegible]
Present the same officers of last adjournment when Major ^ Thomas ^ Gibson + Major Gillison appeared after taking the oath prescribed by law took their seats [next word is illegible and appears to be scratched out]. The court Martiall then [next two words illegible] Compleat [sic] proceedings to business.

The accused by his Counsel delivered a Travuse [sic] to the court, in these words "The answer +C.

The Counsel for the Accused required the Separate Charges exhibited ag^t him and the time at which they [word illegible] committed as follows.

1st For disobe[y]ing orders. On the 5th day of September last in the town of Dumfries, In riding into the Court house of the county of Prince William, while on duty making a return of Draft Contrary to orders.

2nd For ungentlemanly conduct in raising his sword against his Superior officer.

1807-001 Court-martial Papers of Major Townsend Dade of 2nd Battalion + 36th Regiment (Cont.)
[Page 3]
    3rd For being Intoxicated when on duty. The 5th Day Sept 1807 or on the day of the draft.

Upon Hearing the testimony as well for the Commonwealth as for the accused the Court [next three lines are illegible and lined through] are of opinion that the charges against the said Major Townshend Dade, some of them are frivolous and others not sufficiently supported Therefore he is reinstated.
Ordered that this Court be adjourned untill tomorrow at 9 oClock.
                              (signed) Thomson Mason, B.Gen¹ and Presᵗ, C.M.

[page 4]
Ordered that George Renoe who summoned Sixteen Witnesses receive nine Dollars for his service.

    That Richᵈ Weedon receive Six Dollars for going after the articles of War

    That Philip Dam receive Twelve Dolls for his Service Summoning Witnesses

    That Richᵈ Roy receive for furnishing a Room +c Six dollars

    That the Judge Advocate Received for his Service Forty Dollars

    That the Provost Martial receive for his Service Nine Dollars

The business being done the court was dissolved.

H.R. Campbell, Judge Advocate   Thomson Mason, B. Gen¹ and Presᵗ C.M.

1807-002 Court Martial Muster Fines
- Receipt

Received January the 27th 1807 from Joshua Owens, Clerk of the court Martial for the 44th Regᵗ of Virginia Militia, a list of Muster fines assess'd in said Regᵗ in the year 1806 collectable in the year 1807 amounting to One hundred + ninety Two Dollars ["recᵈ from" is scratched out] + fifty Cents recᵈ of me.
                          (Signed) L. Ashton S.F.C.

Reverse side of Receipt
    Sheriffs Recᵗ for Muster fines for 1806 collectable 1807

- Notice

Mʳ Lawrence Ashton   Sheriff Fauqʳ County
    Take notice that on the first day of the next Court to be held for the County of Fauquier we Shall move said court for a Judgment against you for the amount of muster fines in the 44th and 85th Regiments Virginia Militia, placed in your hands for collection and Collectable in the year 1807.
Fauqʳ Novʳ 13th 1807   (Signed)   Thomas Chilton, Colº of the 44th Regᵗ, Virgᵃ Militia
                                      Thornton Buckner, Colº of the 85 Regᵗ, Virgᵃ Militia
I acknowledge the above Notice.
    (signed) L. Ashton

Reverse side of Notice:
    Notices to Shrff
    Chilton ⎱
    Ashton ⎰   Notice, 1807 Nov. died

1807-003 Major John Gillison's oath as Militia Officer, 85th Regiment, 5th Brigade, 2nd Division
Fauq' County   [Illegible]

John Gillison took the oaths prescribed by law to be taken by a Major of the Militia before the subscriber a Justice of the peace for the County aforesaid this 27th April 1807 in the 85 Reg' 5th Brigade + 2nd Division of the Militia of Virginia

(Signed) Thornton Buckner

1807-004 Ensign George L. Ball's Oath as Militia Officer, 85th Regiment, 5th Brigade
Fauquier Sct

This is to certify that on this day George L. Ball took the oath prescribed by Law to be taken by Militia Officers before me he having been commissioned by the Governor of this State as Ensign in the 85 Reg' 5 Brigade and 2nd Division of the Militia of Virginia   Given under my hand this 25th July 1807

(signed) Thornton Buckner

1808-001 Heirs at Law of Nathaniel Quarles, a Sergeant in the Revolutionary War

At a Court held for Fauquier county the 22nd day of February 1808 – it is ordered to be certified that it appears to the satisfaction of the Court by the oath of **Philip Mallory, a Captain** in the late revolutionary war of said county that **Thomas Humston is the eldest son and heir at law of Susanna Humston the wife of Edward Humston** and that the said **Susanna departed this life in March in the year 1786 and was the heir at law and only sister of Nathaniel Quarles**, who died immediately after his return from the service of the United States in the Continental army during the revolutionary war, in which he had served as a sergeant in the Virginia continental line.

1809-001 Heirs at Law and Certification of service of Joshua Jenkins, a Sergeant in Captain Chilton's Company, 3rd Virginia Regiment

I hereby certify that Joshua Jinkins was a Serjeant in Capt Chiltons Company in the third Virginia Regim' of Continental Troops under my command, and that he was killd in the Battle of Brandywine on the 11th of September 1777. Given under my hand this 26th of March 1780.

(Signed) T. Marshall, formerly Col° of the 3d Virginia Regim'

Reverse side of Certification

At a Court held for Fauquier County the 27th day of March 1780

John Barker made oath that the within was an authentic and true Certificate that Thomas Jenkins was heir at law to the within mentioned Joshua Jenkins and that no right to ["right to" interlined] land has ever been claimed for the Service therein mentioned which was ordered to be certified.

(Signed) H. Brooke

1809-002 John Roach's request to give his discharge to the bearer, Edward Shacklet
Sir.   Please to let the Bearer Edward Shacklet have my discharge and youl [sic] oblige yours

(Signed) John Roach

April the 28 day 1783
to Col° Brooke

1809-003 Stephen Connor's oath to service in Revolutionary War in a Virginia Regiment under Colonel Byrd

At a Court held for Fauquier County the 27th day of March 1780

Stephen Connor made oath that he served as a Soldier in the Virginia Regiment commanded by Col° Byrd til the same was discharged, and that he never before proved or claimed his right to Land for the said Service which was ordered to be certified.

(Signed) H. Brooke

1809-004 Thomas White Jr.'s order to Humphrey Brooke, Clerk of Court, to deliver his discharge for 3 years service in State Artillery to Hezekiah Shacklett
S^{ir} Please to Deliver Hezekiah Shacklett My discharge for 3 years service in the State Artillery and oblige Sir your humble servant.
    Test: John Monroe
                      (Signed)   Thomas White J^r
                                    Novbr 16th 1783

1809-005 Enoch Smith's order to Colonel Brooke to deliver his discharge to Joseph Goddard
Sir please to let the Bearer Joseph Goddard have my discharge and youl [sic] oblige yours ---

April the 29th 1783   (Signed)   Enoch Smith
to C^{olo}. Brooks

1809-006 Judas Levy and Joseph Garners' orders to Clerk of Court to deliver Pension Warrants to Martin Pickett
To the Clerk of Fauq^r Court
    You will please to Deliver to Martin Pickett our Pention [sic] Warrents [sic] as we desire that
    he may Receive the Contents.

                              his
                (Signed) Judas (X) Levy
                              mark

Test   his
Landf^d Dade   Joseph (X) Garner
                              mark
                        April 29th 1789

1809-010 John Athey's order to Clerk of Court to deliver money and tobacco to Martin Pickett & Company
Sir   Please deliver [to] Martin Pickett & Co. [two words illegible] two pound five Shillings + three pence + eight Hundred + thirty pound of Tob^o + Oblige yours
    Allow^d this day by the Court

To the Clerk of   (Signed)   John Athey
Fauquier   24th Novr 1789

1809-011 Reuben Martin's order to Clerk of Court to deliver certificate of his Public Service claim against the County to Martin Pickett & Company
Sir   Please deliver [to] Martin Pickett & Co. a certificate for my Claim against County. Obligi[n]ly Yours

                      (Signed)   Reuben Martin
Clerk of Fauquier   Novr 26th 1789

1809-012 Minor Winn's 1//10/1761 Receipt for a gun for the use of the Fauquier Militia with appraisement of value on reverse side of receipt (for use in French and Indian War)
Rec^d of Minor Winn One Smooth Gun, for the use of the Fauquier County Militia
this 10th Jan. 1761.   (signed)   James Winn
Sent down

Reverse side of Receipt:
We the Subscribers being first Sworn, have appraised the Smooth gun Belonging to Minor Winn, to One hundred and forty four Pounds this 10th day of January 1761.
            (signed) Hezekiah Brady, Robt Combs, Evan Griffiths

		75/114/	1.10
.63	75	75	5
	126	69	2.6
	75	69	4
	51	138	1:17 10

1809-013   Marmaduke Brown's 7/12/1781 Public Service Claim for a saddle for the use of Captain Wm. Triplett's Company of Cavalry
July 12th 1781
    Know I received of Mr Marmaduke Brown one saddle for the use of Capt William Triplett's Company of Cavalry appraissed [sic] to three pounds, specie money   Certifyed by us the appraissers.
            (Signed)   S. Blackwell, Maj^r, Jno Shumate
July 12th 1781

1809-014 Charles Duncan's 7/12/1781 Public Service Claim for a saddle for the use of Captain William Tripletts Company of Cavalry
July 12th 1781
    Know I received of Charles Duncan one saddle for the use of Capt William Triplett's Company of Cavalry appraised to two pounds ten Shillings specied money Certifyed by us the appraisers.
            (Signed)   Saml Blackwell, Maj^r, Jno Shumate

1810-001   A Bond for a Virginia Military Continental Land Warrant for 400 acres for Joseph Chilton found in Court suit papers (for debt) in Jones v. Chilton (Jones, Daniel v. Chilton, Joseph)
Front side of Certificate:
    I do acknowledge my selfe indebted to Danl Jones four hundread [sic] acres of Virginia Military Continental Land Warrent [sic] for which he has my obligation + in consequence of my not having them on hand I oblige my selfe to pay to him or order the price that the warrents can be sold for payable the 1st of September next with Interest in the City of Washington about this date it being certifyed by John Laird of George Town or Genl John Marshall on the Back of this certificate   Witness my hand   April 23th 1802
    Test: John White   (signed) Joseph Chilton

Reverse of Certificate:
    There being no regular market in this Quarter for Land Warrants it is difficult to ascertain the Prise as required within-- -- A Broker in Town holds some for which he asks 30 Dollars p[er] hundred acres, says this is his limit and that they are worth that in Philadelphia --.

1810-001 Court papers from Jones, Daniel v. Chilton, Joseph In Covenant (Cont.)

A Bond for a Virginia Military Continental Land Warrant for 400 acres for Joseph Chilton found in Court suit papers (for debt) in Jones v. Chilton (Jones, Daniel v. Chilton, Joseph) (Cont.)

I presume when there is any demand in the City of Washington that the Prise [sic] is governed by the Philadelphia Market and, if the Brokers information be correct as above stated, that the Price here may be said to be about 30
Dollars.—not exceeding-- -- -- I know that seems years ago. The Warrant viewed current at that Rate in Philad^a
        (signed) John Laird
  Test.   John Murdock   Georgetown 30 April 1802

Bill of Complaint in Court suit papers (in Covenant) in Jones v. Chilton (Jones, Daniel v. Chilton, Joseph)
Fauquier County to wit

     Daniel Jones complains of Joseph Chilton in custody of a plea that he render unto him one hundred and twenty dollars with Interest from the 3rd of April 1802 ["with Interest…" interlined] which to him he owes and from him unjustly detains for that the Deft on the 23rd day of April 1802 at the County aforesaid by his certain note in writing signed with his proper hand and now hereto to the Court shews the date whereof is on the same day and year aforesaid did acknowledge himself indebted to the Plff. Four hundred acres of Virginia military continental Land Warrants for which he obliged himself to pay to the Plff or order the price that the warrants could be sold for in the City of Washington about the date of the said note in writing ["about the date…" is interlined] payable the first of Septr. Then next ensuing with Interest—

The price of said ~~certifi-~~ warrants being certified by John Laird of George Town or Genl. John Marshall on the back of said note And the said John Laird afterwards to wit on the 30th of April 1802 at George Town in the county aforesaid by his certain writing on the back of said note signed with his proper hand did certify that the price of said Land warrants in the City of Washington at the time aforesaid was thirty dollars per hundred acres by reason whereof the Deft became liable to pay to the Plff the said sum of $120 dollars with Interest as aforesaid ["with Interest as aforesaid" is interlined] yet the Deft altho often required hath not paid the said sum of money nor any part thereof…

[Note: This suit was filed in the Haymarket District Court in June 1806 and was not settled until April 1810 when a jury brought a verdict and judgment for the plaintiff.]

1811-001 Lieutenant John Herndon's Certificate for oath as Militia Officer
Fauquier county S^{ct}

    I James Pickett a Justice of the peace for the county aforesaid do hereby certify that this day John Herndon personally appeared before me and made the oaths required by law to the execution of the office of a Lieutenant in the Militia of this commonwealth—Given under my hand the 24th day of August 1811.
            (Signed)   James Pickett

On reverse side of Oath:
    At a Court of Quarterly Sessions held for Fauquier County on the 26th day of August 1811 This Certificate was returned to the court and ordered to be Recorded
                Teste   HR Campbell C.C.
Certificate of John Herndon's Oath
1811 26 Aug^t [Certificate] ret^d + O.R.
        Recorded

1812-001 Mary Kernes, widow of Jeremiah Kerns, War of 1812 Pension Papers
- **Widow's Declaration**

Be it known, that I **Mary Kernes**, do solemnly swear that I am the identical person named in an original pension certificate in my possession, which certifies: **No. 1513**. **That Mary Kernes, widow of Jeremiah Kernes who as a Private Capt. T Jennings's Co. V^a Mil** in the service of the United States, is entitled to pension at the rate of eight dollars per month, to commence on the **14th** day of **February 1871** and to continue during life, unless she shall again marry; in which case the pension is not payable after the date of such marriage.

Dated this **25** day of **January 1872** and signed by B. R. Cowen *Acting Secretary of the Interior* and by J. H. Baker, *Commissioner of Pensions*. That I am the widow of Jeremiah Kernes, above mentioned, and have not intermarried since his death; ...

...

Vouchers:

$77^{33}

Received of A. Washburn, U.S. Pension Agent at Richmond V^a Seventy seven 30/100 dollars, being for 9 months and 20 days' pension due me on pension certificate No. 1513 from the 14th day of February 1871 to the 4th day of Dec 1871 ...

- **Notification of Pension Approval to widow**

(No. 26)
ACT OF FEB. 14, 1871 – WAR OF 1812

Department of the Interior
Pension Office
Washington D.C.   Jany 25th, 1872

Madam:

You are hereby notified that your claim for pension, **No. 1513**, under act of February 14, 1871, has been allowed at eight dollars per month, commencing February 14, 1871, payable at the Pension Agency in **Richmond Va.**

Your pension certificate has been issued and sent to the Pension Agent at **Richmond**, who will forward to you, upon receipt thereof, and quarterly thereafter, proper vouchers for payment thereupon. The note indorsed upon said vouchers will explain when and how they shall be executed by you, and how the payment thereupon will be made.

The fee to be paid your attorney for the prosecution of your claim is $10—

Very respectfully,
(Signed)   J.H. Baker   Commissioner

To **Mary Kernes**
  Bealeton
  Fauquier Co. Va.

- **Oath of Allegiance**

This oath is required from pensioners once, (on the first payment to new ones,) who are native-born, or have been naturalized. If a ward, from the guardian, and whenever there is a change of guardian; if dead, from the person or persons executing the vouchers. When those of foreign birth have not resided in the United States, the magistrate may certify to the same; but if they have, and do not owe allegiance, it should be properly explained. When a pension has been increased, and the oath has been previously furnished, it will not be required again of the pensioner.

I, **Mary Kernes**, a pensioner of the United States, do solemnly **Swear** that I will support, protect, and defend the Constitution and Government of the United States against all enemies, whether domestic or foreign, and that I will bear true faith, allegiance, and loyalty to the same, any ordinance, resolution, or law of any State Convention or Legislature to the contrary notwithstanding; and further, that I do this with a full determination, pledge, and purpose, without any mental reservation or evasion whatsoever; and further, that I will and faithfully perform all the duties which may be required of my be law: So help me God.

[Unsigned and undated]

1812-001   Mary Kernes, widow of Jeremiah Kerns, War of 1812 Pension Papers (Cont.)
- **Partially filled out Form for Arrears due Deceased Pensioners**

[Form has only the name of the heir of Mary Kernes and his relationship to her. Nothing else has been filled out on this form]

Meredith J. Sanford, Heir of Mary Kernes…

1812-002   Elizabeth E. Sangster, widow of Captain Thomas Sangster, 1812 Pension Papers

[These papers are NOT in this folder. The paper that is here contains the above information; the inside portion are payments of judgments to various people, unrelated to Captain Sangster or his widow]

1813-001 Illegal enlistment of Jonas Williams by Lt. John Kincaid in Jones v. Kincaid Suit papers (Hab^s Corp^s) (Jones, Jonas Sr. V. Kincaid, Lt. John W.)

- **Petition Williams v. Kincaid   1813 14: Ap^l Hab^s Corp^s awarded + the said Jonas Williams Jr. Dism^d**

    To the superior court of law for Fauquier County now sitting. The petition of Jonas Williams Senr sheweth that his son Jonas Williams J^r a minor and under the age of twenty one years has enlisted in the military service of the United States under one John W. Kincaid an officer in the service afores^d by whom the said Jonas Williams J^r is unlawfully detained agns^t the consent and without the approbation of your petitioner, who is rightfully entitled to the possession of the person and the benefit of the services of the said Jonas Williams J^r, your petitioner humbly prays your Honor to grant to him the commonwealths writ of *habeas corpus ad subjeciendum* + directed to the s^d Kincaid commanding him forthwith to bring up the body of the said Jonas Williams J^r before you honorable court of Fauquire [sic] that your petitioner may there at receive justice and your petitioner [next 3 words are illegible]

    (Signed) Jonas (X) Williams Senr

- **Williams v. Kincaid   Hab^s Corp^s**

    The Commonwealth of Virginia to John W. Kincaid a Lieutenant in the Army of the United States. We command you that the Body of Jonas Williams Jr. Detained by you and under your custody as it is said together with the day and cause of his being taken and detained by whatsoever name he may be called you have immediately on the receipt of this Writ ~~before the Judge of the~~ Superior Court of Law of Fauquier County now sitting at the Court house of the said County to do submit to and receive all and Singular those things which shall then and there be considered of him in this behalf. And have then there this Writ. Witness Berkeley Ward Clerk of our said Court at the Courthouse afs^d the 14- of April 1813 in the 37 year of the Com^o (signed) B. Ward

    The within named Jonas Williams Jr. Voluntarily enlisted as a soldier in the Army of the United States for which Cause I detain him + for no other.
    (Signed) John W. Kincaid

- **Oath of Jonas Williams Sr. as to unlawful enlistment of son Jonas Jr.**

    Fauquier County to wit

    Personally appear'd Jonas Williams Senr before me a justice of the peace for the county aforesaid and made oath that he hath good cause to suspect + ["hat good cause to suspect +" is interlined] doth verily believe that his son Jonas Williams Junr is unlawfully detain'd in custody by John W. Kincaid a Lieutenant of the Army of the united states, and that he the said Jonas Senr hath applied to the said Kincaid for a certificate of the cause of the detention of the said Jonas, Junr and that the said Kincaid refused to grant it Given under my hand this 14th of April 1813.
    (Signed)   James Morgan

1813-002 Assault on George Pursley, a soldier in the US Army detailed in Commonwealth v. Blackaby (Commonwealth v. Blackaby, Wm.)

- **Appearance and Peace Bond**
    State of Virginia   Fauquier County to wit

Be it remembered that on this the 13th day of April in the year of our Lord 1813 personally appear'd Greg Blackaby and George Munroe and James Cowles before me the subscriber one of the Justices of the peace of the said state and for the County aforesaid and acknowledge themselves to owe and stand Justly bound with James Barber ["James Barber" is interlined] the Governor of Virginia that is to say the said Greg Blackaby in the sum of two hundred dollars current money of Virginia and the said George Munroe and James Cowles each in the sum of one hundred dollars current money of Virginia which said respective sums they and every of them acknowledge shall be respectively made and levied of their and every of their [word illegible], goods, chattels, lands and tenements to and for the use of said State if the said Greg Blackaby shall fail in performing the condition hereunder written.

The condition of the recognisance is such that if the above bound Greg Blackaby shall personally appear at the next court to be holden in and for the county of Fauquier aforesaid, to to [sic] and receive what shall then and there be injoined him by the said Court, and in the mean time shall keep the peace and be of good behaviour towards the said state of Virginia ["Maryland" crossed out] and all its citizens and especially towards George Pursley of said County and now soldier in the service of the United States then the said recognisance shall be void or else remain in full force.

(Signed) Wm Horner

- **Justice's summons for Gregory Blackaby and Wm. Blackaby to answer complaint of George Pursley**
    Fauquier County to wit

Whereas George Pursley a Soldier in the army of the United States hath this day Come before me Thomas Chilton a Justice of the Peace for the County aforesaid and hath made oath that Gregory Blackaby and William Blackaby did on the Night of the 12" ins^t assault and beat the said George Pursley, These are therefore to require You to apprehend the Said Gregory Blackaby and William Blackaby and bring them before me or Some other Justice of the Peace for the said County of Fauquier to answer the premises and further to be dealt with according to law. Given under my hand and Seal this 13 day of April 1813.
To the constable to Execute + make Return   (signed) Thomas Chilton (seal)

1815-001 Receipt for Camp Equipage from Samuel F. Adams, Quartermaster 36th Regiment, Virginia Militia to William Obannon, Captain of 36th Regiment of Virginia Militia

I hereby acknowledge to have receiv'd of Captn William Obannon of the 36 Reg^t V^a Militia lately in the service of the United States the following Camp Equipage namely articles of the following description:

Common Tents:	6	Camp Kettles:	7
Wall Tents:	2	Skillets:	Not Given
Mattocks or Pick axes:	4	Ovens:	5
Felling Axes:	3	Griddles	Not Given
Shovels:	4	Bread Basketts:	Not Given
Spades:	4	Scales:	1
Iron Pots:	9	Weights:	6^{lb}
Mess pans	20	Ovenleads:	8

I acknowledge to have received the above.
Test: Peter Holmes first Lieut.   Saml F. Adams
            Charles Duncan   Q^{r}Master 36 Reg^t V^a Militia
I do hereby certify that the above is a true copy from the original now in my possession
        Given under my hand this 23rd day of May 1815.
Test: Thos B. Jennings   (Signed) William Obannon Capt of the 36 Reg^t V^a Militia

1816-001   Roll and Minutes of 2 Mounted Rifle Companies attached to 2nd Battalion of 85th Regiment, Fauquier County at Morrisville

- **Roll of Company of Mounted Riflemen, attached to 2nd Battalion of 85th Regiment, T. Brown Capt**

We the Subscribers do agree to associate our Selves into a Company of (Mounted) Riflemen, to be attached to the 2nd Battallion of the 8thth Regiment of Fauquier County—When forty names shall have been obtaind, a Meeting shall take place at Morrisville to elect officers, of Which due Notice Shall be given, -- Thirty five Votes Shall be necessary to Constitute an election either present or by proxy –

1. Tho: Brown
2. James Keith
3. William Blackwell
4. Chas B. Ficklin
5. Robert N. McConckie
6. N S West
7. Alex^r Child
8. William Jones Jn^r
9. Abijah Embry
10. Benjn West
11. Daniel Embry
12. James C. Stephens
13. Thomas Brown Jn^r
14. Joseph Brown
15. Sydnay F. Chapman
16. Hosea Hickerson
17. David Wickliff
18. Chas Edrington
19. John Cave
20. James Cave
21. William Cox
22. Charles Cox
23. Benjn Edwards J^r
24. John Cox
25. Francis Stone
26. Leonard Courtney
27. Marshall Parker
28. Joseph Teagle
29. George Embry
30. William O. Ransdell
31. William Hefling
32. Philip Harding
33. Nathl H. Saunders
34. Mathias Fox
35. James Marshall
36. Hyram Hickerson
37. Charles Day
38. William W. West
39. Elijah Ennis
40. Bryant Stephens
41. Patrick H. Pollard
42. Zephiniah Watson
43. James Smith
44. Alexander McConckie
45. Charles Beale
46. Richard Luckett
47. William E. Gibson
48. Benjn Corbin
49. Thomas Oliver
50. Thomas Tharp
51. Elijah Baker
52. John Cummings
53. John Kendall
54. Daniel King
55. Moses Baker
56. John Cooper
57. John Combs
58. Zachariah Crimm
59. Conileas Oliver
60. Hezekiah Oliver
61. Rhodam Eskridge
62. Richard Claxton

1816-001   Roll and Minutes of 2 Mounted Rifle Companies attached to 2nd Battalion of 85th Regiment, Fauquier County at Morrisville

- **7/13/1816 Minutes of Proceedings, Company of Mounted Rifleman attached to 2nd Battalion, 85th Regiment of Fauquier County, at Morrisville**

At a Meeting of the Volunteer Company of (Mounted) Riflemen, to be attatched to the 2nd Battallion of the 85th Regiment of Fauquier county – at Morrisville, on Saturday the 13th July, 1816. Agreeably to Notice; for the purpose of electing Officers

Present

Thomas Brown[1], James Keith[2], William Blackwell[3], Charles B. Ficklen[4], Robert H. McConckie[5], N. S. West[6], Alexander Child[7], William Jones Jn^r[8], Abijah Embrey[9], Benjamin West[10], Daniel Embrey[11], James C. Stephens[12], Thomas Brown Jn^r[13], Jo^s Brown[14], Sydnay F. Chapman[15], Hosia Hickerson[16], David Wickliff[17], Charles Edrington[18], John Cave[19], James Cave[20], William Cox[21], Charles Cox[22], Benjamin Edward Jn^r[23], John Cox[24], Francis Stone[25], Leonard Courtney[26], Marshall Parker[27], Joseph Teagle[28], George Embrey[29], William O. Ransdell[30], William Hefling[31], Philip Harding[32], Nathl: H. Saunders,[33] Ja^s Marshall[34], Hyram Hickerson[35], Charles Day[36], William W. West[37], Elijah Ennis[38], Bryant Stephens[39], [name is illegible][40], Richard Luckett[41], Thomas Tharp[42], Elijah Baker[43], John Cummings[44], Daniel King[45], Moses Baker[46], John Cooper[47], John Combs[48], William E. Gibson[49], Charles Beale[50], Benjn Corbin[51]

1816-001 Roll and Minutes of 2 Mounted Rifle Companies attached to 2nd Battalion of 85th Regiment, Fauquier County at Morrisville

- 7/13/1816 Minutes of Proceedings, Company of Mounted Rifleman attached to 2nd Battalion, 85th Regiment of Fauquier County, at Morrisville (Cont.)

N S West was chosen Secretary and on counting the Votes
    Thomas Brown, was unanimously elected Captain
    Sydnay F. Chapman was elected 1st Lieutenant
      Charles B. Ficklin   "   "   2   Ditto
    James C. Stephens "   "   3   Ditto

They are therefore respectfully offered to the Worshipful County court of Fauquier, as propper [sic] persons to be recommended to the Executive, to be commissioned as above.
    (Signed) N S West Secretary

1816-002 Lieutenant Henry D. Hale's certificate for oath as officer of 44th Regiment, 5th Brigade, 2nd Division of Militia of Virginia   Jany 1816 Produced + Ordered to be filed.

Fauquier County [abbreviation is illegible]
    I James Pickett a Justice of the peace for the county aforesaid do hereby certify that Henry D Hale this day personally appeared before me and took the oaths required by Law to execute the office of a Lieutenant in the forty fourth Regt fifth Brigade and second Division of the Militia of Virginia – Given under my hand the 11th day of January 1816.
    (Signed) James Pickett

1816-003 Eppa Hunton recommended as replacement for Troop of Cavalry lately commanded by Captain Wm. R. Smith, resigned.

To the County court of Fauquier
    In behalf of the Troop of Cavalry lately commanded by Capt William R. Smith, we recommend Eppa Hunton as a proper person to fill the vacancy as ocasiond [sic] by his resignation, -- who has been duly elected by the members of the Troop.
Octo 28th 1816 --   (Signed)   J.B. Hunton – 1st Lieut.
                                        John Hampton – Cornet

---

1816-004 Officer Recommendations for Captain Eppa Hunton's Cavalry Troop

To the court of Fauquier County
    Martin E. Carter recommended as 1st Lieut. In room of Silas B. Hunton resigned.
    John Walden, do, Second Lieut. In room of Martin E. Carter promoted.
    Alexander Edmonds, do, Cornet in room of John Hampton resigned.

The above Gentlemen were duly elected by the Troop of Cavalry I command and are recommended by Eppa Hunton.

1816-005 Agreement of Samuel Warner to be substitute for Samuel Gordon for 6 months service and other papers in Warner v. Gordon's Breach of Contract Suit papers

- **Bill of Complaint**

Fauquier county to wit

Saml Warner complains of Saml Gordon in custody +c of a plea of breach of covenant. For that whereas heretofore to wit on the 30th day of July 1814 at the county aforesaid by a certain agreement in writing then and there made, between the pltff of the one part and the defendant of the other seal'd with the seals of the defend^t and the pltff and now hereunto the court shewn, the date whereof is on the same day and year aforesaid, the pltff agreed at the special instance and request of the defendant to perform as a substitute for the defendant a tour of Militia duty which the defendant had been call'd on to perform in consideration whereof the defendant then + there bound himself to pay to the pltff twenty dollars p^r month for the time the pltff should continue as a substitute as aforesaid, and the defendant still further provided by his covenants as afores^d that he the defend^t would pay the pltff for the whole six months service at the rate of twenty dollars p^r month if there should be a peace, or the said pltff should be discharged before the expiration of the said six months;

And it was still farther provided by the covenant afores^d that if before the expiration of the said six months the s^d pltff should be call'd in which case the s^d defd^t would be compelled to go in the place of the s^d pltff, that then from the time the s^d pltff should be so afores^d call'd, his pay as afores^d should cease.

And the pltff avers that he will and truly performd the defd^{ts} tour of duty until therefrom discharg'd by the proper officer, by means of which discharge the defd^t was relievd from the performance of the tour of duty, and the said pltff saith that [word illegible] truly and sufficiently perform'd every thing containd in s^d covenant to be perform'd, and that Neither the pltff nor any other person for him was call'd on to perform his own tour of duty during the continuance of the afores^d six months.

Nevertheless the defendant hath altogether faild to perform his covenants and agreem^{ts} in said covenant contain'd, but the same hath altogether broken, in this that he hath not paid the pltff for three months and a half at the rate of $20. A month and the s^d defd^t his covenant afores^d hath altogether broken to the damage of the pltff $120. + therefore he brings suit +c.   Moore p.q.

- **7/30/1814 Covenant between Samuel Gordon and Samuel Warner**

Know all men by these presents that Mr. Saml Gordon of the one part and Saml Warner of the other part have agreed as followeth that I Saml Warner have agreed and do hereby agreed to perform a tour of Militia duty as a substitute for Saml Gordon who has been call'd on, said term of service suppos'd to be six months.

- **7/30/1814 Covenant between Samuel Gordon and Samuel Warner**

And the said Saml Gordon for and in consideration of the s^d promise and agreement agrees to pay to said Saml Warner twenty dollars per month for the time the s^d Saml Warner may continue a substitute as afores^d but if before the expiration of the said six months, Saml Warner should be call'd in which case Saml Gordon will be compelled to go in the place of the said Saml Warner then + from that period the pay of the said Saml Warner is to cease.

1816-005 Agreement of Samuel Warner to be substitute for Samuel Gordon for 6 months service and other papers in Warner v. Gordon's Breach of Contract Suit papers (Cont.)

If there should be a peace or the said Saml Warner is discharg'd before the expiration of the said six months then and in that case the pay is not to stop but continue on until the [word illegible] end and term of six month in part of the said twenty dollars p^r month.[He?] hereby binds himself to pay immediately fifty dollars, the s^d Saml Warner, not to bound untill the s^d fifty are p^d witness whereof the s^d Saml Warner hereto sets his seal, and the s^d Saml Gordon and [space left blank] his security for the faithful performance of the several matters and agreed to by the said Saml Gordon bind themselves. July the 30th 1814.

     (signed) Samuel Warner (Seal)
Test   Saml Gordon   (Seal)
 Peyton R. Grimsley   (Seal)

I do hereby promise + bind myself to pay to Saml Warner or his afsigns the Amount that may be due him in the service of the [word illegible; crossed out] U States. Now under the Command of Capt Wm. Dooling.
     (signed) Saml Gordon
Test   1st Augt 1814
 Peyton R. Grimsley

It is my wish, in case I should fall in the Service of the U States in place of Saml Gordon that My Sister Matilda Bose shall [word illegible] and inherit all the money, Debts, or property of any kind that may be ["be" interlined] due or pofsefsd by me at the time.
Teste   (signed) Samuel Warner
 Saml Gordon
 Peyton R. Grimsley
 Thomas G. T. Gordon

- **Warner vs. Gordon} In Cov^t**
  1816 March   Cont^d
  1816 29 August W. Enq^{ry} set aside covenant not broken + join^d
      A Jury Verdict for Plt + Judgment according to
      Verdict + for costs

  $1251.

 Fifa issued
 Moore pq
We the Jury find for the pltff + asses his damages at seventy dollars being the prin^l [word illegible] due + that Ints is to commence thereon from the first day of February 1815
    (signed) Walter A. Smith

1817-001 Order for Justices to convene to consider Militia Recommendations
At a Court of Quarterly Sessions held for Fauquier County the 24th Day of March 1817
 It is ordered by the court that the Sheriff of this county Summon the Justices of the Peace of said county to attend on the Second day of April court next for the purpose of Nominating + Recommending to the Executive of this Commonwealth fit and proper persons to fill vacancies in the Militia officers command in this County.
 A Copy
  Test
   Danl Withers C Cl

1817-002 Memorandum of Agreement and other papers in Suddoth v. Martin Breach of Covenant Suit Papers
- **Bill of Complaint and Verdict of Jury**
Fauquier County to wit

Lewis Suddoth complains of William Martin in custody +c of a plea of covenant broken for that on the 8th day of Sept. 1814 in Camp near the White House on the River Potomac to wit in the County aforesaid by a certain memorandum and agreement made and entered into by and between the said Pltf and defendant sealed with the seals of the said Pltf + Deft. and to the court now here shewn the date whereof is on the same day and year aforesaid it was agreed by and between the said Pltf and Deft. that the said Deft. should pay to the Pltf two hundred Dollars to take his the said Martins Place and perform his Tour of duty under Capt William Dulin or any officer he may be required to serve under untill the tour of service expired;

And a discharge for the said Martins Tour should be procured and the said Pltf agreed to perform the said Deft. Martins Tour as above for the aforesaid sum to be paid to him on his return except sooner called for or to his heirs Executors Administrators or assigns in case said Pltf should not call in person and the Pltf avers that he did well and truly perform the said Martins Tour of service under Capt. William Dulin and such other officers as he was required to serve under untill the term of service expired and he was duly discharged and did thereby from the day and year first mentioned entirely exonerate and discharge the said Deft from all service his Tour of duty + service aforesaid and hath in all things kept and performed the covenants and agreements afores^d on his part to be performed;

But the Deft. hath not kept and performed the covenants aforesaid on his part to be performed but hath broken the same in this that he the said Deft did not pay to the said Pltf on his return from the said Tour of duty the aforesaid sum of two hundred Dollars nor any part thereof but the same to the Pltf to pay although often required hath not paid but he [word illegible; crossed out] entirely refused and still doth refuse to the damage of the Pltf $500. And therefore he brings suit +c.

(Signed)   Scott [word illegible]

We of the Jury find for the Pltf and assess his damages to the sum of one hundred and seventy Dollars the principal sum due and Interest is to commence thereon on from the 1st day of Jany 1815. All which we assess for his damages.
(Signed)   Wm White

Sudduth vs. Martin} Nar[rati]^o, tc.	1817 Ap^l Cont^d
1816 13 Apl. Contd. Decl[ation]	9 Sept. Geo. Martin Sp[ecia]^l bail.
13 May Decl[ation] Filed C.O. vs. Deft. [word illegible]	Jury verd[ict]+ Jud[gment] $11:68
13 June R. to plead	
13 July C.O. conf[irme]^d + W[rit] of Inq^{ry}	

1816   10 Sept In[-]^y set aside
Cov[enan]^{ts} perf[orme]^d by [word illegible] J^d Contd.

- **9/8/1814 Memorandum of Agreement between William Martin and Lewis Suddoth**
Memorandum between William Martin + Lewis Suddoth both of the County of Fauq^r + State of Virginia, Now in Camp near the white House on the River Potowmac.

The said Martin agrees to pay the said Suddoth Two hundred Dollars, to take his (the said Martin's) place, and perform his Tour of duty under Capt. Wm. Dulin or any officers he may be required to serve under until the term of Service has expired + a discharge for the said Martin's Tours is procured.

1817-002   Memorandum of Agreement and other papers in Suddoth v. Martin Breach of Covenant Suit Papers (Cont.)
- **9/8/1814 Memorandum of Agreement between William Martin and Lewis Suddoth**

The said Suddoth agrees to perform the aid Martin's Tour as above, for the aforesaid Sum, to be paid to him on his return, except sooner called for, or to his heirs Executors Administrators or assigns, in Case said Suddoth should not call in person. In testimony whereof both parties have hereunto set their hands + seals this 8th Sept. 1814.
    (signed)   Wm Martin (seal)
                 Lewis Suddoth (seal)
Teste
  Wm Thompson

1814 Sept.8th Rec^d of Wm Martin Thirty Dollars in part of the within Contract.
    (Signed) Lewis Suddoth

- **Lewis Suddoth's Discharge from Service signed by Captain Wm. Dulin**

Lewis Suddith a private in my Company in the service of the United States has honourably discharged a tour of duty for William Martin in the year 1814.
    (Signed) William Dulin   Capt of 36 R[rest of word illegible], of Virginia Militia
    (Signed) Enoch Renne Senr Col^o of the 36 Reg^t

1817-003   Papers from slander suit filed by Wm. Thompson against James English
- **Bill of Complaint**
Fauq^r County   to Wit –
William Thompson complains of James English in Custody +c of a pleas of Trespass on the case for this to wit that whereas the said William Thompson is a good true honest citizen of this Commonwealth and as such hath always conducted himself and [word illegible] the committing of the several grievences [sic] by the said James English as herein after Mentioned was always reputed esteemed and respected by and among all his Neighbours and other good and Worthy Citizens of this Commonwealth to whom he was in any wise known to be a persons of good name fame and Credits to wit at the county aforesaid and whereas the said William Thompson hath not ever been guilty or until the time of committing of the said several grievances by the said James English as hereinafter mentioned been suspected to have been guilty of the offences and Misconduct hereinafter mentioned to have been charged upon and imputed to the said William Thompson or of any other such offences or Misconducts –

By means of which said premises he the said William before the committing of the said several grievances by the said James English as hereinafter Mentioned had deservedly obtained the good opinion of all his Neighbours and other good + Worthy Citizens of this commonwealth to whom he was in any wise known to wit at the County aforesaid and whereas also before the commitment of the several grievances by the said James English as hereinafter Mentioned he the said William was Selected and deputed to superintend a drawing of certain numbers or Ticketts [sic] for the clothing and organization of the Militia of the County aforesaid for public service and on such drawing he the said William did attend and superintend as Manager + conducter [sic]thereof –

1817-003   Papers from slander suit filed by Wm. Thompson against James English
- **Bill of Complaint** (Cont.)

To wit at the County aforesaid – Yet the said James English well knowing the premises but greatly injuring the happy state and condition of the said William and contriving + wickedly and maliciously intending to injure the said William in his good Name fame and Credit and to bring him into public Scandal infamy + disgrace with and among all his Neighbours and other good Worthy Citizens of this commonwealth and to cause it to be suspected and believe[d] by those Citizens and Neighbours that he the said William had been and was guilty of conducting the ordering the aforesaid fraudulently and dishonestly in concert with a certain John Smith in order to clear and acquit the said John Smith of the foot service and that he the said William had an understanding with the said John previous to the drawings aforesaid that he the said William would fraudulently and dishonestly acquit the said Smith of the service aforesaid to the great injury of the public service aforesaid.

[H]e the said defendant on the   day of [space blank] at the County aforesaid in the presence and hearing of diver good Citizens of this Commonwealth did Speak Utter and publish of and concerning the Plaintiff divers false scandalous + malicious Words purporting that he the said William conducted the ordering aforesaid fraudulently + dishonestly and ["conducted the ordering...dishonestly" interlined] had an understanding with the said John Smith previous to the drawing aforesaid in order to fraudulently and dishonestly to acquit the said John Smith of the foot service aforesaid to the great injury of the public service aforesaid and that he the said William acted in concert with the said John to effect the fraudulent + dishonest drawing aforesaid—

By means of the committing of which said several grievances by the said James English as aforesaid he the said William hath been and is greatly injured in his said good name fame + credit + brought into public scandal infamy and disgrace with and among all his Neighbours and other good + Worth Citizens of this Commonwealth insomuch that divers of those Citizens + Neighbours to whom the innocence + integrity of the said William in the premises were unknown have or occasion of the committing of the said grievances by the said James English as aforesaid for thence hitherto suspected and believe and still do suspect + believe the said William to have been and to be guilty of the offences + Misconduct aforesaid and have by reason of the committing of the said grievances by the said James English as aforesaid from thence hereto wholly still do refuse to have any transaction acquaintance or discourse with him the said William as they were before used and accustomed to have and otherwise would have had.

To the damage of the Pltf of One thousand dollars + therefore he brings suit.

Pledges to prosecute   Scott pq
John Doe,
Rich Roe

[Jacket of suit papers:]
Thompson vs. English} Na^r
1814   14 Sept. Oct. Nov. + Dec. Contd. Decl.
1815   Jan^{ry} Decl. Filed
       Feby R to plead
       March   C.O.   Conf^d + Jury
       April   W. of Inq^{ry} set aside + not guilty j^d -- -- Moore
       July + Sept.   Cont^d
1816   Ap^l + Sept. Cont^d
1817   Ap^l Cont^d

1818-001   Return to Court of Election of Carola G. A. Jennings as Cornet with recommendation by Captain Eppa Hunton endorsing election
Carola G. A. Jennings was elected by the Troop of Cavalry to supply the vacancy of Cornet, in room of Robert N. Norris resigned. I unite with them in recommending him to the Court of Fauquier Cty.
                (signed) Eppa Hunton Capt.
                    23ᵈ Nov 1818

1818-002   April through May 1818 Orders for Justices to convene to consider Militia Recommendations [NOTE: only one summons is presented here]
Sct. Fauquier April Court 1818
    Ordered by the Court that the Sheriff of this County Summon the Justices of said County to attend on the first day of the next term for the Purpose of Recommending Militia Officers.
            A Copy
                Teste
                    D Withers

1818-003 Thomas Groves' Pension Declaration for service in Revolutionary War with affidavit of Captain Daniel Marr regarding Groves' service
    Thomas Groves of the county of Fauquier made oath in open court of said county that **in the fall of 1779 or eighty** he does not precisely remember which **he enlisted as a private in the continental army of the Unite Sates for three years**, that as such he first **march'd to Richmond** then to the county of chesterfield where he remain'd about **six months under Col° Davis** – from **thence to Cumberland Court House** in the sᵈ State of **Virgᵃ where he remained some two or three months** – from thence he was march'd to York town in Vᵃ at which place he acted as a soldier during the siege – that he was **during the sd siege attached to a body of troops call'd Poseys detachment after which he was march'd as a soldier thro the Carolina's into Georgia – that he remained in the South as a soldier about two years that he was finally discharg'd in Richmond Vᵃ in the year 1783** – That at the period of his discharge + for some time **previous he belonged to a company commanded by Capᵗ Alexʳ Parker of Westmoreland.**

    He the said Thoˢ Groves further stated upon oaths that he is **upwards of fifty years of age, has a wife + children**, that he is in very reduced circumstance and needs the assistance of his country.

    Capᵗ Danˡ Marr of the county of Fauquier made **oath in open court that in the year 1779 or 1780 he belong'd to a class of militia** of the said county in the state of Virginia which class **was required to furnish one man as a soldier for the continental army** – And that the said Class did furnish the aforenamed Thoˢ Groves whom he always understood + believes was recᵈ as the said class was discharg'd upon their furnishing the said Thoˢ Groves – that he always understood and believes that the said Thoˢ Groves continued as a soldier until about the end of the war – He farther states that the sᵈ Thoˢ Groves is in ~~needy~~ indifferent circumstances + has a wife + children and needs the aid of his country.   (signed)   Daniel Marr   (Seal)

The foregoing statements of Thoˢ Groves and Danˡ Marr were severally sworn to in open court this 27 of March 1818.
            Jn° A.W. Smith D.C.   F.C.C.

1818-003 Thomas Groves' Pension Declaration for service in Revolutionary War with affidavit of Captain Daniel Marr regarding Groves' service (Cont.)

It appearing to the satisfaction of the court from the affidavits of Thos Groves petitioner of Capt Danl Marr and from the reputation prevalent in this county that the sd Thos Groves served as a soldier on the continental establishment in the revolutionary war with Great Britain for at least three years next before the conclusion thereof and that he is now in such reduced and distress'd circumstances as to require the aid of his country for a support

It is ordered that the foregoing affidavits and proceedings thereon be certified to the Secretary of the Department of War for the United States.

    Groves, Thomas} Affidavit   27 March 1818 Ordered to be certified

---

1818-004   David Ball's Pension Declaration for service as a soldier in 3rd Virginia Regiment in Captain John Blackwell's Company

David Ball of the county of Fauquier and State of Virginia in order to obtain the benefit of the late act of Congress entitled "An Act to provide for certain persons engaged in the land and naval service of the United States in the Revolutionary War" appeared in the Court of the said county and made oath that he **enlisted on the 18th of February 1778 in the service of the United States under Capt John Blackwell attached to the third Virginia Regiment commanded by Col. William Heath.**

[T]hat he was in **an engagement at Monmouth as a continental soldier**; that he was **discharged on the 19th day of February 1779 at Middlebrook New Jersey by Capt Jno Blackwell** - making a term of service of one year as a Soldier in the revolution—that he has lost his discharge and has no other ["no other" is interlined] evidence of his having been a soldier in the continental establishment but his own affidavit ^ + the affidavits of Jno + Jos: Blackwell ^ that he is in reduced circumstances and needs the aid of his country for support –

    (signed)   David (X) Ball

22nd June 1818
Sworn to in Open Court
    Jno A.W. Smith D.C. F.C.C.

Colo Joseph Blackwell made oath in open court that **he well remembers to have seen** the aforenam'd **David Ball during the revolutionary war, serving as a soldier on the continental establishment** tho he cannot state how long he remain'd as a soldier   sign'd by sd   Jo Blackwell

Sworn to in Open Court 22nd June 1818
    Jno A.W. Smith D.C. F.C.C.

1818-005   Pension Declaration of John Powell, a soldier attached to 1st Virginia State Regiment
District of Virginia S^{cfs}

On this [space left blank] day of [space left blank] 1818 personally appeared in open court, being a court of Record for the county of Fauquier in said district **John Powell, aged Sixty two years**, resident in said county in said district, who being first duly sworn according to law, doth, on his oath declare, that he served in the Revolutionary war as follows:

That he the said John Powell **enlisted as a private under Capt Thomas Ewell of the county of Prince William** in said district, more than three years before the end of said War, and **was attached to the first State Regiment of Virginia, Commanded by Colo Gibson** – Afterwards transfered to the Regt commanded by **Colo Blueford** after its defeat, and **marched to the South** – **was taken sick and left at Hillsboro N. Carolina** – Marched from thence and **joined Genl D. Morgan on the field just at the time he had secured his victory at the Cowpens** –

1818-005   Pension Declaration of John Powell, a soldier attached to 1ˢᵗ Virginia State Regiment (Cont.)

[He] **returned to Virginia and was attached to the first Regᵗ commanded by Colᵒ Dabney; was at the siege and capture of Lord CornWallis;** and continued in the said service of the United States til the declaration of Peace and he ["he" is interlined] received his discharge – that his former declaration was made in the Month of May 1818, and Nᵒ marked on his **Pension Certificate 1.398.**

And I do solemnly swear that I was a resident citizen of the United States on the 10ᵗʰ day of March 1818; and that I have not since that time, by gift, sale, or in any manner, disposed of my property, or nay part thereof, with the intent thereby so to diminish it, as to bring myself with in the provisions of an act of Congress, entitled "An act to provide for certain persons engaged in the land and naval service of the United States in the Revolutionary War" passed on the 18ᵗʰ day of March 1818; and that I have not, not has any person in trust for me, any property or securities, contracts, or debts due to me; nor have I any income, other than what is contained in the schedule hereto annexed, and by me subscribed—

Schedule

Real estate, none – Personal estate, one hog worth five Dollars, one broad ax $2.50 – 2 narrow axes $40.00 handsaw $1.67 – draw knife $1. – 2 froes 1.25 1 Chissel .33 – 2 hoes .67—debts due me, less than 20. Dollars— His occupation, a rough carpenter, but little bodily strength to pursue it – **No family, a wife aged fifty seven years (and sickly) One daughter, named Frances, aged about thirteen years, (sickly) a son, Robert aged eleven years and grand daughter Kitty, aged three years—**

Sworn to in Open Court this 24ᵗʰ July 1820. (signed) J.A.W. Smith D.C.

1818-006   William Thayer's Pension Declaration for services as Private, Corporal and Sergeant attached to 5ᵗʰ Virginia and then to 3ʳᵈ Virginia, Revolutionary War

District of Virginia Scfs

On this 26ᵗʰ day of July 1818 personally appeared in open court being a court of Record for the County of Fauqʳ in said District **William Thayer aged sixty nine** years resident in the said County of Fauquier in said District who being first duly sworn according to Law doth on his Oath declare that he served in the revolutionary War as follows:

That he the said William Thayer **enlisted** in the said Service (to the best of his recollection) ^ **in the autumn of 1775 with a Captain Burgess Ball** ^ who was afterwards promoted to Col Ball **in the County of Lancaster** in said District **for the term of two Years and was attached to the fifth Virginia Regiment at the expiration of** said Term He enlisted under Captain Henry Fantleroy who was killed at the Battle of Monmouth of the same Regiment **for the term of Three years** that before the expiration of said time **he enlisted under Captain John Blackwell of Fauquier county** in said District **for the term of during the War and was attached to the third Virginia Regiment**.

That during the said service he was **at the Battles of Brandywine Germantown and Monmouth**. That he was **at the capture of the Hessians at Trenton and was engaged against the enemy** on the first and Second of January, following **at Trenton and Princeton. That he was with General Green at the Battle of the Euland Springs and Genˡ Morgan at the Cow pens. That he was at the siege and capture of Cornwallis in Virginia after which he marched to the South with a regᵗ commanded by Colonel Thos Possey [sic] and cont[inued] in the South until the proclamation of Peace in Savanna.**

That he was [word illegible] from Charleston S.C. to Richmond Virginia where he received his discharge. That exclusive of the before mentioned engagements he was in a variety of skirmishes in both the Northern and Southern States. That he was **seven years and ten months in** said **service during which time he served as a private, Corporal, Sergeant, + Sergeant Major.**

1818-006 William Thayer's Pension Declaration for services as Private, Corporal and Sergeant & Sergeant Major, attached to 5th Virginia and then to 3rd Virginia Regiments, Revolutionary War (Cont.)

And I do solemnly swear that I was a resident citizen of the United States on the 18th day of March 1818 and that I have not since that time by gift sale or in any manner disposed of any property or any part thereof with intent thereby so to diminish it as to bring myself within the provisions of any Act of Congress entitled "An Act to provide for certain persons engaged in the Land and Naval Service of the United States in the Revolutionary War["] passed on the 18th day of March 1818. And that I have not nor has any person in trust for me any property or securities contract or debts due to me nor have I any income other than contained in the Schedule hereto annexed and by me subscribed.

Schedule of Property of Wm Thayer

Real Estate - None – Personal Estate Six Shoates 2 pegs worth $3.00 carpenter tools - 1 Broad ax $1.25 1 narrow ax 1.75—2 augurs 75—4 chissels 1.—making in all Twelve dollars and Seventy five cents Debts due me None but owing money

(Signed) Wm Thayer

The said William Thayer also mentions his **occupation** to be that of a **coarse carpenter** that in common he enjoys good health and considering that the addition of less than three months will finish his seventieth Year under these circumstances he leaves to others to judge of his ability to pursue his avocation.

That he **married a wife in January 1781** who is now living with him who has brought him Nine living sons and seven ^ daughters ^

That **in the late conflict with the British Government one of his sons entered the United States Cavalry under Captain Littlejohn two others the Virginia Militia one of whom died at Norfolk.**

His present family by the aforementioned **wife aged about fifty two Years (infirm) sons Hiram, 18 years; Albert, 9 years; Taliaferro, near 8 Years; Older Daughter, Betsy 12 Years; and Francis 11 Years old.**

That his original declaration was made before Robert White in the second Week of April 1818 and his own **pension certificate** date the 4th day of May 1818 and marked on the back **317**.

(Signed) Wm Thayer

1818-007 Recommendations for Officers in Captains Ball and Nashes Company

In Capt Balls Company
 Joseph Caldwell is recommended to suply the Vacancy occasioned by the Resignation of Lee^t Armsted Kemper
 A Braham Millan as Ensign to supply the place of Ensign John ["John" interlined] Marr Resigned.

In Capt Nashes Company
 Ensign Stewart is recommended as Lee^t in the place of Dudley Fitzhugh who refus^d to serve
 ~~William Thornberry} Candidates for the Ensigns commission~~
 John Hampton} is appointed by the Court Ensign in the room of Stewart promoted.

1819-001   Pension Declaration of John Bell for service as a waggoner for artillery
Fauquier County, State and District of Virginia

On this 25th Novbr 1819 before the County court of Fauquier State and District of Virginia personally appeared **John Bell aged fifty eight years** resident in the County, State and District aforesaid who being first duly sworn according to law, doth on his oath, make the following declaration in order to obtain the provisions made by the late Act of congress entitled an Act to provide for certain persons engaged in the land and naval service of the United States in the Revolutionary War

That **in January 1782 in the County of Prince William and State of Virginia he enlisted** as a ~~waggoner~~ **under Henry Margaram a Conductor of the artillery with the rank and pay of Captain, for the term of 12 months**, that the said **Margaram was under the Command of col. Wadsworth and Carter who superintended the transportation of the artillery from York in Virginia to Boston and belonged to Rochambeau's Brigade**,

That the said John **Bell was employed as a waggoner** in the same service that **he served two months longer than the term of his enlistment on continental establishment** for the whole time from January 1782, that bout the beginning of the year 1783 he **received a written discharge at Sheffield in Massachusets by Major Aliott**,

That he has **since lost his discharge**, that the only evidence in his power is the **annexed affidavit of Capt Chs Atwell a conductor of the artillery in the revolution and a resident of the County of Fauquier and State of Virginia**,

That the said John Bell is in reduced circumstances and stands in need of the assistance of his Country for support, as will satisfactorily appear from the annexed affidavit of Nathaniel Grigsby, Baylis Grigsby and Peter Adams.

- **Affidavit of Need by Nathaniel Grigsby, Baylis Grigsby and Peter Adams**

Fauquier County to wit.
This 24th November 1819 Nathaniel Grigsby, Baylis Grigsby and Peter Adams credible witnesses of full age, appeared in open Court and made oath that John Bell a petitioner for a pension from the Unites States is aged and infirm, that he has a family of children, is a man of truth and respectability and is in such reduced and indigent circumstances as to stand in need of the assistance of his County for support.

Sworn to in Open Court this 24th day of November 1819. (signed) Jno A.W. Smith D.C.

- **Affidavit of Charles B Atwell, formerly a conductor of the Artillery in the Revolutionary War with rank and pay of Captain**

Fauquier County.
This 25th Novbr 1819 Charles B. Atwell a credible witness aged 55 years says that **he [is] well acquainted with John Bell the petitioner that he has known him since they were boys, that in the year 1782, the affiant was a conductor of the artillery in the revolutionary [war] with the rank and pay of a Captain, that in the year 1782 the said John Bell enlisted as a soldier for the term of 12 months, under Henry Margaram a conductor of the artillery, with the rank and pay of a captain in the said war**

That they served under Colo Wadsworth and Carter in transporting the ammunition and artillery from York in Virginia to Boston

1819-001 Pension Declaration of John Bell for service as a waggoner for artillery (Cont.)

- **Affidavit of Charles B Atwell, formerly a conductor of the Artillery in the Revolutionary War with rank and pay of Captain**

That the affiant served with the deponent from January the time of Bell's enlistment to December 1782 when they were separated, that he believes that the Deponent served two months longer than his enlistment and was discharged at Sheffield, Massachusetts that he was a good and faithful soldier.

Sworn to in Open Court this 25th day of Noveb^r 1819 (signed) Jn° A.W. Smith D.C.

1819-002 Certification of David Ball's service in Revolutionary War as soldier in Captain John Blackwell's Company, 3rd Virginia Regiment
Fauquier County Virginia 9th March 1819

I do certify that **David Ball inlisted [sic] in my Company of the 3rd Virginia Regiment on Continental establishment during the war of the Revolution, sometime in the early part of** the Year **of seventeen hundred and seventy eight, to serve one year which service he performed faithfully**, He was a brave peaceable and a good Soldier. **He is now blind**, he therefore deserves assistance from the government. Given under my hand the date above.
    (Signed) John Blackwell

Fauquier County to Wit, Genl John Blackwell, late a captain in the Revolutionary army, personally appear^d before me, a Justice of the peace for said County + made oath that the foregoing Certificate contains the truth to the best of his knowledge. Given under my hand this 5th day of August 1819.
    (Signed) Wm Thompson

1819-003 Three 4/27/1819 summons to Justices to recommend Militia Officers for Fauquier County [NOTE: Only one summons appears here]
At a Court Continued and held for Fauquier County the 27th day of April 1819
It is ordered by the Court that the Sheriff of this County Summon the Justices of said County to attend on the first day of July Court Next for the purpose of Recommending Militia Officers in this County.
    A Copy
        Teste
            (Signed) Daniel Withers CC

1819-004 Three 9/28/1819 summons to Justices to recommend Militia Officers for Fauquier County [NOTE: Only one summons appears here]
At a Court continued and held for Fauquier County the 28th day of September 1819
Ordered that the Sheriff summon the Justices of this County to attend on the first day of the next Court for the purpose of Recommending Militia Officers for this county.
    A Copy
        Teste
            (Signed) Danl Withers

1819-005 Election of Militia Officers
George H. Payne Lieut.
James English Ensign in Capt. Ball's Company of the 85th Reg^t V^a Fauq^r Cty

Armistead Utterback was elected Cornet in my company on the 2nd Saturday in October to fill the vacancy occasioned by the resignation of Cornet Chew.   (signed) Martin E. Carter Capt V. M.

1820-001 John Horrell's Pension Declaration as soldier in 1st Maryland Line

Fauquier county District of Virginia

On this 27th day of March 1820 personally appeared in open Court being a Court of record for the s[d] County; being a Court of record made so by the Constitution and laws of Virginia and possessing an unlimited Common Law and Chancery Jurisdiction and pofsefsed also of the power of fine and imprisonment **John Horrell aged upwards of sixty years** resident of the County afors[d] in s[d] District who being first duly sworn according to law; doth on his oath declare that he served in the revolutionary war as follows.

That he the s[d] **John Horrell served in the first regiment of the Maryland line under Colonel Peter Adams** commander of the s[d] regiment and that he **enlisted under Capt. William Bruce**. That he **enlisted in** the year **seventeen hundred and seventy eight for the duration of the war**; that he was **discharged in** the year **seventeen hundred and eighty three at the house of General Smallwood in Charles County State of Maryland**; that he is unable to state the date of the original declaration proved before the Hon. Lee Robert White Judge of the Superior court of Law for the County afors[d]; a record of which he has not preserved; that he has rec[d] his pension up to the 4th of March 1820 and that the **number of the pension Certificate is 15.301.**

I, John Horrell do solemnly swear that I was a resident citizen of the United States on 18th of March 1818 and that I have not since that time; by gift; sale; or in any manner; disposed of my property; or any part thereof; with intent thereby so to diminish it; as to bring myself within the provisions of an Act of Congress entitled; "An Act to provide for certain persons engaged in the land and naval service of the United States; in the Revolutionary War" passed on the 18th of March 1818; and that I have not; nor has any person in trust for me; any property or securities; contracts or debts due to me; nor have I any income other than what is contained in the schedule hereto annexes; and by me subscribed.

The following is a schedule of the property of the s[d] John Horrell
    3 head of horses, 13 old sheep, 7 lambs; 7 head of Cattle, 22 hogs;
    4 pair of Gears, one lot of tools, one lot of ploughs and a wagon;
    6 chains, a table and a chest; 2 wheels and 2 bee stands, kitchen furniture.

Debts owing by the s[d] John Horrell amounting in all to eighty eight Dollars.

The declarant also states that he is a **Farmer on rented land**; that he is quite unable to pursue his business; that **he is nearly blind; and disabled in his shoulder; that he has nine children; four of which live with him and are minors; whose names are John, Peter, Nancy, Isaac;** two of which are able to help him in some things, tho very little.

                                                his
                  (Signed) John (X) Horrell
                           mark

Sworn to and declared on the 27th day of March 1821
Fauquier County   27th March 1821
    Sworn to in Open Court   (Signed) Jn[o] A.W. Smith   Clk. F.C.C.

1820-001 John Horrell's Pension Declaration as soldier in 1st Maryland Line (Cont.)

- **Charles Chinn's Affidavit as to Need of Petitioner**

Fauquier County Virginia

This 27th March 1821. Charles Chinn a credible witness of full age appeared in open Court and made oath that he has for several years been well acquainted with the above named John Horrell, that he is in needy and indigent circumstance and cannot support himself without public or private charity.

(signed) Chas Chinn

Fauquier County 27th March 1821

Sworn to in Open Court.   (signed) Jno A.W. Smith Clk. F.C.C.

- **John Horrell's Schedule of Property**

The Amount of John Herral's Propperty

To three head of horses		$82.50	To one Waggon	$25.00
To thirteen oald Sheap and seven Lambs		$20.00	To Six Chears [Chairs]	$ 2.00
To seven head of Cattle		$46.00	To one table	$ 4.00
To twenty two head of hogs		$27.50	To one Chest	$ 2.00
To four pare of geear	[gear]	$15.00	To two Wheals +c	$ 6.00
To one Lot of Twols	[tools]	$ 5.00	To the Kitchen furniture	$ 5.00
To one Lot of plows		$ 9.50	To two bee stands	$ 4.00

[total] $253.50

Debts owing by the said Herald   88

the Property Valeyed By John Strother, Lewis Strother, Armsted Bannon

$165.50

1820-002 Spencer Anderson's Pension Declaration

Fauqr County—State + District of Virginia

On this 29th day of August 1820 personally appeared in open court, in the county of Fauquier + State of Virginia, being a Court of record, made so by an act of assembly invested with common law, + Chancery Jurisdiction, unlimited in point of amount, + with the power of fine + imprisonment, keeping also a record of its proceeding; **Spencer Anderson Senr in his seventieth year**, resident in the said county who being first duly sworn according to law, doth on his oath, declare that he served in the Revolutionary War as follows—

That he **inlisted** ^ in the year 1776 ^ as a soldier for ^ the ^ term of **two years under Capt Philip Lee, of the 3d Virginia Regiment continental establishment** which Regiment was ^ then ^ **commanded by Col Thomas Marshall, afterwards by Col Wm Heath, from whom he obtained an honorable discharge**, at the expiration of the time for which he inlisted, which **discharge was lost while he was on a Militia tour in 1778**—

That he was **in the battles at Brandy Wine + German Town, had a wound over the eye at Princeton**, where he was also in a battle; That his original declaration was made as well as he can recollect in the Spring of the year 1819, and the **number of his pension Certificate is 12.459**—

And the said Spencer Anderson Senr doth solemnly swear that he was a resident citizen of the United States on the 18th day of March 1818, and that he hath not since that time, by gift, sale, or in any manner disposed of his property, or any part thereof, with intent, thereby so to diminish it, as to bring himself within the provisions of an act of Congress entitled an act to provide for certain person[s] engaged in the land and naval service of the United States in the Revolutionary War passed on the 18th day of March 1818 and that he has not, nor has any person in trust for him, any property or securities, contracts or debts due to him, nor has he any income other that what it contained in this Schedule hereto annexed + by him Subscribed.

1820-002 Spencer Anderson's Pension Declaration (Cont.)

That he is **by occupation a coarse carpenter**, but that from his age, the failure of his eyesight, and pains, he is unable to ^ do ^ half the work of an able bodied man, and what he does do, is not done in workman like manner.

That he has a **Wife named Susan in her seventy sixth year, that they live with their son,** on whose hospitality they are entirely dependant.

      Schedule of the property of the said Spencer Anderson Senr
        A Sett of coarse carpenters tools}
        a Square black walnut table   } $7.00
        a Garden hoe   }
                                  his
           (signed) Spencer (X) Anderson Senr
                         mark

Witness: Thos Hampton
Sworn to In Open Court

1820-003 David Ball's Pension Declaration as a private in Captain John Blackwell's Company of 3rd Virginia Regiment, Revolutionary War

Fauquier county State + district of Virginia

On this 29th day of August 1820 personally appear'd in open court of the County of Fauquier Virginia, being a court of record made so by act of Assembly, invested with common law and chancery jurisdiction unlimited in point of amount and with the power of fine and imprisonment keeping also a record of its proceedings David Ball in his <u>sixty second</u> year resident in the said county who being first duly sworn according to law doth on his oath declare that he serv'd in the revolutionary war as follows

That he **enlisted in Feb'y 1778 under Capt Jno Blackwell of the 3rd Virginia Reg^t on continental establishment commanded by Col Heath** ; that he **enlisted as a private soldier for twelve months and serv'd the s^d twelve months in the s^d Reg^t and was honorably discharg'd.**

That he **serv'd as a private soldier in the said reg^t at the battle of Monmouth**—That he was **discharg'd at Middlebrook in Jersey, which discharge he hath since lost**—that the evidence of his services will more fully appear by a reference to his declaration filed in the war office of the United States made in the county court of Fauquier on the 28th December in the year 1819 and that the **date of his pension certificate is 4th of May 1820 and the number thereof 16.835** and that he hath not rec^d anything on account thereof—

I David Ball do solemnly swear that I was a resident citizen of the United States on the 18th of March 1818 and that I have not since that time by gift sale or in any manner disposed of my property or any part thereof with interest thereby so to diminish it as to bring myself within the provisions of an act of congress entitled an act to provide for certain persons engaged in the land and naval service of the united states in the revolutionary war pass'd on the 18th March 1818 and that I have not nor has any person in trust for me any property or securities contracts or debts due to me nor have I any income other than what is contain'd in the schedule hereto annexed and by me subscribed—That is to say –**a life interest in about eighty acres of broken land in the county of Fauquier**—

1820-003 David Ball's Pension Declaration as a private in Captain John Blackwell's Company of 3rd Virginia Regiment, Revolutionary War

That he hath a small mare, for which he hath ^ been ^ unable to pay and for which he is still in debt—one cross legg'd walnut table half dozen ^ pewter ^ plates, knives + forks—three or four stools and benches, one cow and calf and a bull and four hogs and five shoats

That I have no trade or profession whatsoever and that I am **entirely blind**

That **all my children are grown but are destitute** or nearly destitute of property or of obtaining their own subsistence without labour.
                    (signed) David Ball
Sworn to in Open Court
    Thos C. Kelly De. C.

The court proceeded to value David Balls property as contained in his Schedule as follows to wit:

80 acres of land	$20.00 p annum
1 mare	nothing
1 walnut table	1.50
6 pewter plates	2.00
6 knives + forks	1.00
Stools + Benches	1.50
1 Cow + Calf	15.00
1 Bull	8.00
4 hogs + 5 shoats	12.00
	$ 61.00

1820-004 James Arrow Smith's Pension Declaration, as a soldier in Captain Wm. Washington's Company and then drafted into Colonel John Willis's Regiment, Revolutionary War.

Fauquier County, State and District of Virginia

On the 23 day of Oct^o 1820 personally appeared in open Court in the county of Fauquier Virginia, being a Court of Record made so by Act of Assembly, invested with Common Law and Chancery Jurisdiction, unlimited in point o Amount and with the power of fine and imprisonments, keeping also a Record of its proceedings, James Arrow Smith age seventy two years ["years" interlined] resident in the said county who being first duly Sworn according to Law doth on his oath declare, that he served in the Revolutionary War as follows—

That he **enlisted in Stafford county Virginia for the term of two years under Captain William Washington** who enlisted a **company of foot soldiers and marched to the North** –

That **after he served the two years to the North and was discharged he returned home when he was drafted for eighteen months and marched into service under Col^o John Willis, served the eighteen months under Col^o John Willis to the south, and was discharged at Cumberland Old Court House in the state of Virginia by General Scott**—

That the annexed is his **Certificate of Pension numbered 3590**, that he has received his Pension under it up to the 4th day of March 1820

1820-004 James Arrow Smith's Pension Declaration, as a soldier in Captain Wm. Washington's Company and then drafted into Colonel John Willis's Regiment, Revolutionary War. (Cont.)

I James A. Smith do solemnly swear, that I was a resident citizen of the United States on the 18th of March 1818, and that I have not since that time by gift, sale or in any manner disposed of my property or any part thereof with intent thereby so to diminish it, as to bring myself within the provisions of an Act of Congress entitled an Act to provide for certain person engaged in the land and naval service of the United States in the Revolutionary War passed the 18th March 1818, and that I have not nor has any person in trust for me any property or securities contracts or debts due to me—

Nor have I any income other than what is contained in the Schedule hereto annexed and by me subscribed that is to say, one horse eleven or twelve years old, two cows on calf and three yearlings, three small sows and seven pigs, tow old ploughs, two aces, four old hoes, on grubbing hoe, one old pair of plough gears, some few old Irons Tc belonging to an old Waggon, two very indifferent beds, one old table, three old chairs, tc and debts due to me doubtful as to solvency, amounting to eighty five dollars—that I live on poor land rented from year to year

That I am scarcely able to do any work myself from the weaknefs and infirmities of age and from a wound received in my right ancle [sic] which causes a weakness and lameness—

That my **family consists of myself and wife Levinia aged forty six years**

That all my property in the aggregate including the eighty five dollars in doubtful debts amounts to about one hundred and fifty three dollars and seventeen cents [and] that my circumstances require the aid of my Country for my support.

         His mark
  (Signed) James (X) A. Smith

Sworn to in Open Court ["in Open Court" interlined] and declared on the 23rd day of October 1820 before the County Court of Fauquier, Virginia. (signed) Jn° A. W. Smith D.C. F. C. C.

1820-005 William Drone's Revolutionary War Pension Declaration as soldier in Captain John Rodolph's Cavalry Company and then in Legion of Light Dragoons commanded by Colonel Henry Lee.

Fauquier County, State and District of Virginia
  On this 29th Day of August 1820 personally appeared in open Court in the county of Fauquier Virginia, ... **William Drone, aged fifty nine years**, resident in ...[Fauquier] county, who being first duly sworn according to Law, doth on his oath, declare that he served in the Revolutionary War as follow:

That **he enlisted in Leesburg, Virginia for the term of the War under Stephen Lewis, a Cornet in a Troop of Cavalry, commanded at that time by Capt John Rodolph + afterwards by Capt Farthing ONeale, belonging to the Legion of Light Dragoons commanded by Col. Henry Lee.**

That he **served upwards of four years and six months when he was discharged at Charlston South Carolina**, by a public order

That he was **in the Battles of Guilford, Enticus [?] and in [at] the capture of several forts and [in] various skirmishes.**

That the evidence of his services will more fully appear by a reference to his declaration and the **affidavit of Lieut. Wm Harrison, filed in the War Office of the United States.**

1820-005 William Drone's Revolutionary War Pension Declaration as soldier in Captain John Rodolph's Cavalry Company and then in Legion of Light Dragoons commanded by Colonel Henry Lee. (Cont.)

That his original declaration was made in the county Court of Fauquier Virginia on the 28th Day of May 1818.

That the annexed is his **certificate of pension, numbered 1051**. That he has received his pension under it up to the 4th Day of March 1820.

I, William Drone do solemnly swear that I was a resident citizen of the United States on the 18th March 1818 and that I have not since that time, by gift, sale or in any manner disposed of my property or any part thereof....and that I have not, nor has any person in Trust for me any property or securities, contracts or debts due to me, nor have I any income other than what is contained in the schedule hereto annexed and by me subscribed...

[Schedule:] two horses, six head of sheep, six hogs, two shovel plows, three hoes and one ax, seven chairs and one table +c.

I [the next word is scratched out and illegible] a **piece of land rented from year to year. I have been unable to work for three or four years past, from the numbness and infirmities of age attended by a painful complaint in the Breast**...

My family consists of my wife (her name is illegible], 54 years old and three sons, ... Richard, Henry and Thomas, aged sixteen years, fourteen years and ten years; and one daughter Eleanor, age twenty years. [My daughter] is afflicted with a palsy and is able to perform a little house work occasionaly [sic] at the [next two words are illegible] intervals of her disease.

... the support of [Wm. Drone], his wife, daughter and sons depends upon the labor of two of the last... their support is scant and is partly derived from the kind assistance of their neighbors... his circumstances require the aid of his County for his support.

                                            his
                            (Signed) William (X) Drone
                                           mark

Amount of Property $109.24

Sworn to and declared on the [blank] Day of [blank] 1820 before the County Court of Fauquier Virginia.
    (Signed) Jn° A. W. Smith   D. C. F. C. C.

Fauquier County, State and District of Virginia

Wm. B. Smith and French Utterback, credible witnesses of full age, appeared in open Court and made oath that they are neighbors f Wm. Drone, that he is considered a man of truth, that the annexed is a correct schedule of his property shown to them on the place where he lives... [T]hey believe the situations of his family to be such as he has above described. Signed and sworn in open Court this 29th August 1820.
    (Signed) Wm. B. Smith
              French Utterback
Sworn to in Open Court this 29th Day of August 1820.
    (Signed)   Jn° A. W. Smith   D. C. F. C. C.

1820-006 William Stribling's Revolutionary War Pension Declaration
Fauquier County, State and District of Virginia

On this 15th Day of September 1820, personally appeared in open Court... **Wm. Stribling, aged about sixty three** years, resident in ... [Fauquier] county... who being first duly sworn according to law; doth on his oath declare that he served in the Revolutionary War as follows:

That he first **enlisted early in ... 1778 under Capt John Francis Mercer of Fredericksburg, Spotsylvania County, Virginia.**

That **at the close of the year [17]78, he re-enlisted in the same company ^ for during the war ^ at that time commanded by Lieutenant Auther Lynn, of the third Virginia regiment on continental establishment ^** which Regiment was commanded by Col. Heath ^ **[A]t the close of the year 1778, he returned home on furlough, and rejoined the army in the spring of 1779.**

That he was **marched to the south and then attached to the second Virginia** detachment of new levies **commanded by Heath and Wallace.**

That he was **taken prisoner at the siege of Charlston** + that **when he was discharged from his captivity he returned home with Genl Scott.**

That **shortly after his return he was sent for to join a small party at Fredericksburg, com[an]ded by Capt. Barbour + marched from thence to Cumberland old C^t House, from whence he was sent to take charge of some prisoners, back of Winchester where he remained until he was finally discharged.**

That he was ^ **in the service** ^ **from the time of his first enlistment until the end of the war...** He was in the **battles of Molmouth [Monmouth] in Jersey and at the siege of Charleston.**

That he made his original declaration, before the hon. Robert White... he received his pension up to [the] 4th of March 1820... **his Certificate of Pension is dated the 22nd of December 1818 and numbered 5.015.**

I, Wm. Stribling do solemnly swear that I was a resident citizen of the United States on the 18th March 1818, and that I have not since that time by gift, sale or any other manner disposed of my property... I have not, nor has any person for me in trust, any property or securities, contracts or debts due to me, nor have I any income, other than what is contained in the schedule hereto annexed and by me subscribed.

[Word is illegible] nothing except his wearing apparel... **[H]e employs himself in attending to the business of a Widow sister, with whom he lives** ^ and from whom he has derived his support for several years ^ ... **he has neither wife nor children living with him**... [H]is support is very narrow and insufficient for ordinary comfort.. from his age, he cannot, without private or public aid, support himself.
                (Signed)   William Stribling

Subscribed, sworn to and declared by the aforesaid Wm. Stribling on this 15th Day of September 1820, before the Jud[ge] of the Superior Court of ...[Fauquier] county...

15 September 1820. Sworn to in Open Court.
                (Signed) D. Rodes   D^y C.   F. S. C.

1820-007 Philip Lynor's Revolutionary War Pension Declaration
Fauquier County, State and District of Virginia

On this 29th August 1820 personally appeared in open Court in the County of Fauquier, Virginia… **Philip Lynor, upwards of seventy years old**, resident of … [Fauquier] County … who being first duly sworn according to law, declare[s] that he served in the Revolutionary War on continental establishment as follows:

That **he enlisted in the infantry under Capt John Chilton, of the 3^d Virginia Regiment, commanded by Col. Mercer and Col. Weedon.**

That [he] **enlisted at first for [a] term of two years… and served his time**

That he **afterwards enlisted under Captain Elias Edmonds in [Fauquier] County for [a] term of three years, of the Artillery and served until Gates defeat when he was taken prisoner**

And that he was afterwards **discharged at Richmond, Virginia, having made his escape from the enemy.**

That he was **in the Battles of Brandywine, Princeton, Trenton, Germantown and Gates defeat**

That the evidence of his services will more fully appear by a reference to his declaration and the affidavit of Alexander Patton filed in the War Office of the United States… his own declaration was made before the Honorable Robert White…annexed is his **certificate of pension, numbered 8.580**… he has received his pension up to [the] 4th March 1820.

I, Philip Lynor do solemnly swear that I was a resident citizen of the US on the 18th March 1818 and that I have not since that time by gift, sale, or in any manner disposed of my property or any part thereof…I have not, nor has any person in Trust for me, any property or securities, contracts or debts due to me, nor have I any income, or property of any description whatsoever except my wearing apparel.

…I am **by profession a shoemaker and [I] live at the Poor House of Fauquier, Virginia. I have five children: Polly, Peggy, Nancy, Betsey and Thomas, a Millright living at a considerable distance from me,** from neither of which I obtain any aid… from lameness [and] the weakness of old age and want of sight I am unable to work at my trade… my wife is at the Poor House with me.

… I am entirely dependant upon public and private charity for support and need the assistance of my Country.
    (Signed) Philip Lynor
Sworn to and declared on the 27th August 1820 before [the] County Court of Fauquier, Virginia.
    (Signed) Jno A. W. Smith D.C. F. C. C.

1820-008 John Laws' Revolutionary War Pension Declaration

Fauquier County, State and District of Virginia

On this 29th August 1820, personally appeared in open Court for the County of Fauquier, Virginia **John Laws... in his sixty third year**, a native and resident of [Fauquier] county... who being first duly sworn according to Law, doth on his oath declare

That **on the 1st August 1776, he enlisted in the Musketry under Captain Thomas Ransdell and Captain William Blackwell of the 11th Virginia Regiment, commanded by Col. Daniel Morgan and Col. Feebecker for the term of three years**

That **after the resignation of Cap'Blackwell, he served in the same Company under Captain John Marshall** (the present Chief Justice) **for the full term of [his] enlistment**

That he was **discharged in the State of New Jersey in 1779**... he was **in the Battles of Germantown and Stony Point**

That the evidence of his service will more fully appear by a reference to his declaration and the affidavit of John Marshall filed in the War Office of the United [States] and also the affidavits of Samuel Elliott and Joseph Parker filed there... his original declaration was made before the Hon. Robert White, in [Fauquier, Virginia]... annexed is his certificate of pension, numbered 7001... he has received his pension up to [the] 4th September 1819.

I, John Laws do solemnly swear that I was a resident citizen of the United States on the 18th March 1818 and that I have not since that [time] by gift, sale or in any manner disposed of my property or any part thereof... I have not, nor has any person in Trust for me, any property or securities, contracts or debts due to me, nor have I any income or property of any description whatsoever, except that which is contained in the Schedule annexed and by me subscribed ...   1 Bay Mare tc.

... I am **a Farmer by Trade and live upon a piece of land ^ rented ^ from Year to Year at forty dollars per year... my family consists of a wife Margaret Laws, aged forty years and two children, Sally aged four years and John H. aged eighteen months...** my wife is unable to labour and capable only of light domestic employments...they [i.e. wife and children] are solely dependant upon my labour for subsistence... their support is scant and ... I need the assistance of my County for myself and [my] family.

(Signed)   John Laws

Sworn to and declared on the 29th August 1820 before the County Court of Fauquier, Virginia.

(Signed) Jnº A. W. Smith   Dy Clk F. C. C.

1820-008 John Laws' Revolutionary War Pension Declaration: Papers in File

A List of Mr John Laws property Valued by Thomas L. Maddux & Craven Maddux, Augt 25th 1820.

		$	
	Bay Mare sixteen years old	30.	00
Horses	Sorrel colt one years old	17.	00
Cows	two old Cows + Calf	25.	00
	1 Heifer + two yearlings	18.	00
Hogs	three Small Sows + Barrow @ $3.	12.	00
	Five small shoats @ $1.	5.	00
	Ten head Sheep @ $1.20	12.	00
	Three Bead [beds] and furniture @ $15.	45.	00
	One old Chest and Trunk @ $1.	2.	00

1820-008 John Laws' Revolutionary War Pension Declaration: Papers in File (Cont.)

A List of Mr John Laws property Valued by Thomas L. Maddux & Craven Maddux, Augt 25th 1820.

Two old Tables and Six old Chairs	3. 20
old Cupboard and Small parcel Earthenware	2. 00
one set k[n]ives + forks	0. 75
Two old pewter Dishes, three Small Rasors and twelve old puter plates	3. 00
one wool and flax wheel @ $1.	2. 00
Three old pots, oven and Skillet	4. 00
three pare pot hooks, Laddle, Fresh forks + Skimmer	1. 50
pare plough Gear and Stone Crock	2. 33
one ax, two hoes and old Lumber	2. 50
	$187.28
Flat irons and wodden ware	1. 66
	$188. 94

Monies Due by Mr Lawes   1st January 1821

Land Rent to Bernard Hooe Senr	40.00
Tax on Land	3.12 ½
Bond due French Flowerrees Adm^s	8. 50
Bond Due for hire of old Negro woman	10. 00
Bond due Jo^s Carr	
	$61.17 ½
	$188.06

        (Signed)   John Laws

List of John Laws property
    One Mare + Colt, 2 cows and one Calf
    One Heifer and two yearlings, ten head sheep
    Nine head of hogs, three beads [beds?] and furnature [sic]
    Two tables, one Chest, 1 trunk, 1 cupboard with some Earthenware
    Three Pots, one oven, one skillet, Flesh forks, Ladle + knives
    Pot hooks, 6 cairs [chairs?], 2 pewter Dishes, 3 small Pewter basons
    12 Ditto [pot hooks], 2 Flat irons, 1 Stove, Pot and 2 Jugs
    1 woolen wheel, 1 Flax wheel + 1 Reel, 1 set of Plow Gear
    1 set water vessels

Notes on John Laws' Revolutionary Service

John Laws enlisted 1 Augt 1776. Company commanded by Capt^t Wm Blackwell – 3 y^s—afterwards commanded by Capt John Marshall (Now CJ--) 11th Virginia Reg^t commanded by Co^l Danl Morgan – afterwards Co^l Feebecker == Honorably discharged == afterwards served in Virg^a Militia + was in the service at the surrender of Cornwallis—Germantown ["Pensy^a" is interlined] – Stony point – Ap^t 3-4 Jany 1821.

    Wife Margaret ~~twice mar~~^{d} – aged about 40 – 2nd Wife – Name of Children: Sally Ann, upwards of 3, John Horton, 18 months, 20 [next word is illegible]

    N^o of Certificate 7001 – before Judge Robt White

1820-008 John Laws' Revolutionary War Pension Declaration: Papers in File (Cont.)
John Laws' Account with Joseph Carr

Mr Jno Laws	To Joseph Carr	D^r
To Note		$109.50
In^t on same to July 4th 1817=13 Years, 1 Mon.		86.41
		$195.71
deduct Payment made July 4th 1817 –		30.00
		$165.71
In^t on balance to Ap^l 20th 1820 –		27.35
		$193.26
deduct Payment made Ap^l 20th 1820 –		50.00
		$143.26
In^t on balance to this time = 2 months –		1.43
		$144.69
To Note Laws + Norriss	$15.00	
In^t on same to Octr 1st 1809, 10 Years --	9.00	
	$24.00	
deduct bal. Due on Old Books on 1st Octr 1809 --	7.88	
	$16.12	
In^t on bal. To this time = 10 years 9 Mon.	9.60	
	$25.72 =	$25.72
to Note	$11.25	
In^t 8 ¼ Years	5.44	
	$16.69 =	$16.69
Balance on new Books [word illegible] tc p^r son Saml in 1812 --		.96
Am^t due Jos Carr		$188.06

Augt 7th 1820   p^r Caldwell Carr, p^r Joseph Carr

Note $109.50 dated May 12th 1804
Ditto $ 15.00 dated Sep^t 1799
Ditto $ 11.25 dated Ap^l 21st 1812

1820-009 James Lyon's Revolutionary War Pension Declaration
Fauquier County, State and District of Virginia
    On this 29th Day of August 1820 personally appeared in open Court in the County of Fauquier Virginia… **James Lyons, in his sixty fifth year**, resident in … [Fauquier] County, who being dully sworn according to law, doth on his oath declare that he served in the Revolutionary War as follows:

    That he **enlisted as a soldier for the term of 2 years under Captain Gustavus Brown Wallace, of the 3^d Virginia Regiment on continental establishment, commanded by Col. Mercer + Lieut. col. George Weedon, at Falmouth, now in Stafford County, Virginia.**

1820-009 James Lyon's Revolutionary War Pension Declaration

That he **served under Captain Wallace** ^ one year + ten months ^ **and Captains Lowe** ^ two months, making together ^ in the Musketry the term of two years

That he was **discharged at Philadelphia, by Captain Lowe… he has lost his discharge**

That he was **in the Battles of Harlem Heights and the White Plains**

That the evidence of his service will more fully appear by a reference to his declaration and the affidavit of Robert Randolph filed in the War Office of the United States… his original declaration was made in the County Court of Fauquier Virginia on the 22nd Day of ["June 1818" is interlined]… the annexed **is his certificate of pension, numbered 5259**.. He has received his pension under it up to 4th March 1820.

I, James Lyon do solemnly swear, that I was a resident citizen of the United States, on the 18th March 1818 and that I have not since that time by gift, sale or in any manner disposed of my property or any part thereof…

That I have not, nor has any person in Trust for me, any property or securities, contracts or debts due to me, nor have I any income other than what is contained in the schedule hereto annexed and by me subscribed…

One shop Board, one goose, a pair of [word is illegible] and scissors, a set of tea cups and saucers and six tea spoons, one looking glass, a shaving Box and a Razor and one earthen Bowl…

I am, **by profession, a Taylor… I have no wife and three children, John, James and Nancy, aged forty years, thirty-seven years and thirty-three years… none of them live with me…** [and] I obtain no assistance from either of them.

[I am] **afflicted with Rheumatic Pains,** [and am] too infirm and unable from defect of sight to support [my]self by [my] trade…

[James Lyon] is a **boarder in a private family** and … from his pension … draws his support solely and contributes as much as he can to the comforts of the family in which he lives [next two words are crossed out and illegible] by participating with them in such things as his pension affords… he is unable to support himself without the assistance of his Country or private family.

                    (Signed)   James Lyon

The foregoing property [is] estimated at $4.30

Sworn to and declared on the 29 Day of August 1820 before the County Court of Fauquier, Virginia
                    (Signed) Jno A. W. Smith   D^y Clk,   F. C. C.

1820-010 Thomas Groves' Revolutionary War Pension Declaration

Fauquier County, State and District of Virginia

On this 30th August 1820, **Thomas Groves** personally appeared in open Court... who being first duly sworn according to law, doth on his oath declare that he served in the Revolutionary War as follows:

That he **enlisted for the term of three years** at the Court House of ... [Fauquier] County... as a soldier in the Musketry

That the first Captain under whom he served was **Captain Charls [?] Chilton of the 11th Virginia Regiment, commanded by Col. Davis.**

That he was, **in a month, transferred to a detachment commanded by Major Posey**

That **at the end of the three years, he enlisted again [for] during the War under Captain Alexander Parker of Virginia, in South Carolina, also under the command of Major Posey... he served until the end of the War and was discharged at Richmond, Virginia by Gen¹ Lincoln**

That he was **at the siege of York [town], and a skirmish at Petersburg Virgᵃ and the defeat of the Indians near Savannah.**

That his original declaration was made before the Hon. Robert White, one of the Judges of Virginia ... the annexed is his **certificate of pension, numbered 520**... he has received his pension up to the 4th March 1820.

I, Thomas Groves, do solemnly swear that In was a resident citizen of the United States on the 18th March 1818 and that I have not since that time by gift, sale or in any manner disposed of my property or any part thereof...

I have not, nor has any person in Trust for me, any property or securities, contracts or debts due to me, nor have I any income other than what is contained in the schedule hereto annexed and by me subscribed...

1 Iron Pot, 1 Dutch Oven, six knives and Forks, 1 Chest, 1 Pine Table, two axes, 2 Hoes, 3 Augurs, 3 Chizzels [sic], 1 Shoe Hammer, 1 pair of Pincers, 5 or 6 Aniles, 6 plates, 1 small Dish, 1 Coffee Pot, 2 small Tin buckets

I live on a small piece of rented land consisting of a Garden with a House for which I pay a rent of forty dollars, in making and mending Plow, 3 Stocks, making and mending shoes and doing repairs to the Houses of my Landlord.

My **family consists of a wife named Milly, aged about seventy years and one child named Lucy aged sixteen years, residing with me**... My **wife is infirm**, she occasionally spins, makes and [word is illegible] and works in the Garden. My **daughter is very sickly** and has, ever since her childhood, has been under a Doctor ['s care] ... **since May last, I have had a disease supposed to be a white swelling which obliges me to Walk upon a Crutch**... I am unable to support myself and family without the assistance of my Country.

    (Signed) Thomas Groves

Subscribed, sworn to and declared in open Court by Thomas Groves on the 30th August 1820.
    (Signed) Thoˢ C. Kelly   Dʸ C. F. C. C.

1820-010 Thomas Groves' Revolutionary War Pension Declaration (Cont.)
Fauquier County, Virginia

This 30th August 1820, Robert Green appeared in open Court and made oath that he has been acquainted with Thomas Groves [for] many years, that he is very poor and in destitute circumstances, that he lives on a rented lot and that none are more in need of assistance for the support of himself and family than … Thomas Groves.

Sworn and subscribed by
       (Signed)   Robt Green

Subscribed + sworn to by Robert Green this 30th Day of Augt 1820.

$ 8.   (Signed) Thos C. Kelly   D^y Clk

1820-011 Rust Hudson's Revolutionary War Pension Declaration
Fauquier County, State and District of Virginia

On this 30th Day of August 1820 personally appeared in open Court… **Rust Hudson, aged sixty seven years in January last,** resident in … [Fauquier] County… who being first duly sworn according to law doth on his oath, declare that he served in the Revolutionary War as follows:

That he **enlisted in … 1775 for the term of two years under Ensign Thomas Catlett and Captain Samuel Hanes in the County of Caroline, Virginia, of the 2nd Virginia Regiment commanded by Col. William Spotswood**

That **at the end of his term at Valley Forge, he enlisted under Cornet Presley Thornton until the end of the War, of the 3d Virginia Regiment of Cavalry commanded by Col. George Baylor, and afterwards by Col. William Washington**

That he was **discharged at Nelson's Ferry in 1783 by Gen. Green**

That he was **in the battles of Brandy Wine, Germantown, Cowpens, Guilford Court House, Campdens [?] and Eutaw Springs**

That his original declaration was sworn to before the Hon. Robert White, one of the Judges of Virginia… he has received his pension up to the 4th September 1819… his **certificate of pension** is hereto annexed, **numbered 7.249**.

I, Rust Hudson do solemnly swear that I was a resident citizen of the United States on the 18th March 1818… I have not since that time, by gift, sale, or in any manner, disposed of my property or any part thereof… I have not nor has any person in Trust for me, any property or securities, contracts or debts due to me; nor have I any income other than what is contained in the schedule hereto annexed and by me subscribed…

1 Sow, six pigs [number illegible] Shoats, 1 Axe, 2 hilling hoes, 1 Dutch Oven, 1 Shoe Knife, 1 Case Knife, 2 forks, 4 Spoons, 1 plate, 2 dirt pans, 1 Dirt Pot

I live upon a piece of Land free from Rent, holding it at the pleasure of James Marshall Esqr and cultivate as much as I can with my own hands.

1820-011 Rust Hudson's Revolutionary War Pension Declaration (Cont.)

My family consists of a **wife name Anne, aged sixty five years**, she is a sickly woman, supposed to be in a consumption; a **daughter named Elizabeth aged thirty-two years** and **a Grand Daughter named Ursa, aged seven years**, Elizabeth helps ~~me in~~ cultivating the land. She also attends to the House and takes care of her mother and niece...

[I am] unable to support [my]self and family without the assistance of [my] Country.
    (Signed)   Rust Hudson

Signed, Sworn to and declared in open Court on the 30th August 1820 by Rust Hudson.
    (Signed) Thos C. Kelly   D^y C   F. C. C.

Fauquier County, State of Virginia
    This 30th August 1820, Nimrod Farrow appeared in open Court and made oath that he has been acquainted with... Rust Hudson [for] many years, that he is very poor and infirm and unable to do much, that his family and its situation is such as he has represented in the above declaration.
    (Signed) N. Farrow
$11.37
    Subscribed and Sworn to in open Court by Nimrod Farrow on the 30th August 1820.
    (Signed) Thos C. Kelly   D^y C   F. C. C.

1820-012 Benjamin McKnight's Revolutionary War Pension Declaration
District of Virginia, S^{ct} Fauquier County, S^{cf}

On this 30th Day of August personally appeared in open Court... for the county of Fauquier... **Benjamin MacKnight, aged Sixty four years**, resident in ... [Fauquier] county... who being first duly sworn according to law, doth, on his oath, declare that he served in the Revolutionary War as follows:

... That he... **enlisted in the service of the United States in the Revolutionary war in August 1776 for the term of three years under Capt. Abraham Shepperd, who was under the command of Col^o Rollins in the Brigade of Genl Mercer.**

That **after the capture of Fort Washington, he was attached to the Rifle Regiment commanded by Col^o Danl Morgan.**

That after the promotion of Col^o D. Morgan to Genl, he served **under Col^o Wm Buttler in the company of Capt. Gabriel Long.** During [his]... service, he was **at the capture of the Hessians at Trenton**; at the **battle of Princeton, at the capture of Genl. Burgoine** and under the command of Col^o Buttler, was at the **burning of two Indian towns: on the Susquehanna and Onieda Lake.**

That after the expiration of the ... three years, he served in the Militia, and was **at the capture of Lord Cornwallis.**

That his former declaration was made before Judge Holmes, he thinks in November 1818; and the **Number marked on his Pension certificate [is] 7300.**

1820-012 Benjamin McKnight's Revolutionary War Pension Declaration (Cont.)

... I do solemnly swear that I was a resident... citizen of the United States on the 10th Day of March 1818 and that I have not since that time by gift, sale, or in any manner, disposed of my property, or any part thereof, with intent thereby so to diminish it...

That I have not, nor has any person in trust for me, any property or securities, contracts, or debts, due to me; nor have I any income other than what is contained in the Schedule hereto annexed, and by me subscribed.

Schedule: Real Estate   None.   Personal Estate due me on open accompt from a deceased brother's estate about eighty Dollars and Sixty cents.

                        his
(Signed)   Benjamin **O** McKnight
                     mark

... Benjamin McKnight has **no family** and latterly has resided at the house of [his deceased] ...brother.

... His occupation is a labouring agriculturalist, which he performs in much pain at times, in consequence of a broken belly. (Necessity requiring the labour).

                      his
(Signed)   Benjamin **O** McKnight
                    mark

Signed, Sworn To and declared in Open Court on this 30th Augt 1820.

(Signed)   Thos C. Kelly, Dy C.   F. C. C.

1820-013 John Smith's Revolutionary War Pension Declaration
Fauquier County, State and District of Virginia

On the 29th Day of August... 1820, personally appeared in open Court... **Jno Smith, aged Sixty seven years,** resident in Fauquier County, ... who being first duly Sworn according to law, doth on his oath, declare that he served in the Revolutionary War as follows.

That in ... **1777 he inlisted [sic] in Philadelphia as a soldier for three yrs under Capt Colbert, in the Second Pennsylvania Regiment, Continental establishment, commanded by Col Flowers.**

That he **served two years in the company commanded by ... Capt Colbert in the [2nd Pennsylvania]... Regiment, commanded by ... Col Flowery.**

That he was **transfered [sic] to the Company of Artificers commanded by Capt Sparks in the City of Philadelphia, under whom he served ou the balance of the time for which he enlisted** and was then afterwards **honorably discharged, which discharge he has since lost in the City of Baltimore.**

That **during his... service he was in the battles of Brandy Wine, German Town + Monmouth and recd a wound in the right leg at German Town.**

That his Original Declaration was made (as well as he can recollect) in April 1818, and the **number of his Pension certificate is 237.**

1820-013 John Smith's Revolutionary War Pension Declaration (Cont.)

... Jn° Smith doth solemnly Swear that he was a resident citizen of the United States on the 18th Day of March 1818 and that he hath not since that time, by Gift, Sale, or in any manner disposed of his property, or any part thereof with intent thereby so to diminish it ... he has not, nor has any person in Trust for him, any property or securities, contracts or debts, due to him, nor has he any income other than what is contained in this Schedule, hereto annexed, and by him Subscribed.

That he is, **by occupation, a coarse shoe maker**, but that from his age, the failure of his eye sight, and occasional pain from the wound he received, is not able to do half the work of an able bodied man.

That he has a **wife named Leanner, aged 45 years; a daughter named Sally, aged 15 years; and a son named Joseph aged between 13 and 14 years; another son named William, aged 11 years + a daughter named Mary, aged 9 years; all living with him.**

That they have no trade, nor greater capacity to contribute to their support than is common to persons of their age + are a cause of expence [sic] to him.

Schedule of Jn° Smiths Property

A Sett coarse shoe Makers tools, a sow + three pigs, one axe, one Spade, one broad Hoe, one black Walnut table, one pine table, six flag bottom chairs, two iron pots, one tea kettle, one dutch oven, two water tubs + two piggins.

                his
(Signed)   Jn° X Smith
                mark

Sworn to in Open Court the 29th of August 1820.
    (Signed)   Jn° A. W. Smith   D. C.   F. C. C.

1820-014 John Roach's Revolutionary War Pension Declaration
Fauquier County, State and District of Virginia

On this 31st August 1820, personally appeared in open Court... **John Roach, aged sixty years in June last,** resident in the County of Fauquier Virg^a... and previous to January last a resident in the County of Prince William, Virg^a, who being first duly sworn according to law, doth on his oath declare that he served in the Revolutionary War as follows.

That he, **in ... 1777... enlisted for the term of three years in the County of Fauquier Virginia under Lieut. John Green of the Artillery of the 1st Virginia Regiment, commanded by Col. Harrison and Col. Carrington of Virginia. He served the term of three years**... [W]hen he joined the Regiment, [it] was commanded by Capt Thomas Batrop [?]. ... he was **discharged in 1780 at Morristown, New Jersey by Col. Edward Carrington**.

That he was **in the Battle of Monmouth and various small skirmishes**.

That his original declaration was sworn to before the Hon. Wm A. G. Dade of Prince William, one of the Judges of the General Court of Virginia and of the Circuit Court.

1820-014   John Roach's Revolutionary War Pension Declaration (Cont.)

That his **pension certificate** is hereto annexed, **numbered 8.653**.

That he has received his pension up to the 4th September 1819.

... I John Roach do solemnly swear that I was a resident citizen of the United States on the 18th March 1818 and that I have not since that time, by gift, sale, or in any manner, disposed of my property, or any part thereof, with intent thereby so to diminish it... I have not, nor has any person in trust for me, any property or securities, contracts or debts due to me; nor have I any income other than what is contained in the schedule hereto annexed and by my subscribed...
    1 old Mare, 1 Sow and 7 Pigs, 3 Shoats ^ 1 Cow ^

I am by occupation a farmer and live upon a lot of land containing forty five acres for which I have agreed to give the sum of three hundred and fifty dollars. I have paid no part of this money. The land is encumbered with a Deed of Trust for the payment of it. I purchased it with a [word illegible] of paying for it out of its products and such part of my pension as I should be able to save after supporting myself and family.

My family consists of a wife named Patty, aged sixty years in September; and one son named Gerard, aged five or six and twenty; and two daughters named Letty and Polly, aged twenty years and nineteen years. My son sometimes works with me but generally for himself, my daughters live with me, they are fed by me, they [next 2 words are illegible] and work for themselves, without contributing at all to my support and my wife's.

My wife is a weakly woman and from her age can only perform light domestic duties.

The furniture in my house, such as it is, belongs to my children I [word illegible] it at their will and pleasure, **I am unable to work steadily and without the aid of my Country; from a hurt received in the shoulder, I cannot support myself and wife.**

Sworn to, declared and subscribed in open Court this 31st August 1820.

    (Signed)   John + Roach
    (Signed)   Jn° A. W. Smith   D. C.   F. C. C.

Fauquier County, Virginia
    Allen Stewart and Thomas Stewart, credible witnesses of full age appeared in open Court and upon their oaths, say that they are near neighbors of ... John Roach.
    That the above is a correct list of his property.

That it is not worth more than forty four dollars.

That his circumstances are very indigent and that the condition of himself and family [rest of sentence is on the fold and illegible]

(Signed)   Thomas Stewart, Allen Stewart

Sworn to in Open Court this 31st day of August 1821
    (Signed) Jn° A. W. Smith   D. C.   F. C. C

1820-015   John Bell's Revolutionary War Pension Declaration

On this 26th December 1820, personally appeared in open Court... **John Bell, aged fifty nine years**, a resident of this County, who being first duly sworn according to Law, doth on his oath, make the following declaration, in order to obtain the provisions made by the Acts of Congress of the 18th March 1818 and the 1st May 1820.

That... **John Bell in January 1782, in the County of Prince William... enlisted as a soldier for the term of twelve months under Henry Margaran, a Conductor of the Artillery with the rank and pay of a Captain. Margaran was under the command of Col. Wadsworth and Col. Carter, both of whom commanded in the transportation of the Artillery from York in Virginia to Boston. They belonged to Rochambeau's Brigade.**

That... **John Bell acted as waggoner in this service [and] served two months more than... his enlistment and [was] on [the] Continental establishment for the whole time... in 1783 he received a written discharge at Sheffield in Massachusetts from Major Alcott,** which he has since lost.

That the only evidence in his power is the **annexed affidavit of Capt' Ch' Atwell**, a conductor of the Artillery in the Revolution and made in this Court on the 25th November 1819.

That the evidence of his indigent and destitute circumstances is the annexed affidavit of Nathaniel Grigsby, Baylis Grigsby and Peter Adams, made in this Court on the 24th November 1819... the declaration to which these affidavits were annexed [is here]because at the succeeding session of Congress, the pension law was materially changed and he was advised that an application under this declaration would be unsuccessful.

... John Bell was in no battle during... his service.

...[H]e is now and has hitherto since his first declaration been unable to procure the attendance of his witness Cap' Ch' Atwell.

In pursuance of the Act of the 1st May 1820, I do solemnly swear that I was a resident citizen of the United States on the 18th March 1818... I have not since that time, by gift, sale, or in any manner, disposed of my property or any part thereof with indent thereby so to diminish it... I have no nor have any persons in trust for me, any property or securities, contracts or debts due to me, nor have I any income other than what is contained in the schedule hereto annexed and by me subscribed.

I have no property of any description except my wearing apparel. I am by trade a cooper. I am crippled and very weak and inform, a waggon having run over me and disabled me.

I have no wife. I have four children. James, aged twelve years; Landy, aged fourteen years; Moses, aged sixteen years; Mary Ann, aged eighteen years. My sons have been bound out to trades; my daughter lives with Landy Calvert. I derive no assistance from either and obtain subsistence by working at my trade when I am able.

                    his
(Signed)   John + Bell
                    mark

Fauq' County to wit:
Sworn to in Open Court this 26th Day of December 1820.

1820-016 William Hughlett's Revolutionary War Pension Declaration
State of Virginia, Fauquier County, SS.

On this twenty ninth Day of August 1820 personally appeared in open Court,... **William Hughlett, aged sixty three years**, resident in [the]... County of Fauquier... Virginia, who being first sworn according to law, doth on his oath, declare that he served in the Revolutionary War as follows:

In the second Virginia detachment ^ on Continental establishment ^ commanded by Colonel John Green and afterwards by Lieutenant Colonel Samuel Haines, and afterwards by Major --- Sneed ^ and was in the battles of Guildford Court House, Camden, Eutaw Springs and siege of '76^

This declarant's first declaration was dated April 28th 1818 ^ as he believes ^ and his ^ **pension** ^ **certificate [is] numbered 3591**

... I do solemnly swear that I was a resident citizen of the United States on the eighteenth of March 1818, and that I have not since that time, by gift, sale, or in any manner, disposed of my property, or any part thereof, with intent thereby so to diminish it... and that I have not, nor has any person in trust for me, any property or securities, contracts or debts, due to me, nor have I any income other than what is contained in the schedule hereto annexed + by me subscribed.

Schedule:
One lease for three lives on fifty acres of land In Fauquier County, one life believed to be expired. One mare fourteen years old; one weavers loom + gear; one axe, two hoes, one shovel plough + gear; two pots, one dutch oven; two pine tables, four flag chairs, one poplar chest; half dozen knives + forks, one dish (pewter); half dozen pewter plates, half dozen earthen plates + 1 dish; five ewes + five lambs; one sow + eight pigs; twenty bushels of rye; one looking glass.

The whole amount [of his schedule of property is] estimated at $100.00

This declarant is a **farmer without any trade, and is troubled frequently with rheumatic pains.** [He] has **a wife, aged fifty four years, two daughters, one of ^ them ^ aged twenty seven + the other, twelve years; two grandsons, whose parents are dead; one of the grandsons, aged about two years + the other, eight months**; all living with this declarant + to be supported entirely by him.

This declarant has no debts due to him and owes more than two hundred dollars.

    (Signed)   W. Hughlett

Sworn to and declared on the 29th Day of August 1820 before the County Court of Fauquier, Virginia
    (Signed)   Jno A. W. Smith   D^y Clk F. C. C.

1820-017 Gideon Johnston's Revolutionary War Declaration Papers
Fauquier County, State and District of Virginia

On this 29th August 1820, personally appeared in open Court... **[Gideon Johnston], aged seventy one years**, resident in [Fauquier] County, who being first duly sworn according to law, doth on his oath, declare that he served in the revolutionary war [as follows]:

1820-017 Gideon Johnston's Revolutionary War Declaration Papers (Cont.)

[He served] first as a volunteer under Captain ^ Richard ^ K. Meade of Virginia... [then]soon after the second Virginia Regiment was raised, ... he enlisted [in that regiment]... as a regular soldier under Captain Richard K. Meade...[He] was afterwards transferred to a Company of Artillery, commanded by Capt Arundel who was killed on Gwinn's Island in York River, Virginia.

That ... a Regiment of Artillery was raised by order of Congress, to which the Company to which he belonged was attached... this Reg^t was commanded by Col. Charles Harrison.

That he received the Commission of a Lieutenant in this Regiment and served as such at Norfolk and Portsmouth, two or three years and was there employed in the erection of forts and other military works.

That he then received the Commission of a Captain in a Regiment of Artillery commanded by Col. Thomas Marshall at Lieut. Col. Elias Edmonds, and was employed in active service until Gate's [sic] defeat.

That upon the reduction of this Regiment, he was a Junior Captain [and] became a supernumerary.... He remained with the Army until the Surrender of Lord Cornwallis at York Town, Virginia... in the siege of Yorktown, he lost his horse by the Batteries of the enemy and the American Army, it being exposed to both...

That all his other property was destroyed by the enemy... the loss of his house [horse?] is proved by the annexed affidavit of Corbin Griffin and Larr. Gibbons.

That... Gideon Johnston has hitherto received a pension under the Act of Congress of the 18th March 1818...the annexed is his **certificate of pension, numbered 232**... the date of his original declaration he can only ascertain by a reference to the Pension Office in Washington, the Judge the Hon. Robt White or the Clerk of this Court, having preserved no record of the declaration, with the affidavits thereto annexed and the proceeding had thereon.

I, Gideon Johnston do solemnly swear that I was a resident citizen of the United States on the 18th March 1818 and that I have not since that time by gift, sale, or in any manner, disposed of my property or any part thereof, with intent thereby so to diminish it...

That I have not, nor has any person in trust for me, any property or securities, contracts or debts due to me; nor have I any income other than what is contained in the schedule hereto annexed and by me subscribed.

[Schedule:] one negro woman aged eighty three years; two walnut Tables, one walnut side Board, one Bureau, one domestic Carpet, one flax wheel, one Cotton Wheel, one Pine Table, one spade, one shovel and a few old Tubs and Barrels, ^ sundry small articles in his shop ^ ... the debts from me exceed the debts ^ due ^ to me...the former consist of unsatisfied Judgments and Bonds, the latter with the exception of a small sum, of open Accounts of which I have no evidence but my own personal knowledge.

... **I have two children, Elizabeth and William**... [William] lives in a store and by that means supports himself. [Elizabeth] is the wife of William Thompson, in whose House I board, he being the keeper of a **public House.**

... I am **by Trade a Tailor**... from defect of sight, the consequence of age, I am unable to pursue it.

1820-017 Gideon Johnston's Revolutionary War Declaration Papers (Cont.)

... I am supported partly by the business of a [next seven words are crossed out and unreadable]...Without the pension which I have received for two years past, the profits of this business would be inadequate to my support.
       (Signed)   Gideon Johnston

Signed and Sworn to and declared in Open Court this 30th Augt 1820.
       (Signed)   Thos C. Kelly   Dy C

- **Affidavits in Gideon Johnston's Pension Declaration Papers**

Fauquier County, Virginia

This 30th August 1820, William McNish and Henry L. Y. Pope, credible witnesses, appeared in open Court and made oath, that they have examined particularly the articles in the Shop of Gideon Johnston; they believe that upon the most favorable estimate that [the articles] are not worth more than one hundred and twenty five dollars.
    Sworn to and subscribed in open Court.
       (Signed) Wm McNish, H. L. Y. Pope
    Sworn to in open Court this 30th Day of Augt 1820.
       (Signed)   Thos C. Kelly   Dy C

Fauquier County, Virginia

This 30th August 1820, James English and William Thompson, credible witnesses, of full age, appeared in open Court and made oath that the articles particularly enumerated in his schedule are worth at a proper estimate, no more than fifty seven dollars.
       (Signed)   Wm Thompson, Jas English
    Sworn to in Open Court this 30th Day of August 1820.
       (Signed)   Thos C. Kelly   Dy C

- **Schedule of Gideon Johnston's Property**
    2 walnut Tables
    1 Walnut Side Board
    1 Bureau   1 Carpet   1 Flax Wheel
    1 Cotton Wheel
    1 Pine Table
    1 Spade
    1 Shovel
    Tubs + Barrels

Being call'd in by Capt G. Johnston, We are of opinion that the above articles are worth fifty seven dollars.

Given under our hands, this 29th Day of Augt 1820.
    (Signed)   Wm Thompson
    (Signed)   Jas English

Reverse side of Gideon Johnston's schedule:

We were called on to say what amount of Goods Capt Gideon Johnston had on hand. We suppose the amount to be one hundred and twenty five Dollars.
    Given under our hands this 15th July 1820.
       (Signed)   Wm McNish
       (Signed)   H. L. Y. Pope

1820-018 Wm. Thayer's Revolutionary War Pension Declaration

At a Court Continued and held for Fauquier County the 25th Day of July 1820.
District of Virginia, S^{ct}

On this 25th Day of July 1820, personally appeared in open Court... **William Thayer, aged Sixty nine years,** resident in the County of Fauquier... who being first duly sworn according to Law, ... declare[s]

That I... **enlisted in... service... in the autumn of 1775 with a Captain Burgess Ball (who was afterwards promoted to Colonel Ball), in the County of Lancaster... for the Term of Two years and was attached to the fifth Virginia Regiment**

At the expiration of [my] Term, I enlisted under Captain Henry Fauntleroy, who was killed at the battle of Monmouth, of the Same regiment for the Term of three years... before the expiration of [this] term, I enlisted under Captain John Blackwell of Fauquier County... for the Term of during the War and was attached to the third Virginia Regiment

That during [my] ...service, **I was at the battle of Brandy Wine, Germantown and Monmouth... I was at the Capture of the Hessians at Trenton and was engaged against the enemy on the first + second of January following, at Trenton and Princeton... I was with General Green at the battle of Eawtaw [sic] Springs and [with] General Morgan at the Cowpens... I was at the siege + Capture of Lord Cornwallis in Virginia, after which I marched to the South in a Regiment Commanded by Colonel Thomas Posey and Joined General A. Wayne in the State of Georgia and continued in the South until the Proclamation of Peace in Savanna.**

... I was **Cartelled from Charleston South Carolina to Richmond Virginia where I Received my discharge**... exclusive of the before mentioned engagements, I was in a Variety of Skirmishes in both the Northern and Southern States.

... I was **seven years and Ten months in... Service, during which time I served as a private, Corporal, Sergeant and Sergeant Major...**

I... solemnly swear that I was a Resident Citizen of the United States on [the] 18th day of March 1818 and that I have not since that time, by Gift, Sale, or in any manner disposed of my property, or any part thereof with intent thereby to diminish it...

That I have not nor has any person in Trust for my any property or securities, Contracts or Debts due to me no[r] have I any Income other than what is Contained in the schedule hereto annexed and by me subscribed to wit:

Four head of Horned Cattle, owned by my children living with me; one old mare, [a] Bill of Sale on the same to James Pickett to secure payment; six hogs owned by my children ^ ~~living with me~~ ^ ; one plow, two hods and two axes, some Coarse Carpenters Tools, a debt due me by my deceased son, about Sixteen dollars of Six years Standing, debtor considered insolvents; which articles so as aforesaid Enumerated, the Court doth appraise to the sum of ninety nine dollars.

1820-018   William Thayer's Revolutionary War Declaration (Cont.)

I do further declare that **my occupation is that of a coarse carpenter**, that in, common, [I] Enjoy good health and Considering that the addition of less than three months will finish my Seventieth Year, under these circumstances I leave to others to Judge of my ability to pursue my avocation.

… **I married a wife [in] January 1786**, who is now living with me and who has, through me, **nine living sons and seven Daughters.**

… in the late Conflict with the British Goverment [sic] [the **War of 1812**], **one of my sons entered the United States Cavalry, under Captain Little John, two others, the Virginia Militia, one of whom died at Norfolk.**

My present family, the fore mentioned Wife, aged about fifty two years (infirm0; Sons Hiram, aged 18 years; Albert, aged 9 years; Taliaferro, aged near 8 years; Daughters Betty, aged 12 years; + Francis, Eleven Years.

… That my original Declaration was made before Judge Robert White in the Second Week of April 1818 and my **Pension Certificate is dated the 4th day of May 1818 and numbered on the back thereof 317.**

Sworn to in open Court.
   A Copy   Teste   (Signed)   Daniel Withers

1820-019   Joseph Blackwell's Pension Declaration
At a Court held for Fauquier County the 24th day of July 1820, District of Virginia, Fauquier County, to wit:

On this 24th day of July 1820, personally appeared in open Court… **Joseph Blackwell, aged sixty three years in August next**, resident in the County of Fauquier… who, being duly Sworn according to Law, doth on his oath declare That he served in the Revolutionary War as follows:

I enlisted in the 3^d Virginia Regiment on Continental Establishment, commanded by Captn John Ashby, as a Cadet – afterwards … about the Beginning of the year 1777, **I was appointed a Lieutenant in the 10th Regiment on Continental Establishment, commanded by Co^l Edward Stevens**, in which Regiment I continued until the Virginia Regiments were reduce. When the 10th became the Sixth and was Commanded by Col. John Green

I was **appointed a Captain in the Sixth Regiment in which I Continued until the end of the War**.

I was **in the following battles, Viz: Harlem Hights [sic] + White Plains in the State of New York; Brandy Wine + Germantown in the State of Pennsylvania; Monmouth, in the State** of New Jersey; and the Siege of Charlestown in the State of South Carolina (where I was taken prisoner), besides many little skirmishes in different places.

… I made my original Declaration in the County Court of Fauquier… the **number of my pension certificate is (27).**

1820-019   Joseph Blackwell's Pension Declaration (Cont.)

... I do solemnly Swear That I was a resident citizen of the United States on the 18th day of March 1818 and I have not since That time, by Gift, Sale, or in any other manner, disposed of my property or any part thereof, with intent thereof so to Diminish it... I have not, nor has any person in trust for me, any property or Securities, Contracts or Debts due to me. Nor have I any income other than what is contained in the schedule hereto annexed and by me subscribed. To wit:

A claim ag^t Thomas Chilton which is unliquidated, and Which I gave up Some months Since when I took the oath of an insolvent Debtor. It is uncertain whether the aforesaid claim will yield enough to pay the debt under which I swore out.

I have no property, real, personal or mixed.

(Signed)   Jo   Blackwell

I am **by occupation a farmer, but in Consequence of being Crippled in my right hand and from my weakness in My Knees**, am unable to pursue it.

I live upon a piece of rented land, very poor, at the rate of L20 per annum.

Mrs. Brent, my mother in Law, lives with me and makes me a present of the Use of two Negroes or I could do Nothing on the Land, the proceeds of which affords Nothing like a support for my Family.

My family consists of my Wife... Mary ... who is in very delicate health; Sarah, my Eldest Daughter, about fifteen Years of age; Mary, aged about Nine Years; Christopher, aged about five years or thereabouts... my Family, so far from aiding in my Support <u>are</u> a charge upon me.

Sworn to and Declared in open Court this 24th day of July 1820.

A Copy.   Teste   (Signed) Daniel Withers   C C

Virginia
Fauquier County, to wit:
I, Daniel Withers, Clerk of the County Court of Fauquier... do hereby certify That the foregoing oath and the schedule thereto annexed and truly copied from the Records of the said Court and I do farther certify That it is the opinion of the... Court That the total amount in Value of the property exhibited in the aforesaid Schedule is [blank]

1820-020   John Franklin's Revolutionary War Pension Declaration

Fauquier
Virginia, ~~Stafford~~ County Court, to wit:
November
On this 26th Day of ~~August~~ 1820 in open Court, being a Court of Record, made so by law, personally appeared John Franklin, aged about seventy-two years, resident in Fauquier County, who being first duly sworn according to Law, doth on his oath declare, That he served in the Revolutionary War as follows:

[That he **served**] in the third Regiment of Light Dragoons under Colo" George Baylor

That the **number of his certificate of pension, which commenced the first Day of May 1818 is 12.495**

1820-020 John Franklin's Revolutionary War Pension Declaration (Cont.)

... I [John Franklin] do solemnly sear That I was a resident citizen of the United States on the 18th Day of March 1818, and That I have not since That time by gift, sale or in any other manner, disposed of my property, or any part thereof with intent thereby so to diminish it...

... I have not, nor has any person in trust for me, any property or securities, contracts or debts due to me, nor have I any income other than what is contained in the schedule h[paper torn; word illegible] annexed and by me subscribed, necessary Bedding +n cloathing [sic] excepted, to wit:

One Cow, two chairs, two spoons, three knives + forks + three Bowls, one house pig, one bed +c, four pewter plates + one pewter dish, one small pot, one dutch oven + one chest, Valued by the Court at twenty seven dollars + ninety-five cents.

He also makes oath That his **occupation is that of a common Labourer** [sic] without much ability, owing to his age + the debility consequent thereon; he has **no other family than his wife Elizabeth Franklin, aged sixty-eight years,** who is scarcely able to work.

[The rest of the writing in this record is x'd out.]

1820-021 Andrew Green's Revolutionary War Pension Declaration

District of Virginia, Sᶜ

On this 29th Day of August 1820 personally appeared **Andrew Green**, before the County Court of Fauquier... in open Court... **aged fifty seven years**, resident in the County... who, being first duly sworn according to Law, doth on his Oath declare That he served in the Revolutionary War as follows:

He... enlisted for the term of three years on the [blank] Day of **February 1779** in the State **of Virginia, in the Company commanded by Captain John Chapman, in the Regiment commanded by Colonel Joseph Crockett, in the Line of the State of Virginia on the Continental establishment.**

That he **continued to serve** in the ... Corps **until** the [blank] Day of **September... 1782** when he was **discharged** from the... service **at the Falls of Ohio** which was then in the... State of Virginia.

That he was **wounded on Bear Grass Creek, three miles above the Falls of the Ohio, in a skirmish with the Indians upon which occasion... Captain John Chapman was killed.**

That he made an original declaration to this effect in June 1818, upon which he has received a pension ^ up to the 4th of September 1819 ^; the **number of the pension Certificate being 4.531.**

And I do solemnly swear That I was a resident Citizen of the United States on the 18th Day of March 1818 and That I have not, since That time, by gift, sale, or in any manner, disposed of my property or any part thereof, with intent thereby to diminish it... I have not nor has any person in trust for me, any property or securities, contracts or debts due to me, nor have I any income other than what is contained in the Schedule hereto annexed and by me subscribed.

I have no Article of real or personal Estate whatever, except some Carpenter tools to the value of about fifteen dollars: Landy Waters owes me about ten Dollars.

1820-021 Andrew Green's Revolutionary War Pension Declaration (Cont.)

I am, by occupation, a Carpenter and Joiner but from age, infirmity and the wound received in the War, I am unable to do but little at the trade.

I have **no family living with me at this time**, my wife being dead someyears ago and several of my Children living in the State of Pennsylvania.

    (Signed)   Andrew Green

Sworn to in open Court.
    (Signed)   Thos C. Kelly   D^y C

1820-022 John Herndon's Oath as Major in the Virginia Militia
Fauquier County   S^c
    To the Clerk of said county

I, James Pickett, a Justice of the peace for the county aforesaid, do hereby certify That **John C. Herndon** personally appeared before me in the county aforesaid and **took the oaths prescribed by law, to execute the office of a Major in the Militia of the commonwealth of Virginia.**

As witness my hand and seal this 7th Day of October 1820.
    (Signed)   James Pickett   (Seal)

1821-001 Missing from Box

1821-002 Daniel Boyd's Revolutionary War Declaration
Fauquier County, State + District of Virginia   S^{ct}

On this 24th Day of September 1821, personally appeared in open Court... **Daniel Boyd, aged eighty four years**, who being first duly sworn according to Law, doth on his oath, make the following declaration, in order to obtain the provision made by the Acts of Congress of the 18th March 1818 and 1st May 1820.

That **he ... enlisted for the term of eighteen months** on the [blank] **February 1779 in the county of Loudon** [sic]... **Virginia, in the Company commanded by Colonel Buford or Bluford, in the line of the State of Virginia on the Continental establishment**.

That **he continued to serve in the ...Regiment till** [sic] **it was defeated in South Carolina by Col^o Tarlton in the month of May or June 1780, when he joined the Regiment commanded by Colonel George West of the Continental Establishment in which he served at the Battle of York** and till [sic] the **conclusion of the War, when he was discharged at Noland's ferry in the State of Virginia**.

That he was **at the Battle in which... Col^o Bluford was defeated and in the Battle of York** which were the only Battles of consequence in which he was engaged.

That he has no other evidence now in his power [next two words are illegible] his ... services except the **affidavits of W^m McClanaham** and Charles Owens + Alex D. Kelly.

1821-002 Daniel Boyd's Revolutionary War Declaration (Cont.)

I do solemnly swear That I was a resident citizen of the United States on the 18th Day of March 1818, and That I have not since That time by gift, sale, or in any manner, disposed of my property or any part thereof, with intent thereby so to diminish it… I have not, nor has any person in trust for me, any property or securities, contract or debts due to me, nor have I any income other than what is contained in the schedule hereto annexed and by me subscribed – to wit:

one Bed, one Pewter dish + four pewter plates, half dozen knives + forks ^ half dozen cups + saucers, one Coffee Pot ^ , two pots, one skillet and a Bread pan, two axes, two hoes, two Mattocks, one Spade, one shovel, one stone hammer + two hogs.

I owe some small debts but nothing is owing to me.

My family consists of a ~~family~~ **wife fifty one years old and two Children, the one aged seven; the other, nine years** who render me no aid in making out a subsistence.

… I, from wounds and the Palsy, am unable to support myself without the assistance of my Country.

                        his
(Signed)   Daniel X Boyd
                        mark
Sworn to and declared in open Court this 24 September 1821.
    (Signed)   Jnº A. W. Smith   C. C.

Wm McClanaham and Charles Owens, this 24 September, personally **appeared in open Court and made oath that Daniel Boyd**, who made the foregoing declaration, **was a soldier in the Revolutionary War…** They served with him in the Regiment commanded by Colonel Buford or Bluford until his defeat in south Carolina by Colo: Tarlton, all from February 1779 – till [sic] 29th May 1780… from that time, they had no knowledge of him till [sic] within a short time past.

    (Signed)   Wm McClanaham
                         his
    (Signed)   Charles X Owens
                        mark
Sworn to in open Court this 24th of September 1821.
    (Signed)   Jnº A. W. Smith   C. C.

Alexander D. Kelly ^ a Justice of the Peace for the Coty of Fauqr ^, Personally appeared in open Court this 24 September 1821 and made oath that he has known Daniel Boyd, who made the foregoing Declaration, for the last twenty years and that … Boyd has (so far as … Kelly hath known him) supported a good character as to honesty and truth.
    (Signed)   Alexander D. Kelly
Sworn to in open Court this 24 of September 1821.
    (Signed)   Jnº A. W. Smith
$55.35 cts

Military Records from Fauquier County Virginia Clerk's Loose Papers, Military Records Series 1759-1825

1821-002   Daniel Boyd's Revolutionary War Declaration (Cont.)
Fauquier County, State and District of Virginia   S^{ct}

On this 26th Day of November 1821, personally appeared in open Court… Daniel Boyd, aged Eighty four years, being the same Daniel Boyd who made the Declaration of a Pensioner with said Court on the 24th Day of September 1821, and being first duly sworn according to Law, doth on his oath declare that on the 24th Day of September 1821, he was a resident citizen of the County afores^d and State and District afores^d and that he still remains a resident citizen thereof.

                              his
(Signed)   Daniel X Boyd
                             mark

~~Fauquier County, to wit,~~
Subscribed, Sworn to and declared in open Court, this 26th Day of November 1821.
(Signed)   Jno A. W. Smith   C. F. C. C.

1821-003   John Horrell's Revolutionary War Pension Declaration
S^{ct}
Fauquier County,
         District of Virginia

On this 24th Day of April 1821, personally appeared in open Court… **John Horrell, aged upwards of sixty years**, resident of the County afores^d… who, being first duly sworn according to Law, doth on his oath declare that he served in the revolutionary War as follows:

… He …served in the **first regiment of the Maryland Line under Colonel Peter Adams, commander of the … Regiment.**

… That **he enlisted under Capt Willm Bruce.**

… That **he enlisted in … seventeen hundred and seventy eight for the duration of the War.**

… That he was **discharged in … seventeen hundred and eighty three at the house of General Smallwood** in ^ the ^ State of **Maryland, Charles County.**

That he is unable to state the date of the original declaration proved before the Honourable [sic] Robert White, Judge of the Superior Court of Law for the County afores^d, a Record of which he has not preserved.

That he has rec^d his pension up to the 4th of March 1820 and that the number of his pension Certificate is 15.301.

I, John Horrell, do solemnly swear that I was a resident Citizen of the United States on the 18th of March 1818 and that I have not since that time, by gift, sale or in any manner disposed of my property, or any part thereof with intent thereby so to diminish it…

1821-003 John Horrell's Revolutionary War Pension Declaration (Cont.)

... I have not, nor has any person ~~for~~ in Trust for me, any property or securities, contracts or debts due to me nor have I any income other than what is contained in the schedule hereunto annexed and by me subscribed.

The following is a Copy of the schedule of ... John Horrell:
Three head of horses and thirteen old Sheep, seven Lambs, seven head of cattle and Twenty two head of hogs; four pair of gear and one Lot of Tools; One Lot of Ploughs and one waggon; Six chairs and one table and one chest; Two wheels and two bee stands; Kitchen furniture

Debts owing by ... John Horrell amounting in all to eighty-eight Dollars.

The Declarant also states that he is a Farmer on rented land; that he is quite unable to pursue his business; that he is nearly blind and disabled in his shoulder.

... **He has nine children; James Horrell is the eldest, who is about twenty nine or thirty years old**. [James] is married and lives to himself; **Will Horrell is about twenty seven years of age**, is married and lives to himself; **John Horrell is about twenty five years of age** who works for himself and aids me but little. Peter Horrell is about twenty two and works for himself and aids ~~him~~ me but little.

Nancy Horrell is in her Twenty first year, she lives with me and weaves and spins in my house but gets most of the profits of her labour. **Isaac Horrell is about eighteen years of age**, lives with me and assists me. **Matthew Horrell is about fifteen years of age**, lives with and assists me. **Hugh Horrell is about twelve years of age** and is just able to do a little work. **Patsa [Patsy?] is about nine years of age** and is unable to render me any assistance.

That his **wife is old and infirm** racked with pain and a dead expense to him, and that he is unable to support himself without the aid of his Country.

Sworn to and declared on this 24th Day of April 1821 in Open Court.

    (Signed)   Jno A.W. Smith   C.F.C.C.

Fauquier County, Virginia

This 24th Day of April 1821, William Urton, a credible witness of full age appeared in open Court and made oath that he has for several years been well acquainted with ... John Horrell, that he is needy and ^ in ^ indigent circumstances and cannot ^ in the opinion of this Affiant ^ support himself without public or privat charity.
    (Signed)   Wm Urton

Fauquier County 24th of April 1821. Sworn to in open Court.
$165. (Signed)   Jno A. W. Smith   C.F.C.C.

Military Records from Fauquier County Virginia Clerk's Loose Papers, Military Records Series 1759-1825

1821-004 Joseph Anderson's Revolutionary War Declaration

Fauquier County, State and District of Virginia

On this 24th Day of April 1821, personally appeared in open Court ... **Joseph Anderson, aged sixty five** years, and a resident of said County and State, who being first sworn according to law, doth on his oath, make the following declaration, in order to obtain the provisions made by the Acts of Congress of the 18th March 1818 and the 1st May 1820.

That ... **Joseph Anderson on the 12th September 1779, enlisted as a soldier for the term of eighteen months in a company of Foot, commanded by Captain Richard Stevens in the 11th Virginia Regiment, commanded by Col. Thomas Hawes of Caroline County, Virginia.**

That he was **on Continental establishment.**

That he **received a dangerous hurt which rendered him incapable of duty while he was attached to [the] regiment... he remained in the hospital [for] some time without mending and was afterwards sent home on furlough, for recovery**... his inability detoured him at home until the end of the War and has ever since rendered him unfit for labour... He **did not receive a formal discharge.**

... He has no other evidence than the annexed ~~affidavits of General John Blackwell, who was Captain in the Revolutionary War and~~ of William Skinker and William Thompson... [he] was in no Battle of the Revolution.

In pursuance of the Act of the 1st May 1820, I Joseph Anderson, do solemnly swear that I was a resident citizen of the United States on the 18th March 1818 and that I have not since that time, by gift, sale or in any manner disposed of my property or any part thereof, with intent thereby so to diminish it... and that I have not, nor has any person in trust for me, any property or securities, contracts or debts due to me; nor have I any income other than what is contained in the Schedule hereto annexed and by me subscribed.

1 Negro man, aged nearly seventy years, ~~200 Acres of Poor land entirely unproductive~~, 1 Horse, 6 Head of Cattle, 7 Hogs and 12 [word illegible], 12 sheep, 6 chairs, 2 Tables, 1 Cupboard, 2 Chests, ½ Dozen plates, ½ dozen Cups and saucers, ½ Dozen Spoons, 2 Dishes, ½ Dozen Knives and Forks, 2 Bowls.

I live upon a small piece of rented land. I am entirely unable to cultivate it from the injury sustained by me during the revolution, in the abdomen, and in the falling of my intestines on both sides of the rim of my belly and also from the debility of age.

I have a **wife aged fifty seven years**, who is feeble but in other respects healthy. She contributes to the support of my family by waiting upon females in their confinement.

I have **six children: Thomas, twenty three years old; Milly, eighteen years old; and William fourteen years old, who live with me.** Thomas receives the beneficial shares of his carrings [?]; Milly spins and assists my wife in cooking. Milly does not aid me. Thomas ploughs and assists in the support of my family.

I have three children besides; **Daniel, aged twenty eight; Joseph, twenty five; Jenny, aged twenty one**. They are [all] married and live to themselves, the provide me no assistance.

I have an old negroe [sic] named George, nearly seventy years old who is an expense and burthen to me.

1821-004 Joseph Anderson's Revolutionary War Declaration (Cont.)

My wife has a daughter by a previous marriage and a grandchild Sally Freeman and her son John. …One [is] aged twenty one, the other, [aged] nine. Sally [word illegible] and spins occasionally for the family but princibally [sic] for herself and [word illegible] when she can get employment.

I am in needy circumstances and unable to live in humble comfort or care without public or private aid. I owe several debts and am unable to pay them. My property is not sufficient for that purpose. I have been permitted to keep it by the money of my landlord and creditors.

                     his
   (Signed)   Joseph + Anderson
                     mark

Sworn to and declared in open Court this 24th April 1821.
   (Signed)   Jno A. W. Smith   C.F.C.C.

William Skinker, a Justice of the Peace for the County of Fauquier, this 24th April 1821 appeared in open Court and made oath that ten or twelve years ago, **Thomas Hord, a respectable citizen of Stafford County, Virginia, since deceased, appeared before him as Justice of the Peace and made oath that during the Revolutionary War with Great Britain… Joseph Anderson ^ enlisted ^ for eighteen months in a Regiment commanded by Col. Thomas Hawes of the United States Army.**

That … Joseph Anderson received a hurt which disabled him; the Affiant also states that … Anderson has never recovered from it, that he is a steady, sober, industrious man, [he] is too infirm to labour, [he] has a large family and is in very needy circumstance ^ that he owes more than he is worth ^ ; that the certificate of … Thomas Hord was obtained to [word illegible] the Declarant Anderson is an intended [applicant] for a pension, that it has been lost.

   (Signed)   Wm Skinker

William Thompson, a Justice of the Peace for the County of Fauquier, appeared in open Court and made oath that he has been acquainted with Joseph Anderson for twenty years; that he is reputed to be an honest, industrious, sober man, that he has **attended him as a physician, that he has a rupture or Hernia of such a nature that it prevents him for labouring** ^ that he is poor and is largely indebted ^

Sworn to in open Court this 24th April 1821.
   (Signed)   Jno A. W. Smith   C.F.C.C.
   (Signed)   Wm Thompson

1821-005 Lieutenant Hiram Rookard's Oath as Militia Officer

Fauquier County   Sc

I, James Picket, a Justice of the peace for and in the county aforesaid, do hereby certify that Hiram Rookwood of said county personally appeared before ~~and~~ me, and took the oaths prescribed by Law to execute the office and commission of a Lieutenant in the Militia of the Commonwealth of Virginia. Given under my hand this 28th Day of May 1821.

   (Signed)   James Pickett

1821-006 Warner Sullivan's Commission as Ensign, 44th Rgt. (See page 113. This commission is in the Military Records Historical Signature Folder.)

1821-001 Timothy Bray's Petition for an Increase in his Pension

To the Senate and House of Representatives of the United States of America in Congress assembled.

The Petition of Timothy Bray of the County of Fauquier and State of Virginia humbly sheweth;

That he was a **soldier in the last War between Great Britain and the United States and was enlisted by Lieutenant John Kincaid of the Artillery in the County of Fauquier and State of Virginia**…

That during his stay in s^d County under his Lieutenant, he was **unfortunately wounded by the bursting of a Cannon while celebrating the Anniversary of our Independence;** that he … was **wounded in the bones of the** ~~right~~ **left forearm which were fractured to so great a degree that it is now impossible for him to use his** ~~right~~ **left arm with any effect in the ordinary business of his trade.**

… [He] further states that he is, at this time, enrolled as a Pensioner of the United States on the Pension list roll of the Virginia Agency at the rate of two dollars per month as will more fully appear by a reference to a Certificate of [next two words illegible], the original being now in his possession…

Although the present pension that he received has assisted him in his embarrassed condition, yet he hopes he will not be disappointed when he calls upon congress to increase his pension to the sum of eight Dollars per month and this he humbly asks of his Country because the wound which he rec^d as above mentioned has injured him so much of late that he is unable to support himself by his trade (which is that of a wheelwright) and the present pension not being sufficient to relieve his wants and distress.

[He] … begs leave further to state that he is a man of **family consisting of a wife and two children, both of which are under seven years of age**… He lives on rented ^ land ^ and has no property of any consequence. …He is involved in debt and verily believes that his property is not sufficient to pay and discharge him from his debts; which property consists of one heifer, one bed and bedstead and furniture, Chairs, one sow and seven Pigs, one set of wheelwrights [sic] tools, one walnut table.

Believing himself therefrom from his poverty and afflictions entitled to the further aid of his County, he humbly asks that he may be inscribed in the Pension List Roll at the rate of eight Dollars per month and as the wisdom of Congress may deed fit and suitable and your Petitioner will ever pray +c.

    (Signed)   Timothy Bray

Sworn to and declared on this [blank] Day of January 1822 in open Court…

Fauquier County Virginia

[Jeremiah Strother's Affidavit:]
This 20th of January 1822, Jeremiah Strother, a credible witness of full age personally appeared in open court and made oath that he has, for several years, been acquainted with… Timothy Bray, that he is in needy and indigent circumstances and cannot, in the opinion of this Affiant, support himself without the aid of his
Country.
    (Signed)   Jeremiah Strother
Sworn to in open Court

1821-001 Timothy Bray's Petition for an Increase in his Pension (Cont.)
[Doctor's Certificate:]

I hereby Certify that the injury, on account of which Timothy Bray of this County, was placed on the U.S. pension list, continues; and that from the nature of the injury, there is every reason to believe that the disability is full as great as ~~every~~ it then was, and is not likely to become less. It Being **a fracture of the bones of the forearm, which never reunited.**

    (Signed)   John E. Cook   MD
    Warrenton, Fauquier County
    Dec 29, 1821

    I certify the above statement to be correct.
    (Signed)   Thos T. Withers   MD

Fauquier County, to wit; Jno E. Cooke, one of the above subscribers, personally came before me, a Justice of the Peace for the County aforesaid, on the 29th Instant + solemnly affirmed that the allegations in the foregoing certif8cate are true. And Thomas T. Withers made oath on this Day that the allegations contained in the said certificate are true. Given under my hand this 31st Day of December 1821.
    (Signed)   Thos O. Jennings

1822-002 John C. Herndon's Oath as Colonel in the Virginia Militia
Fauquier County S^{ct}

This Day personally appeared before me, a Justice of the peace, for said County, **John C. Herndon** and took **the Oaths** prescribed by Law, to the execution of the Office **of a Colonel in the Militia** of the commonwealth of Virginia.

    Given under my hand this 26th Day of August 1822.
    (Signed)   James Pickett

Herndon } Certificate
Jno
1822
Augt 26   Ordered to be filed.
[Note: This information appears on the reverse side of the JP's certification of John Herndon's oath.]

1822-003 Burr Comb's Oath as Lieutenant in the Virginia Militia
Fauquier County S^{ct}

I James Pickett, a Justice of the peace for s^d county, do hereby certify that **Burr Combs** this Day came before me in said county and **took the Oaths prescribed by Law to a Lieutenants commission of Light Infantry in the Militia** of the commonwealth of Virginia.

    Given under my hand this 17th Day of August 1822.
    (signed)   James Pickett

Combs}   Certificate
Burr
1822
Augt 17   Ordered to be filed.
[Note: This information appears on the reverse side of the JP's certification of John Herndon's oath.]

1822-004   George Purcell's War of 1812 Pension Declaration

State of Virginia   Fauq[r] County, to wit:

On the 30th Day of March 1822, personally appeared in open Court... **George Purcell, aged fifty-three years**, resident in the County of Fauquier ..., who being first duly sworn according to Law, doth on his oath declare that he was in the regular service of the United States as follows:

... in the early part of the late War between the United States and Great Britain, he **enlisted under Lieutenant John W. Kincaid for the period of five years**

That about ^ a year after ^ he **marched under Captain Ritchie into Canada** about one year, during which time he was **engaged in the Battles of Chippeway, Bridgewater** and ~~Black Hawk and~~ **Fort Erie**

That in the **Battle of Bridgwater [sic] he rec[d] a severe wound in the back of his neck and a cut in the head occasioned by a sword**

That in the **Battle of Fort Erie, he rec[d] a severe wound in the thigh from a shot in the thigh... which...** [happened when] [he] **laid on some planks on which the cannons of the Fort were worked. ... whilst on those planks a Bombshell of the Enemy struck the sill on which the planks were laid and so jarred [them] that his arm became entangled in the planks and [was] broken. The wounds so disabled him as to render him unfit for service** ... he **lay in the hospital from the time of the wound [he received at Fort Erie] till after a peace was concluded, when he was discharged by Captain Fanning**, under whom he served after the Battle of Bridgwater [sic] till he was discharged.

... He ... is from [these] wounds, ... utterly unable to support himself ^ + family ^; ... from his neccessitous [sic] circumstances, he has been compelled to sell the Land he rec[d] for his services afores[d]. He owns no property whatever. His family consists of a wife, about forty-five years of age and three children and one son in Law who is sickly. His family render him no aid in supporting themselves.

                    his
(Signed)   Geo **X** Purcell
                    mark

Sworn.
Subscribed and sworn to in open Court this 30th March 1822.
    (Signed)   Jn[o] A. W. Smith   C.F.C.C.

State of Virginia   Fauquier County, to wit:
   We, **Thomas T. Withers and James W. M. Wallace, practicing physicians** in the county afores[d], having diligently **examined the wounds of George Purcell**, said to have been received in Canada, do hereby certify that **his left thigh ^ + leg ^ have several scars ^ upon them ^ , one of which was, to all appearance, occasioned by a Ball.**

His ... thigh ^ + leg ^ have lost much of their size & steming [?] power, his right shoulder is dislocated and consequently, its uses much impaired. He seems generally enfeebled, His disabilities are likely to continue.

    (Signed)   Tho[s] T. Withers   M.D.
                 J. W. M. Wallace M.D.

Subscribed and sworn to in open Court this 20 March 1822
    (Signed)   Jn[o] A. W. Smith   C.F.C.C.

1822-004 George Purcell's War of 1812 Pension Declaration (Cont.)

I Jn° A. W. Smith, Clerk of the County Court of Fauquier, do hereby certify that the foregoing Declaration and certificate were duly subscribed and sworn to in open Court [word illegible] in pursuance of the order of the s^d Court.

I do hereby certify that Thomas T. Withers & James W. M. Wallace ^ who subscribed the foregoing certificate ^ are practicing physicians in the County and State aforesaid.

In testimony whereof I have hereunto set my hand and affixed the seal of my office this this 30 March [1822].

1822-005 Thomas R. Hampton's Oath as a Lieutenant in Virginia Militia

Fauquier county S^c

I James Pickett, a Justice of the peace for the county aforesaid, do hereby certify that Thomas R. Hampton came before me in the county aforesaid and took the oaths prescribed by Law, to execute the duties of a Lieutenant of a Company of Light Infantry in the first Battalion of the forty fourth Regiment, fifth Brigade and second Division of Virginia Militia.

Given under my hand this 15th Day of January 1822.

(Signed) James Pickett

Hampton} Certificate
Thomas R.
1822
Jany 15 Ordered to be filed.
[Note: This information appears on the reverse side of the JP's certification of John Herndon's oath.]

1824-001 Papers in the Proceedings of the General Court Martial of Colonel John Kemper, held at Fauquier Court House

[Note: This is an extensive file and also occasioned a trial for slander brought by Colonel Kemper against the officers of his Battalion in civil court.]

1. February 10, 1818 Letter from the Adjutant General's Office in Richmond by C.W. Gooch Adjutant General to Colonel John Kemper of 85th Regiment

Adjutant Genl Office
Richmond 10th Feby 1818

Sir

A memorial from the Officers of a Troop of Cavalry Commanded by Cap. E. Hunton attached to your Regiment, complaining of the illegality of an order of the Court of enquiry of the 85th Regiment, designating the place at which the said Troop is to muster, has been submitted to the consideration of the Executive, by whom I am instructed to inform you that the Court of Enquiry of your Regiment have transcended their authority in fixing up on the Muster ground of Capt. Huntons troop; inasmuch as the law directing the Regimental Courts to designate the places for the Musters of Companies of Militia & for the light Companies, does not include either Cavalry or Artillery.

It is considered that they ^ are ^ not embraced under the denomination of <u>Light troops</u> – And although there seems to be ^ an ^ omission in the Law in this respect, and the authority, in reference to other denominations of troops, is expressly given to the Court of Enquiry, it does not necessarily follow that that authority ought to be excersised [sic] in relation to Cavalry and Artillery.

Military Records from Fauquier County Virginia Clerk's Loose Papers, Military Records Series 1759-1825

1824-001 Papers in the Proceedings of the General Court Martial of Colonel John Kemper, held at Fauquier Court House

1. February 10, 1818 Letter from the Adjutant General's Office in Richmond by C.W. Gooch Adjutant General to Colonel John Kemper of 85th Regiment (Cont.)

If, however, such a power had been given in express terms to the Court, it might reasonably have been expected, that acting <u>discreetly</u> and <u>impartially</u> they would have considered the wishes of the troop in the selection of their muster ground. More is expected, and indeed more is required, of Volunteer Companies, than of the ordinary Militia.

In consideration of this, they are justly entitled to more privileges, provided they be reasonable in their nature. In fact, it is presumed that in the Selection of the Muster ground of a Company of Infantry of the line, the <u>Convenience</u> of the Men is the only consideration, which ought to be allowed any weight. I mean in ordinary cases. It is hoped that on this subject, the Court of Enquiry could not have been influenced by any other than the above considerations. Under the decision of the ~~Law~~ Executive, the troop will be left to select its own parade ground.

    I have the honor to be
        Very respectfully, your obt. serv^t
           (Signed)   C.W. Gooch   Adj^t Genl

Col. John Kemper
85th Reg^t Fauquier

A Copy: The above is a true Copy of the letter of the Adjutant General to Col: Kemper which is filed with the original record of the proceedings of the Court Martial & with that record, of which its [word illegible] apart, is transmitted to Major Genl Williams
        (Signed)   A. Mason

2. Bound Papers from the Trial of Col. Kemper: Proceedings of a General Court Martial held at Fauquier Court House in the State of Virginia by Virtue of the following Order:

(Page 1)
                      Soldiers Rest, May 23^d 1818
Division Orders
    A Division Court Martial will sit at Fauquier Court House on the 22^d Day of June for the trial of Col^o John Kemper, Com^{dt} of the 85th Reg^t upon charges & specifications exhibited against him by Capt Eppa Hunton.

    Genl Armistead T. Mason will preside. The Court to consist of five members & two Supernumeraries, & furnished agreeable to the following detail:
        1st Brigade 1   Lt Col.   1 Capt Sup^y
        3^d Brigade 1   Major   1 do do
        5th Brigade 1   Lt Col.
        6th Brigade 1   Major   1 Judge Advocate
Major Philip Lightfoot will furnish subpoenas to summons the Witnesses.
        Signed   James Williams   M.G., 2^d Division

By order of the Major General commanding the 2^d Division Virginia Militia.
        Signed   P. Lightfoot   Aid de Camp

1824-001 Papers in the Proceedings of the General Court Martial of Colonel John Kemper, held at Fauquier Court House

2. **Bound Papers from the Trial of Col. Kemper: Proceedings of a General Court Martial held at Fauquier Court House in the State of Virginia**

(Page 2)
June 22^d 1818   The Court met pursuant to the above order.

Present: Genl. A. T. Mason President; Lt Col: Staunton Slaughter, Maj^r Samuel Carr, Maj^r Ch^s Elgin; Capt Geo. Grasty, Members. Supernumerary, Capt Thomas Jones. James Saunders, Judge Advocate.
The Lt Col: detailed from the 5th Brigade did not appear.

The Court being duly sworn in the presence of the prisoner proceeded to the trial of Col^o John Kemper, Commandant of the 85th Reg^t Virg^a Militia, who being previously asked if he had any objections to the members named in the General Order, and replying in the negative, was arraigned on the following Charges & Specifications [word illegible] against him by Capt Eppa Hunton of [word illegible] Cavalry attached to said Reg^t.

Charge 1st Oppressive & Unwarrantable conduct towards the Troop of Cavalry commanded by said Capt Eppa Hunton.
   Specification 1st: In that he [Colonel Kemper], did while acting as president of a Court of Inquiry held for said 85th Reg^t at Germantown on Friday the 14th Day of Novr 1817, move and by argument, endeavor to influence s^d Court to make an Order that ... Capt Eppa Huntons Troop of Cavalry should in future meet for company muster at Elk Run Church, which Order was at his, [the] said Col^o John Kemper's instance by them made and which order is highly oppressive in as much as a majority of the Troop reside near twenty Miles off. Said Order having in its tendency and object the final destruction of said Troop.

(Page 3)
   Spe^c 2^d: In that ... Col^o John Kempers conduct in obtaining the Order was unwarrantable because the Order is contrary to Law, without precedent, and has no regard to the convenience of the Troop.

   Spe^c 3^d: In that the conduct of ... Col: John Kemper was farther unwarrantable because he did say that the Order alluded to above would not have been made if ... Capt Eppa Hunton had met with his Troop at the Battalion Muster held at Elk run Church in fall 1817 as if that was the legal mode of punishing for neglect of duty.

Charge 2^d Duplicity
   Spe^c 1st: In that ... Col^o John Kemper did, while acting as president of said Court, say that his only object in moving the Order was the good of the Militia System, at the same time discovery his prejudice and hostility against said Troop & shewing his object to be their final destruction as a Troop, and altho he averd his object to be the good of the Militia while acting as President of the Court, he did say some short time thereafter that ... Capt. Eppa Hunton could only blame himself, for if he had attended the Battalion muster previous, the Order would not have been made, altho it had been proved previous to his making a motion for [this] order that no notice had been given to ... Capt. Eppa Hunton of s^d Battalion muster.

   Spe^c 2^d In that ... Col^o John Kemper did say at another time when he was told that the Order was oppressive and might probably injure his Election as candidate for the Assembly that he, [Col. Kemper] could not be blamed, for that it was the Order of the Court of enquiry, and that he was Comd^t was bound to have it executed when at the same time he was the Mover of the Order and had at that time an Order from the Adj^t Genl to permit the Capt of s^d Troop to chuse [sic] his muster ground, which order the Adj^t Genl pronounced the Order of the Court of enquiry to be illegal.

1824-001 Papers in the Proceedings of the General Court Martial of Colonel John Kemper, held at Fauquier Court House

2. Bound Papers from the Trial of Col. Kemper: Proceedings of a General Court Martial held at Fauquier Court House in the State of Virginia

(Page 4)

Spe^c 3^d: In that ... Col^o John Kemper did say that this disturbance would not have taken place if ... Capt Eppa Hunton had not been the Commander and that he tryed to get the appointment for Martin E. Carter, now 1st Lieut. in said Troop and endeavoured to justify his own Conduct to... Lieut. Carter & prejudice him against ... Capt. Eppa Hunton.

Charge 3^d Disobedience of Orders and Contempt towards his Superiors in Command.

Spec^n 1st: In that ... Col^o John Kemper did issue an Order to the Officers of said Troop dated the 26th Feby Requiring the most positive obedience to the Order of the Court of enquiry after he had rec^d an Order from the Adj^t Genl to the Contrary, informing him... that the Court of enquiry had no Authority to make such an Order according to the late decision of the Executive on the subject.

Spec^n 2^d: In that ... Col^o John Kemper did threaten that he would arrest the Officers of s^d Troop altho he knew that the Executive has sanctioned them in the course they pursued.

Spec^n 3^d: In that ... Col^o John Kemper manifested great contempt to the Executive Authority as well as the Adj^t Genl, saying that the Order or letter was damned insulting, that they had transcended their authority, that he would teach them their duty, and that he would see all their Heads (meaning the Executive, Adj^t Genl and Officers of the Troops) choped [sic] off before he would be treated in Such a manner.

(Page 5)
Charge 4th: Neglect of Duty
Spec^n 1st: In that ... Col^o John Kemper fail to give Maj^r Seth Combs, Com^{dt} of the lower Battalion in [the] 85th Reg^t legal and timely notice of the Battalion muster in fall 1817, the Very muster Capt Eppa Hunton's neglect of which he says was the cause of the Order made by [the] Regimental Court of enquiry.

Spec^n 2^d: In that ... Col^o John Kemper did permit a Company of Militia formerly commanded by Capt Rice Hooe to exist as a company altho the number of ... Company for the last twelve months has been considerably under that which the Law regulates, thereby defeating the object of the Law.

Spec^n 3^d: In that ... Col^o John Kemper did fail to comply with the Law requireing [sic] a commandant of the Reg^t to a lot [sic] one [word illegible] to each Battalion when there is more than one to a Reg^t by not giving ...Capt Eppa Hunton notice of the allotment previous to the Battalion muster in fall 1817.

(Signed)   Eppa Hunton   Capt of Cavalry attached to 85th Reg^t V. M., Fauquier County, May 23 1818.

To which several Charges & specifications the Prisoner plead **Not Guilty**

1824-001 Papers in the Proceedings of the General Court Martial of Colonel John Kemper, held at Fauquier Court House

2. Bound Papers from the Trial of Col. Kemper: Proceedings of a General Court Martial held at Fauquier Court House in the State of Virginia

(Page 6)
The Court then adjourned to meet tomorrow morning at 9 °Clock.

June 23rd 1818

The Court met pursuant to adjournment.
Present: Genl Armistead T. Mason, President.   Lt Col. S. Slaughter, Maj. Saml Carr, Maj. Ch^s Elgin, Capt Geo. Grasty, Members.   Sup^{ry} Capt Thomas Jones.   James Saunders, Judge Adv^{te}

Capt Wm Bowers of the 85th Reg^t, a witness for the prosecution, being duly sworn, deposeth as follows: that Col^o John Kemper did move the Court of enquiry to confine Capt. Eppa Hunton's Troop of Cavalry to the lower Battalion & stated his object to be the good of the Reg^t

    Quest^n by the J.A. [Judge Advocate]   Did you consider the Order as oppressive to the Troop of Cavalry?
    Ans: I did think so & therefore voted against it but after it was carried I voted for the muster ground being at Elk Run Church.

    Quest^n by the J.A.   did you hear Col^o Kemper say that the Order would not have been made if Capt. Hunton had attended the Battalion Muster at Elk run Church in the fall of 1817?
    Ans: I do not recollect.

    Quest^n by the Pros^r After the Order confining the Troop to the lower Battalion, who made the motion to have the muster ground at Elk Run Church?
    Ans: Col^o Kemper

    Quest^n by Same   How much nearer is Germantown to this place than Elk run?
    Ans: I suppose about 5 or 6 miles

(Page 7)
Maj^r Seth Combs, a Witness for the Prosecution, being duly sworn, says that he rec^d notice from Col^o Kemper, of the Battalion Muster either the Day before or a few days after the time prescribed by Law.
    Quest: by the Pros^r Did you give me notice of the Bat^n Muster in the fall 1817.
    Ans: I did not.

    Quest: by Same   Was there a Motion made before the C^t of enq^y to fine me for not attending the Bat^n Muster?

    Ans: There was; & I informed the C^t I had not notifyed [sic] you.

    Quest: by Same   Was this make known to the Court before Col^o Kemper made the motion to change my muster ground?
    Ans: I believe it was.

1824-001 Papers in the Proceedings of the General Court Martial of Colonel John Kemper, held at Fauquier Court House

2. Bound Papers from the Trial of Col. Kemper: Proceedings of a General Court Martial held at Fauquier Court House in the State of Virginia

(Page 7)

Major Seth Combs' Testimony (Cont)

Quest: by same   Did I not endeavor to impress upon the Court the inconvenience the Troop would encounter by mustering at Elk run & at the same time declare my preference for Germantown?
Ans: I believe you did.

Quest. by same   Do you believe a Troop of Cavalry could be raised out of the lower Battalion without injuring some of the Companies?
Ans: I don't believe it could.

Quest. by the same   Do you not believe that by carrying the order into effect it would break up the Troop no com^d by me?
Ans: I do not because if a part of the Troop withdrew I believe their places might be supply^d in the lower Bat^n

Quest: by the Accused   Is Th^s Brown a member of Capt Hunton's Troop?
Ans: I do not know. The prosecutor admitted he was a member of his Troop

---

(Page 8) [**Major Seth Combs'** Testimony continues:]

Quest: by the Accused   How far does Thos Brown reside from Warrenton?
Ans: I believe 20 miles or upwards.

Quest. by the accused: What is the General Character & conduct of Col Kemper as a Militia Officer?
Ans: I believe the Col has always conducted himself with ^ the utmost ^ propriety as an Officer.

Quest. by the pros^r: Is not Col: Kemper reputed to be a men of violent prejudices?
Ans: I have heard such a Character of him but have no knowledge of it myself.

Quest. by the accused: Did you serve with Col Kemper during the late War?
Ans: I did, about two months.

Quest. by the same: Was he prompt & active in the discharge of his duties?
Ans: He was.

Ques^t by the Court: Did Col: Kemper in his conduct on the Court of Enquiry appear to be actuated by motives of hostility towards Capt Hunton & his Troop or did he appear ton have for his object the good of the Reg^t?

1824-001 Papers in the Proceedings of the General Court Martial of Colonel John Kemper, held at Fauquier Court House

2. Bound Papers from the Trial of Col. Kemper: Proceedings of a General Court Martial held at Fauquier Court House in the State of Virginia

(Page 8)
[**Major Seth Combs'** Testimony continues]

Ans: I heard him declare that his object was the good of the Reg^t & I have no reason to believe to the Contrary.

Quest. by the accused: Did you concur in the opinion that the good of the Reg^t required the Order, & what are your reasons for that opinion?

Ans: I thought it perfectly right because I thought the Troop of Cavalry attached to the lower Bat^n should parade in it.

Capt. Bowers was then again brought before the Court for further examination.

Quest: by Pros: Did Col Kemper in his conduct on the C^t of enquiry appear to be actuated by motives of hostility towards Capt. Hunton and his Troop, or did he appear to have for his object the good of the Reg^t?

(Page 9)
[**Capt. Bowers'** Testimony:]

Ans: I believe his object was the destruction of the Troop.

Quest. by the Accused: What circumstance induced you to think that such was my object?
Ans: from its being a Very old Troop & no attempt having been previously made to my knowledge of confining it to the lower Battalion together with the a[n]xiety which Col. Kemper displayd in his efforts to have the order made.

Quest. by the Same: Are there not two Troops of Cavalry attached to the 85th Reg^t and is not the other older than Capt Hunton's?
Ans: There are two & the other is older than Capt. Hunton's.

Quest. by the Same: Has not the elder Troop com^d by Capt Diggs been for a long time attached to the first or upper Battalion?
Ans: I do know to a certainty but I believe it has.

Quest. by the ~~pros:~~ Court: Have you any reason to believe that Capt. Hunton could not keep up his Troop if confined to muster in the lower Battalion?
Ans: I do not believe he could because his Troop is principally composed of his neighbours & acquaintance and because of the distance they would have to travel to muster.

The Accused then admitted that he issued an Order to Capt. Hunton & his Officers requiring obedience to the Order of the Court of enquiry after he had rec^d a letter from C. W. Gooch dated Richmond 10th Feb: 1818, which letter was produced by the accused & at his request is filed as a part of this record.

David James, Adj^t of the 85th Reg^t, a Witness for the prosecution, being duly sworn, was examined as follows: The prosecutor first admitting that the witness resided within the limits of the 2nd or lower Battalion.

1824-001 Papers in the Proceedings of the General Court Martial of Colonel John Kemper, held at Fauquier Court House

2. Bound Papers from the Trial of Col. Kemper: Proceedings of a General Court Martial held at Fauquier Court House in the State of Virginia

(Page 10)

Testimony of **David James**, Adjutant of 85th Regiment:

> Quest. By the Acc[use]d : From your acquaintance with the men composing the 2d Battalion, are you of opinion that a Troop of Cavalry mustering at a convenient place could be kept up out of it?
> Ans: No doubt of it.
>
> Quest. by the same: What is the Genl conduct and character of Col Kemper as a Militia Officer?
> Ans: It is generally Very good.
>
> Quest. by the Prosr: Do you not believe that raising a Troop of Cavalry out of the 2d Batn would [word illegible] some of the company?
> Ans: Yes I think it would break some of them.
>
> Quest. by the Court: Do you believe that Col Kemper had at any time a will to destroy the troop?
> Ans: Quite the contrary.
>
> Quest. ^ by the Acc[use]d: ^ Do you not know that Colo Kemper issued Orders to the Officers of the Regt to assemble in Order to New Model the company bound[ar]y in consequence of the Reduction of Capt. Hooe's compy?
> Ans: He did issue Orders at two different times for that purpose.

The Prosecution admitted that his Troop had been attached to the 2d or lower Battalion by Colo Kemper's predecessor and that it had ~~generally~~ always mustered with it on Battalion musters.

The accused also admitted that he had never given Capt. Hunton any Notice on the Subject until after the Battalion Muster in the fall 1817.

John Hampton, a Witness for the prosecution, being duly sworn, deposed as follows:

Some few days after the Session of the Court of enquiry I had a conversation with Colo Kemper in which I asked him the cause of the Order relating to Capt. Huntons Troop of Cavalry

He observed it was made for the good of the Militia, that the Regt had been injured by too much Cavalry, that there was then too much Cavalry, by fixing the comp[an]y musters of the Troop in the lower Battalion, a number of its members residing in the Upper Battalion would quit it and consequently fill up the Infty companies.

That if the members living in the extreme part of the upper Battalion thought proper to continue in the Troop, he could not help it, the last observation was made in reply to a remark made by the Witness that he thought the order oppressive.

1824-001 Papers in the Proceedings of the General Court Martial of Colonel John Kemper, held at Fauquier Court House

2. Bound Papers from the Trial of Col. Kemper: Proceedings of a General Court Martial held at Fauquier Court House in the State of Virginia

(Page 11) **John Hampton's** Testimony (Cont.)
... That some other[s] of the Troop ment [sic] to remain in it in any event. The witness further states that Col. Kemper observed that he believed Capt. Hunton would keep up his Troop out of the lower Batt^n.

> Quest. by the Court: Did you believe from the conversation between you & Col Kemper that his object was to destroy the Troop?
> Ans: I had no reason to believe it, only from his expressing a wish to consolidate the two Troops and ^ to ^ haveing but one.
>
> Quest. by the Pros: Have you a particular knowledge of the members of the Troop and how far do they generally reside from Elk run?
> Ans: I have, an think a majority of them reside from 16 to 20 miles from Elk run.
>
> Quest. by the Same: Was it the unanimous wish of the Troop last fall to muster at this place?
> Ans: It was.

Capt. Wm R. Smith, a Witness for the prosecution, being duly sworn, deposed as follows:

> That the Majority of the Troop of Cavalry com^d by Capt. Hunton resided about fifteen miles from Elk run Church when he commanded it about two years ago. He further said that he thinks sometime in 1815, there was a plan proposed to consolidate the two troops of cavalry attached to the 85th Reg^t to which the officers belonging to his troop and himself agreed; part of the officers of the other Troop refused; Col^o Kemper always appeared anxious to him that the consolidation should take place and expressed a wish that if the two Troops were consolidated that he should get the command; before this plan was entirely abandoned, the officers of the other Troop all resigned.

(Page 12)
Captain Wm. R. Smith's Testimony (Cont.)

> The witness mentioned to Col. Kemper that it was a favorable time to reduce the Cavalry, that when a Volunteer Troop was abandoned by the Officers I thought it was dissolved of course, that Col K thought differently & thought the Sergeant could com^d the comp[an]y until the officers then recommended would be commissioned.
>
> The Court was then cleared and decided that it was unnecessary to proceed farther in the investigation of the 1st, 2nd and 4th charges and their specifications, being sully satisfied that in regard to them the Specifications are either irrelevant or not supported by such testimony as to convict the accused of criminality of conduct, & determined therefore to proceed at once to the investigation of the 3rd Charge & its Specifications.

The Court then adjourned to meet tomorrow morning at eight ^{o}Clock.

June 24th 1818
The Court met pursuant to adjournment.
Present: Genl A. T. Mason, Pres^t.   Lt Col: S. Slaughter, Maj. S. Carr, Maj. Ch^s Elgin, Capt. Geo. Grasty,
Members: Capt. Th^s Jones, Super^y. James Sanders J. A.

1824-001 Papers in the Proceedings of the General Court Martial of Colonel John Kemper, held at Fauquier Court House

2. Bound Papers from the Trial of Col. Kemper: Proceedings of a General Court Martial held at Fauquier Court House in the State of Virginia
(Page 12) (Cont.)

Lieut. Martin E. Carter, a witness for the Prosecution, being duly sworn, deposed as follows:
That Col. Kemper told him a few days previous to his arrest that he meant to arrest Capt. Hunton & all his Subalterns, that he (Col Kemper) was apprised of the Order from the Adj^t Genl at the time.

That Col. K. shewed him a letter from the Adj. Genl. and remarked that he took it as a damned insulting letter.

(Page 13)
[Lieut. Martin E. Carter's Testimony]
Quest. by the Accused: Did Col^o Kemper say anything disrespectful of the Executive?
Ans: Col. Kemper said he took the Adj^t Genl's letter as a damned insulting one and that he had written a letter & had paid him in his own Coin; that they had written him that the Court Martial had transcended their Authority, and that he would Shew them that they had transcended theirs. That he had written a damned tough letter which upon reflection he had declined sending and that he had written two others [word illegible] but that he had declined sending either of them, that Col: Kemper observed that he had no doubt but that the Order would be countermanded when they rec^d his letter.

Ques^t by the pros: Were those remarks made by Col Kemper previous to your receiving the Order dated 26th Feb: 1818 requiring your attendance at Elk run church?
Ans: That part of them which related to the Adj Genl's letter were. The witness also stated that Col Kemper observed that if they had turned to the 14th Section of the Militia Law they would have saved themselves all that trouble.

John White, a Witness for the prosecution, being duly sworn, deposed as follows:
That sometime in April last, he heard Col: Kemper threaten to arrest Capt. Hunton & Lt Walden. The Witness asked Col: Kemper if the Governor & Council had not authorized the Troop to muster here, The Col reply'd that they had no right to interfere and in doing so, they had transcended their Authority, that he would shew them so before he was done with it and that sooner than he would suffer such conduct towards him, he would suffer to see their Heads taken from their Shoulders; that the Col said he would arrest Capt. Hunton for Mustering his Troop at this place and Lt Walden for making a Speech to them, & that he would arrest all the Officers if they did not repair to Elk run agreeably to his Orders.

(Page 14)
[John White's Testimony] (Cont)
Quest. by the prosecutor: When did Capt. Hunton muster his Troop at this place, and where did Lt Walden make the Speech?
Answ: On the Second Saturday in April last.

Quest by the same: When did the conversation take place between Col Kemper & yourself?
Ans: Some short time after the muster and previous to the fourth Saturday in April.

1824-001 Papers in the Proceedings of the General Court Martial of Colonel John Kemper, held at Fauquier Court House

2. Bound Papers from the Trial of Col. Kemper: Proceedings of a General Court Martial held at Fauquier Court House in the State of Virginia

(Page 14) (Cont.)

Cornet Robt W. Withers, a Witness for the prosecution, being sworn, deposed as follows:

That a few days before Col Kemper was arrested, he heard him say he would have Capt. Hunton & all his officers arrested. That he heard the Col: say that the order from the Adj: Genl was a Very insulting one and that he would shew them the Law and that the Col: shewed him (the witness) the Militia Law a few days after he had rec^d the Order from the Adj. Genl.

That he (the Witness) asked Col Kemper some short time since what he intended to do as he had two orders, one from the Adj. Genl and one from the C^t Martial, that Col: Kemper reply'd that he should endeavor to carry into effect the Order of the C^t Martial, that he should not mind that from the Adj. Genl more than he would the edicts of Bonaparte.

[Note: Upon reference to the Order of the Reg^{tl} C^t of enquiry, it appears that the time appointed for the Troop to muster at Elk run Church was on the 4th Saturday in April, June, Aug^t & October.]

The evidence in the part of the prosecution [was] closed.

(Page 15)

Thornton Buckner, a witness for the accused, being first duly sworn, deposed as follows:

That sometime ago Col: Kemper shewed him a letter which he had written and addressed to the Governor of V^a; that the witness read the letter, the language of which was very respectful, that the Col; in that letter set forth reasons in a proper & decorous manner why the Order he had rec^d from the Adj. Genl. Should be countermanded, that he, the Witness, had informed the Col: that the Governor would attend to any communication form him on that subject, that some time after seeing the letter above alluded to, he heard the Col; express some surprize [sic] at not receiving an answer to his letter and at the same time, his anxiety to hear from the Governor on the subject previous to the muster of the Troop as appointed by the Court of enquiry in order that all difficulty with the Troop might be done away.

The witness further said that he had a high opinion of Col. Kemper as being a man of high standing as a militia officer, a man of vigorous intellect, great promptitude of action and of unquestionable Bravery. The accused admitted that the information given him by Col: Buckner that the Governor would receive any communication from him respecting the Troop was subsequent to his Order to the Officers of the Troop requiring them to muster at Elk run Church [interlined words illegible] (The affidavits of commodore Rogers & Genl Hungerford were produced & read to the Court)

The testimony on the part of the Prisoner having been heard, the prisoner requested the indulgence of the Court until 2 °Clock P.M. to prepare his final defence which was accordingly Granted.

(Page 16)

At two oClock P.M. the Prisoner, being asked if he were [sic] ready to proceed, made the following defence. [There is hand with pointed finger and this comment: "See the original defence filed as a part of this Record. X see last page." On the last page of this records is another X and the following: "Immediately after the Prisoner made his defence, the Prosecutor delivered a Written reply, the manuscript containing which is sent to the Major Genl Ordering the Court. The prosecutor having omitted to sign his name to the manuscript, it was deemed irregular to admit it as a part of this record. (signed A. T. Mason, President)"]

The Court then adjourned to meet tomorrow morning at 8 °Clock.

Military Records from Fauquier County Virginia Clerk's Loose Papers, Military Records Series 1759-1825

1824-001 Papers in the Proceedings of the General Court Martial of Colonel John Kemper, held at Fauquier Court House

2. Bound Papers from the Trial of Col. Kemper: Proceedings of a General Court Martial held at Fauquier Court House in the State of Virginia

(Page 16)
June 25th 1818
The Court met pursuant to adjournment.
Present: General A. T. Mason, President. Lt Col. S. Slaughter, Maj: S. Carr, Maj^r Ch^s Elgin, Capt. Geo. Grasty, Members.   Capt. Thomas Jones, Supernumerary.   James Saunders, J. A.

The Court being ordered to be cleared and the whole of the proceedings read over to the court by the Judge Advocate, the following sentence was pronounced.

Sentence.
   The Court after mature deliberation on the testimony adduced find the prisoner Lt Col John Kemper **Guilty** of the 1st Spec^n of the first charge but **not Guilty** of any criminality of intention.

   The Court find the prisoner **Not Guilty** of so much of the 2^d Spec^n of the 1st charge as charges him with ^ conduct ^ unwarrantable, contrary to Law and without precedent, but they are of opinion that the Order of the Court of Enquiry had no regard to the convenience of the Troop.

   The Court are of opinion that the 3^d Spec^n of the 1st charge is irrelavent.[sic]

   The Court find the prisoner **Not Guilty** of the first Charge.

(Page 17)
   The Court are of opinion that the 1 & 2^d Spec^{ns} of the 2^d charge are irrelavent. [sic]

   From the Testimony adduced the Court find the prisoner **Not Guilty** of the 3^d Spec^n of the 2^d charge and are   ^ moreover ^ of opinion that said Spec^n is irrelavent. [sic]

   The Court find the prisoner **Not Guilty** of the 2^d Charge.

   The Court find the prisoner **Not Guilty** of the 1st & 2^d Spec^{ns} of the fourth charge, **Guilty** of the 3^d Spec^n of the same charge but acquit him of any censure because his pride upon having aloted one Troop ^ of Cavalry ^ to each Battalion. The Court deem it unnecessary that he should have again acted upon the subject.

   The Court find the Prisoner **Not Guilty** of the fourth charge.

   The Court are of opinion that the accused is **Guilty** of the 1st Spec^n of the 3^d Charge, **Guilty** of the 2^d Spec^n of the same charge, **Guilty** of the 3^d Sepc^n of the same charge, except it appeared in evidence that he use the words that he would 'suffer to see their heads &c" as contained in the Spec^n.

   The Court are of Opinion that the accused is **Guilty** of the third Charge and sentenced him to be **Cashierd**; But in consideration of his high standing, his extraordinary good conduct on all other Occasions as an Officer, and a belief on their part that he honestly mistook the law ^ in this case ^ & did not intend to depart from what he conceived to be his duty, they unanimously and earnestly recommend him to the Executive to be reinstated in his command.

1824-001 Papers in the Proceedings of the General Court Martial of Colonel John Kemper, held at Fauquier Court House

2. Bound Papers from the Trial of Col. Kemper: Proceedings of a General Court Martial held at Fauquier Court House in the State of Virginia

(page 18)

The prisoner upon hearing this sentence pronounced, immediately gave notice that he would appeal from it to the Executive.

The Court then Ordered that the attendance and distance of travelling of the following witnesses be certified and also to be made a part of this Record, their attendance having been first proven on Oath.

Names	No. Days	No. Miles	Names	No. Days	No. Miles	Remarks
Jos D. Smith	4	24	Sydney F. Chapman	2	34	The whole distance of travelling to and from the Court is charged opposite each name.
Rice Hooe	4	20	Seth Combs	4	40	
Rob.t Brent	4	"	Ja.s Combs	2	36	
Jn.o P. Kelly	4	36	Marshall Smith	3	30	
Th.s Brown	4	50	Thompson Smith	3	28	
W.m Thompson	4	36	Eppa Nash	4	"	
Geo: Kemper	4	52	Elias Edmonds	4	4	
Steph: Chilton	4	12	Jn.o Saunders	4	16	
Th.o T. Withers	4	"	Armis.d Utterback	4	6	
Edw.d Digges J.r	4	16	Th.s O. Jennings	4	3	
W.m H. Digges	4	5	Sam.l Chilton	3	36	
W.m Dulin	4	10	Th.s Ingram	3	20	
Rob.t W. Withers	4	"	Rob: Randolph	2	14	
Sam.l Baker	2	40	Thornton Buckner	3	3	
John White	4	5				
Ch.s R. Scott	4	"				
John Smith	4	"				
Martin E. Carter	4	6				
Th.s L. Moore	4	"				
Jn.o Hampton	4	20				
W.m A. Rose	4	6				
David James	3	20				

1824-001 Papers in the Proceedings of the General Court Martial of Colonel John Kemper, held at Fauquier Court House

2. Bound Papers from the Trial of Col. Kemper: Proceedings of a General Court Martial held at Fauquier Court House in the State of Virginia

(page 19)
It was then proved on Oath to the Court that Robert Wallace had necessarily travelled [sic] one hundred and fifty four Miles in summoning witnesses in the case of the Commonwealth and Lt Col: John Kemper, and that Martin E. Carter had necessarily travelled [sic] fifty miles for the same purpose. Whereupon the Court Ordered the same to be certified and made a part of this Record and further decided that ^ in their opinion ^ they ought to receive ten Cents per Mile as a compensation for their services.

The Court then Ordered that it be certified that Daniel Eddy served four days as Prevost [sic] Martial to said Court for which Services the Court decided that he ought to receive three dollars per Day.

It was then Ordered that the attendance and distance of travelling of the members of the Court be certified. The Court then decided that the whole compensation of the Judge Advocate be fixed at Ninety Dollars and that the same be certified and made a part of this record.

The Court then adjourned Sine die.
James Saunders, Judge Advocate, Armistead T. Mason, President Brigadier Genl. V^a M^a

[AUTHOR'S NOTE: There is a second copy of this Trial Proceeding which appears to be a rough draft of the proceedings. It is not entered here as it is all but identical to this copy.]

1824-001 Papers in the Proceedings of the General Court Martial of Colonel John Kemper, held at Fauquier Court House

3. The Petition to the Governor for a new Commanding Officer of 85th Regiment
Jacket:
Contested, Fauquier County
Petition respecting Col° Kempers promotion.
Recd. July 16th 1818

To his Excellency The Governor & Honb^l the Council of Virginia, Richmond

Fauquier   July 16, 1818
To his Excellency the Governor
& The Honorable the Council of Virginia

Gentlemen,
Participating in the general desire of having the office of full Co^l ably filled, & the Lieu^t Co^l who was recommended to fill it, while under arrest, having since been removed, we have thought proper to join in recommending one whose merit and qualifications preeminently deserved, the appointment, we therefore bring before your notice Captain Wm R. Smiths.
We recommend him as being best calculated to ally and reconcile the present disorder of the 85th Reg^t as a Gentleman of conciliating disposition but firm, and decided [word illegible] high as an officer & in whom the utmost confidence might be reposed in times of peril and danger.

1824-001 Papers in the Proceedings of the General Court Martial of Colonel John Kemper, held at Fauquier Court House

3. The Petition to the Governor for a new Commanding Officer of 85th Regiment (Cont.)

We believe if he had the command of the Reg^t, he would obey and respect the higher authorities of the state, and enforce necessary obedience with a due regard to law and justice, without prejudice or partiality, having any influence over his conduct.

We believe that in selecting the officers of his Reg^t, he would look for merit without regard to Politics, which seems lately to have had its influence in recommending the officers of this County and pursue that fair and correct course, which would do justice to all, promote harmony and good government, and steer clear from the consequences which must necessarily result from an opposite course.

Capt Smith commanded a large Troop of Cavalry during the last War and served a tour of duty with much credit. He was, while acting, the oldest officer in the Reg^t except Col Kemper, and did not resign until after the appointment of Major Diggs and Combs, who were junior to him, which may be seen by a reference to the Roster of Officers in the Reg^t.

We are, with great respect, your ob^t Servants &c.

Owen Thomas	James Pickett J.P. F.C.	Jno Edmonds J^r
John Brown	James Payne	Wm Edmonds J^r
Wm D. Fitzhugh	Jno P. Smith	Th: Hunton
Ch^s Hunton		Eppa Hunton
Jno Hampton	Wm Bower	W. L. L. Skinker
A. Edmonds	Jno L. Eastham	
Martin E. Carter		
Joseph Morgan	Tho: Brown	
Robt. Green	Jo^s Blackwell	

1824-001 Papers in the Proceedings of the General Court Martial of Colonel John Kemper, held at Fauquier Court House

4. December 10, 1822 General Orders restoring Colonel John Kemper to his rank as Lt. Colonel of the 85th Regiment of the Militia

General Orders
Promulgated at Richmond Decr 10th 1822.

Lieutenant Colonel John Kemper of the 85th Regiment of the Militia of the line, is declared to be honourably restored to his Rank, place and command in that Regiment, the sentence pronounced against him by a Division Court Martial, upon charges of disrespectful conduct towards his superior in command in parade of the Regiment, and of contumacy before a preceding Court Martial, having been regularly annulled, according to law, upon his appeal to the Executive Department, and no subsequent misconduct whatsoever having been alledged [sic] against that Officer during the lapse of twenty one months since the decision of the Executive, which could justify the institution of further proceedings with regard to him.

Given under my hand on the Day above written.
    (Signed) Thomas M. Randolph, Governor & Commander in chief of the forces of the Commonwealth of Virginia.
Bernard Peyton, Adjutant Genl

1824-001 Papers in the Proceedings of the General Court Martial of Colonel John Kemper, held at Fauquier Court House

5. December 10, 1822 Letter from Bernard Peyton, Adjutant General to Lt. Col. John Kemper

Adj^t Genl Office, Rich^d, 10 Decr 1822

To Lt Col^o John Kemper
    85th Reg^t V^a Militia   Viz:

His Excellency Th^s M. Randolph, Commander in Chief of the Militia of this State, has, this Day issued the subjoined General Order which I forward for your information, & Co^l Smith & Genl Hunton are also furnished with a copy each, as well as the senior officers in the Division, Genl William Madison.

    Very respectfully,
        Your Mo: Obd.
            (Signed)   Bernard Peyton, Adj^t General

1824-001 Papers in the Proceedings of the General Court Martial of Colonel John Kemper, held at Fauquier Court House

6. Two Records from Virginia Council regarding legality of late Court Martial Proceedings

        In Council   March 10th 1821

The Governor again submitted to the board, the records of the trial of Lieu^t Col. John Kemper of the 85th Reg^t.

Whereupon it is advised that the sentence of the Court Martial be annulled and declared void: The Council, being of opinion that the said Court were not properly and legally constituted, and that a General Order issue to the proper Officer, requiring him to convene a Court Martial for the trial of the said Lieut. Col. John Kemper upon the charges and specifications heretofore exhibited against that Officer by Col. Wm R. Smith of the 85th Regiment. The Court to be composed of a number not less than seven, and to be taken from as distant Brigades as the nature of the service and convenience of the members will permit.

    A Copy.   Teste.
        Wm H. Richardson C.C.

        In Council   27th February 1823.

The Governor submitted a letter from Col. Wm R. Smith of the 85th Regiment, Fauquier, inquiring whether a certain general order issued by the late Governor Randolph honorably reinstating Lt Col John Kemper in his command was issued by advice of the Council, whether that order was legal, and whether he ought to respect it as such.

Whereupon it is advised that Col Smith be informed that the General order in question was issued by the late Governor Randolph without the knowledge or advice of the Council, that on the 10th Day of March 1821 when the subject was submitted to their consideration, they advised the Governor to cause to be convened another Court Martial for the trial of Lieu^t Col Kemper, it appearing to the Council that the Court from whose decision he was then appealing had been illegally organized. It is further advised that Col. Smith be informed that the Council do not consider this subject at present before them and that he himself must judge of the legality of the general order in question and of the degree of respect to which it is entitled. And that Copies of the advice of the 10th of March 1821 and of the present advice be forwarded to Col. Smith and Lieut. Col. Kemper.

    A Copy
        Teste
           (Signed)   Wm. H. Richardson   C.C.

Council Chamber
28 July 1823
Sir:

I am instructed to forward the foregoing Copies to you.

    Very Respectfully, Your Ob S^t, Wm. H. Richardson, C.C.

Col. Wm R. Smith

1824-002 Court Papers from John Kemper's Slander suit against Owen Thomas and others for slanderous words while the plaintiff was Lt. Col. of the 85th Regiment, 5th Battalion, 2nd Division, Va. Militia.

[Note: This suit has a Declaration made by the complainant, John Kemper; an answer by the defendents, all officers of the 85th Regiment; Subpoenas, a partial Bill of Exceptions, filed by the plaintiff; and what appears to be testimony by Col. Kemper, taken from his Court Martial along with Captain Eppa Hunton's prosecution summation before the Court Martial. It appears that the latter two were made part of the Slander suit court record. A jury heard the Slander suit.]

1. **The Declaration of Complaint.**

    Fauquier County, to wit

    John Kemper complains of Owen Thomas, John Brown, William D. Fitzhugh, Charles Hunton, John Hampton, Alexander Edmonds, Martin E. Carter, Joseph Morgan, Robert Green, James Pickett, James Payne, John P. Smith, William Bower, John L. Eastham, Thomas Brown, Joseph Blackwell, John Edmonds Jr., William Edmonds Jr., Thomas Hunton & Eppa Hunton in custody &c of a plea &c for that the said Pltf now is a good, true honest and faithfull [sic] citizen of this Commonwealth and as such, hath always from his nativity behaved and governed himself and hath for all the time aforesaid been held and reputed to be a man of good name, fame and reputation and the said Pltf before and at the time or writing and publishing the false, scandalous, infamous and malicious libels hereafter mentioned was Lieut. Colo. Commandant of the 85th Regiment and fifth Brigade and second division of the Militia of this Commonwealth, duly appointed Commissioned and qualified and had, during all the time whilst he held the office aforesaid, had discharged its duties faithfully and without fear, favor or [word illegible] and untill [sic] the writing and untill the writing and publishing the false, scandalous and malicious libels herein after mentioned, never was suspected or accused of want of due obedience and respect to the higher authorities of the State, nor of enforcing obedience without regard to Law or justice, nor of disregarding [word illegible] and being influenced only by the political opinions of those persons whom he selected & recommended as officers for the said Regiment, nor of pursuing the opposite of a fair & correct course which would do justice to all, promote harmony and good government.

    And before the writing and publishing the false, scandalous and malicious libels herein after mentioned, the said Pltf. had been duly recommended to the Executive of this Commonwealth by the County Court of Fauq' as a fit person to be appointed and Commissioned full Colonel of the said Regiment; which recommendation was, at the time of writing and publishing the false, scandalous and malicious libels herein after mentioned, was pending and undetermined before the said Executive of this State; by means whereof the Pltf had [word illegible] gained the good opinion of divers good and faithfull citizens of this commonwealth, to wit, in the count aforesaid.

    Yet the Defendants, well knowing the premises but contriving and intending maliciously intending wrongfully to deprive the Pltf of his said good name, fame and reputation and to bring him into public scandal, ignominy and contempt and to cause it to be credited and believed that the Pltf had been disgraced by the sentence of a Court Martial and Cashiered without reserve or qualification; and that the Pltf whilst exerciseing [sic] the duties of his aforesaid Office had not faithfully discharged the same and had not been influenced by a due regard to Law & Justice and had not yielded due obedience to the Lawfull [sic] authority of his Superiors and had been governed by prejudice and partiality and that in selecting the Officers of [the]… Regiment, he the … Pltf had regarded their political opinions more than their merit.

1824-002 Court Papers from John Kemper's Slander suit against Owen Thomas and others for slanderous words while the plaintiff was Lt. Col. of the 85th Regiment, 5th Battalion, 2nd Division, Va. Militia.

1. The Declaration of Complaint (Cont.)

And with intent to prejudice the ... Executive against the ... Pltf and induce them not to appoint him full Colonel of the ... Regiment, which appointment, from his merit, his grade and the recommendation of the ... County Court he had a [word illegible] to expect ^ to injure him in the opinions of the good citizens of this Commonwealth ^, they the ... Defendants on the 26th Day of June 1818 at the County aforesaid, did falsely and maliciously, willfully & disynedly [sic] publish ^ to divers citizens of the Commonwealth ^ a certain false, scandalous, malicious, ^ insulting ^ and defamatory libel and concerning the Pltf of the [word illegible] following, to wit:

Fauquier June 26th 1818

To his Excellency, the Governor & the Honorable... Council of Virginia
    Gentleman,

Participating in the general desire of having the office of full col. ably filled & the Lieut Col. who was recommended (Meaning the Pltf) to fill it, while under arrest, having since been removed, we have thought proper to join in recommending one whose merit and qualifications preeminently deserved the appointment; we therefore bring before your notice Captain Wm R. Smith

We recommend him as being best calculated to ally and reconcile the present disorder of the 85th Reg^t as a Gentleman of conciliating disposition but firm and decided standing high as an officer & in whom the utmost confidence might be reposed in times of peril and danger.

We believe if he had the command of the Reg^t, he would obey and respect the higher authorities of the State and enforce necessary obedience with a due regard to Law and justice without prejudice or partiality having any influence over his conduct. We believe that in selecting the officers of his Reg^t, he would look for merit, without regard to politics, which seems lately to have had its influence in recommending the officers of this county, and pursue that fair & correct course, which would do justice to all, promote harmony and good government, and steer clear from the consequences which necessarily result from an opposite course.

Capt Smith commanded a large Troop of Cavalry during the last war and served a tour of duty with much credit. He was while acting, the oldest officer in the Reg^t except Col Kemper, and did not resign untill after the appointment of Majors Digges & combs who were junior to him, which may be seen by a re3ference to the Roster of officers in the Reg^t. We are with great respect your ob^t servants &c.

(Signed) Owen Thomas   James Pickett   J. P. F. C.
         John Brown   James Payne
         Wm D. Fitzhugh   John P. Smith
         Ch^s Hunton   Wm Bower
         Jno. Hampton   Jno. L. Eastham
         A. Edmonds   Tho: Brown
         Martin E. Carter   Jo. Blackwell
         Joseph Morgan   Jno. Edmonds J^r
         Robt Green   Wm Edmonds J^r
                                Th: Hunton
                                Eppa Hunton
                                W. J. L. L. Skinker

1824-002 Court Papers from John Kemper's Slander suit against Owen Thomas and others for slanderous words while the plaintiff was Lt. Col. of the 85th Regiment, 5th Battalion, 2nd Division, Va. Militia.

1. The Declaration of Complaint (Cont.)

Meaning thereby that the ... Pltf, by the sentence of a Court Martial, had been Cashiered in an unqualified Manner and thereby disgraced and rendered unfit for the office of full colonel of the ... Regiment; and also that the Pltf did not obey and respect the higher authorities of the State when exercising their Lawfull function; and also that the Pltf, in enforcing necessary obedience, had not a due regard to Law and Justice but was influenced by prejudice and partiality; and also that in selecting the officers of his Regiment, the ... Pltf did not look to the merit of the person selected but to his political opinions and was influenced in recommending person to be commissioned as officers in [the] Regiment by their political opinions; and also that the Pltf did not pursue that fair and correct course which would do justice to all parties and promote harmony and good government but pursued an opposite course.

~~Whereas in truth the sentence of the Court Martial by which the Pltf had been Cashiered was accompanied by an unanimous recommendation from the Court to the Executive that the Pltf should be reinstated in his command, expressed in terms highly credible to the Pltf by which he was expressly acquitted of all criminal intentions or dishonorable conduct and adjudged only to have commited [sic] an error of Judgment upon a legal question and so far from shewing the Pltf to be a person unfit for the appointment of full Colonel [word illegible due to being crossed out] his pretensions to that appointment by the forces, whit it has [word illegible] for him~~ ^all of which was well known to the Defts ^

[A]nd also afterwards, to wit, on the same Day and year aforesaid, at the [word illegible] and county aforesaid, the ... Defe[de]nts, well knowing the premises but contriving and maliciously intending to injure the Pltf. and to deprive him of his good name, fame and reputation and to prevent him from obtaining from the ... Executive the ... appointment of full colonel of the ... Regiment, did cause to be written and published ^ to divers citizens of this Commonwealth ^ a certain other false, scandalous, ^ insulting ^ and malicious libel of and concerning this Pltf ..
[The same letter to the Governor, date June 26, 1818 is again inserted into this record]

Meaning thereby [referring to this June 26, 1818 letter] that the Pltf had been cashiered by the Sentence of a Court Martial without qualification or extenuation and thereby disgraced and rendered unfit for the appointment of full Colonel to the ... Regiment; also that the Pltf was not inclined to obey and respect the higher authorities of this commonwealth when exercising their Lawfull function; and also that the Pltf, in enforcing obedience to his authority as a Militia officer had not a due regard to Law and Justice but was influence by prejudice and partiality; and also that in selecting his officers the Pltf was not influence by the merit but by the political opinions of the person selected and was influenced in recommending persons to be appointed officers of his ... Regiment by their political opinions; and also that the Pltf did not pursue the fair and correct course of conduct which would [word illegible] justice to all parties and promote harmony and good government but pursued and opposite course;

[B]y reason of writing and publishing and causing to be written and published which several false, scandalous and malicious libels the Pltf hath been greatly injured in his good name, fame and reputation and hath been greatly injured in his character and standing as a militia Officer with many good Citizens of this Commonwealth and more especially in the estimation of the ... Executive who appoint and commission Militia Officers.

1824-002 Court Papers from John Kemper's Slander suit against Owen Thomas and others for slanderous words while the plaintiff was Lt. Col. of the 85th Regiment, 5th Battalion, 2nd Division, Va. Militia.

1. The Declaration of Complaint (Cont.)

~~And whereas also afterwards, to wit, on the same Day and year aforesaid at the County aforesaid, the Pltf had been arrested and tried by a Court Martial of which Gen. Armistead T. Mason was president on certain charges and specification exhibited against him by Capt Eppa Hunton; and whereas the ... Court had sentenced the Pltf to be cashiered but unanimously and earnestly recommended him to the Executive to be restored in his command in consideration of his high standing, his extraordinary good conduct on all other occasions as an officer, and a belief on the other part that he honestly mistook the Law in that case, and did not intend to depart from what he conceived to be his duty, which recommendation together with the grounds of it were attached to and made part of the ... sentence. From which sentence the Pltf had appealed to the Executive of this commonwealth~~

...Whereas before the writing and publishing the false, scandalous and malicious libels herein after mentioned, the ... Pltf had been duly recommended by the County Court of Fauq^r to the Executive of this Commonwealth as a fit person to be appointed full Colonel of the aforesaid Regiment, which appointment was before, and at the time of writing and publishing the false, scandalous and malicious libels hereinafter set forth, pending and undetermined before the ... Executive; and whereas the Pltf then was, and always from his youth upwards, had been a good, true, faithful and honest citizen of this Commonwealth and had faithfully and impartially discharged the duties of Lieut. Colo. Commandant of the ... Reg^t.

Yet the ... Defendts, well knowing the premises but contriving and intending to injure the Pltf in his good name, fame and reputation, to prejudice the ... Executive against him and prevent a favourable decision on the ... Appeal and to prevent the Pltf from being appointed full Colonel of the ... Regiment, on the same Day and year aforesaid at the parish and County aforesaid, did write and publish and ~~cause to be written~~ ... to divers citizens of this Commonwealth a certain ^ other ^ false, scandalous, ^ insulting ^ and malicious libel of and concerning the Pltf, containing the false, scandalous, malicious and libellous [next two words illegible] following to wit: [Here follows a third copying of the June 18th Letter to the Governor. This time the letter stopped with the recommendation of Captain Wm. R. Smith as the Colonel for the 85th Regiment]

Meaning thereby that the Pltf had been cashiered by the sentence of the Court Martial aforesaid without qualification or extenuation and thereby disgraced and rendered unfit for the office of full Colo. Of the ... Reg^t; and also the false, scandalous and libellous [sic] matter following to wit: "We Believe that in selecting the officers of his Reg^t he (meaning ... William R. Smith) would Look for merit without regard to politics which seems lately to have had its influence in recommending the officers of this County"

Meaning thereby that the Pltf whilst he commanded the ... Reg^t had not looked to merit in selecting his officers but was influenced by their political opinions; and in recommending persons to be commissioned as officers in the ... Reg^t, he the Pltf, regarded their political opinions rather than their merit; by means of writing and publishing which last mentioned false, scandalous and malicious libel, the Pltf hath been greatly injured in his good name, fame & reputation and also in his standing and Character as a Militia Officer and hath lost the ... office and appointment of full Colonel in the ... Regiment;

1824-002 Court Papers from John Kemper's Slander suit against Owen Thomas and others for slanderous words while the plaintiff was Lt. Col. of the 85th Regiment, 5th Battalion, 2nd Division, Va. Militia.

1. **The Declaration of Complaint (Cont.)**

[A]nd also afterwards, to wit on the same Day and year aforesaid at the County aforesaid, the ... defendants, well knowing the premises, but contriving and intending to injure the Pltf did cause to be published a certain other false, scandalous and malicious libel of and concerning the Pltf, containing the false, scandalous and libellous matter following to wit: [here is yet another copying of the June 18th 1818 letter and another rehashing of Kemper's reasons the letter was libelous, this time regarding his alleged promotion of officers due to their political opinions rather then by merit.]

...The Pltf hath been greatly injured in his good name, fame and reputation and in his character and slandering as an officer and hath lost the said office of full Colonel in the said Regiment. Where for the Pltff saith that he had been injured and sustained damage to the value of $20,000.

2. **The Defendants response**
Owen Thomas et altera   Defd^{ts}
    adv
John Kemper   Pltff

And the defendants Owen Thomas, John Brown, Wm D. Fitzhugh, Charles Hunton, Jno Hampton, Alexander Edmonds, Martin E. Carter, Joseph Morgan, Robert Green, James S. Pickett, Jno: P. Smith, Wm Bower, Jno: L. Eastham, Thomas Brown, Joseph Blackwell, John Edmonds, Jr., Wm. Edmonds, Jr., Thomas Hunton and Eppa Hunton, by their att° defend the wrong and injury when &c. and say that the said Jno: Kemper, the pltff, ought not to have or maintain his said action thereof against them, because for pleas they say that before the writing and publishing of the supposed libels in the pltff's declaration mentioned, the pltff had been recommended to the executive of this commonwealth by the county court of Fauquier as a fit and proper person to be appointed and commissioned full Colonel of the 85th Reg^t of V^a Militia, which recommendation was at the time of writing and publishing the said supposed libels in the declaration mentioned, pending and undetermined before the said executive of the ... state;

[A]nd the ... defendants, desiring to have the ... office of full Col: of the ... reg^t then vacant, fill'd by a fit and proper person and believing that the ... Pltf so, as aforesaid nominated, was not a fit and proper person to fill the ... office of full Col: of the ... Reg^t, did for the better manifestation thereof write and deliver to the Governor and council of the commonwealth afores^d composing the executive of the commonwealth... on the [left blank] Day of [left blank] in the year [left blank] at the county aforesaid, the ... office being still vacant and the ... recommendation being still pending and undetermined before the ... executive, the supposed libels in the pltffs declaration mentioned, according to the custom and by others in such behalf and approved by the ... executive, which is the same writing and publishing of the ... supposed libels whereof the ... pltff hath in his declaration complained.

And this the ... defendants are ready to verify, wherefore they pray judgment whether the ... pltff ought to have or maintain his ... actions thereof ag^t them &c.

3. **There were eleven summons that went out to the defendents and to witnesses to testify for both John Kemper and for James Pickett and the defendents. I have not included those forms here. All witnesses appeared to be officers of the Regiment.**

1824-002 Court Papers from John Kemper's Slander suit against Owen Thomas and others for slanderous words while the plaintiff was Lt. Col. of the 85th Regiment, 5th Battalion, 2nd Division, Va. Militia. (Cont.)

4. **The Replication**
   Kemper vs. Thomas & others
   The ... Deft. by his attorney saith that he ought not to be precluded from having and maintaining his action aforesaid against the Defendants, anything in their second plea alleged because he saith that the publication of the several libles [sic] in the Pltffs. Declaration mention to the Executive of this Commonwealth in the ... plea alleged is not the same publication of the ... several libles [sic] whereof the Pltff in his declaration hath complained.

   ... [T]he ... Pltff in fact saith that the ... Defts. Did on the Day and year in the ... declaration mentioned ^ maliciously ^ letter and publish the several libles [sic] in the declaration mentioned of and concerning the Pltf. to divers citizens and inhabitants... of the county of Fauquier aforesaid, not members of the ... Executive and this he prays may be enquired of by the County.
   (Signed)   Scott, Atty [for the] Pltf.

5. **John Kempers's Testimony in the Suit Papers**

[NOTE: The following testimony appears to be the missing defense of Colonel Kemper offered at his Court Martial and not found in those papers. There is no doubt these remarks are addressed to a Military Court and not the County Court. It looks as if Colonel Kemper was successful in making his Court Martial defense part of his slander trial.]

   A complaint has been preferred against me.

   I was condemned upon the interested representations of my accusers; And by men to who [sic] I believed and trust this Court now think had no authority over the subject. And beg the Court to bear in mind that Capt Hunton and his Officers calculating upon that feature of my disposition, which disqualifies me from patiently submitting to insult or Indignity, had ingeniously contrived to keep alive and increase the irritation caused by the Letter of the Adjutant General.

   That his determination to disobey my Order appeared in broad characters in the Newspapers published at this place. And as if this were not enough, Lieut Walden, Orator and Soldier, addressed the Troop in an inflamatory speech ^ prepared for the Occasion ^ . Thus goaded, I have to felicitate myself that I was not driven to Acts of greater indiscretion.

   But had the Adjutant General, who was made the Organ of communicating the mandate of the Executive, confined himself within the limits of his duty, had he been content to transmit the Executive resolve with out larding it with his own offensive remarks, had he, in short, in making these remarks confined himself to the language due from one Gentleman to another, much as I felt the wrong done me by the Executive, I should have abstained from intemperate language; but when adopting the views of my accusers, he charges the Court of Enquiry & consequently myself in broad terms of having acted <u>indiscreetly & partially</u>, I put it to you as Honourable men to say if tame submission was my duty.

   I hope, Mr President, you do not consider yourself and your Brother Officers in such a stake of vasalage [sic] that because a man is dressed in a little authority, he may heap his insults upon us and it shall be accounted a crime to speak of them in language which they merit.

   I hold it to be the right and duty of every Officer to resent an insult whether it be given by Superior or inferior. If a Contrary doctrine is to prevail, it is time you had stricken Me from your List.

1824-002 Court Papers from John Kemper's Slander suit against Owen Thomas and others for slanderous words while the plaintiff was Lt. Col. of the 85th Regiment, 5th Battalion, 2nd Division, Va. Militia. (Cont.)

5. **John Kempers's Testimony in the Suit Papers**

Under what Law is it that speaking the words of which I am accused is punishable? We are not now under the Rules and Articles of War. And if we were, Article 24 punishes with arrest irritating and insulting words, when spoken <u>to</u> a Superior & not when spoken of him.

But I hold, Sir, that a Militia Officer when not on duty enjoys the Liberty of Speech in as full and ample a manner as any other Citizen, and further maintain that even in a regular Army, an Officer, however low his grade, may complain of a wrong done him by a Superior in terms as bitter as his feelings may prompt.

6. **Further testimony by Colonel John Kemper** [taken from his testimony at his Court Martial and evidently entered into the Slander suit Court record]
   Mr President & Gentleman of the Court

Although I had a perfect willingness to give to the Prosecutor the evident range in the investigation which he proposed of my conduct, as well as it regards matters not embraced in the charges and Specifications which he has adduced against me as those contained in them, and the decision of the Court on a part of those charges has deprived me of the opportunity of introducing Evidence on my part, which would, if possible, place my conduct in relation to them on still higher Ground than it occupies by the Evidence of the prosecutor.

Yet at the acquittal pronounced by the Court must be founded on a Conviction of the absence of all impure Motive on my part, and, I feel a conscious innocence of all bad intentions as well, in relation to those charges; as to the one which now remains for decision, I acquiesce with perfect cheerfulness in the Course taken by the Court. It remains for me to satisfy this Court that there is no ground for attaching to me either criminality or censure in relation to the third charge and its specifications. I beg leave briefly to recapitulate the facts connected with the first specification under this charge.

At a Regimental Court of Enquiry held at German Town at which I presided, on the 14th Day of November 1817, It was Ordered that the future Muster Ground of Capt. Eppa Hunton's Troop be at Elk run church on the 4th Saturday in April, June, August & October in each year. Some time in February in the year 1818, I received a letter from the Adjutant General informing me that a memorial of the Officers of a Troop of Cavalry commanded by Capt E. Hunton attached to my Regiment, complaining of the illegality of the before mentioned Order had been submitted to the Consideration of the Executive, by whom he was instructed to inform me 'that at the Court of Enquiry of my Regiment had exceeded their Authority in fixing on the Muster Ground of Capt Hunton's Troop' & that in [the] future, the Troop should be permitted to select its own parade Ground.

On the 26th of the same month, believing that the Resolution of the Executive had passed without due Consideration, and that it was a Question over which they possessed no authority, I issued an Order to Capt Hunton, requiring obedience to that of the Court of Enquiry.

The first and most important question arising on this branch of the subject is, Was the Resolution of the Executive an Usurpation of Authority or can they legally control the decisions of the Regimental Court of Enquiry. For, if by virtue of a supposed General superintendence, they have a right to reverse the decisions of these Courts because they have transcended the Limits of their Jurisdiction, they must equally possess the right to Reverse their Judgments in all cases where in the Opinion of the Executive they have erred.

1824-002 Court Papers from John Kemper's Slander suit against Owen Thomas and others for slanderous words while the plaintiff was Lt. Col. of the 85th Regiment, 5th Battalion, 2nd Division, Va. Militia. (Cont.)

6. Further testimony by Colonel John Kemper [taken from his testimony at his Court Martial and entered in the Slander suit Court record]

Upon an attentive review of our State Constitution, it will be found that the Executive department possesses <u>limited</u> powers in the strictest sense of the word. And that the maxim which in American Politics is considered a fundamental one: "that a power which is not granted either in express words or by necessary implication cannot be exercised" applies with peculiar force to that Department. The Framers of our Constitution had smarted under the misrule of the Executive of the Mother Country.

They had seen in the History of that Country the liberty of the Subject become a prey to the King and his Ministers by the Exercise of an <u>undefined</u> Prerogative, that the Portion of liberty then enjoyed was the scanty fruit of partial Victories obtained at favorable junctures in the grand struggle between privilege & prerogative; and when liberty seemed to have finally triump[h]ed she was again tramelled [sic] by the more insidious but no less powerful engine Patronage. And thus the power of Parliament, the result of so many arduous struggles between the King & people to which they looked as the Bulwark of their safety was converted into the most effectual means of subjugation.

By the dextrous [sic] management of this all subduing Weapon, they had seen the British parliament equally obsequious to the nod of a Minister as to the mandates of the most imperious Sovereign. They therefor wisely determined to guard against both evils. They secured the Legislature against the corrupting influence of Executive patronage by depriving the Executive of all important appointments and they guarded against the exercise of an <u>undefined</u> Prerogative by declaring that the Governor, with advice of Council "shall exercise the Executive powers of Government <u>according to the Laws of this Commonwealth, and shall not under any pretence exercise any power or Prerogative by virtue of any Law, Custom, or Statue of England.</u>" or in other words ^ that ^ the Executive should exercise no powers but those expressly Given either by the Constitution or by Statute.

It may be contended that as the Governor & Council exercise the Executive powers of Government, such powers as are in their nature Executive appertain to them of course, and that the command of the Forces is of that description. To what consequence would such an enlarged construction of the Constitution lead us. A Question arises whether a particular power claimed by the Executive belongs to that branch or not. Where are we to look for precedents and reasons to aid us in our deliberations? To England whence we borrow our Civil Code. Are we to consult the writers on the Common Law on this as upon Questions of property? The Constitution forbids it. Are we to look into the other and more Despotic Governments of Europe and see how they have parcelled [sic] out the Legislative, Judicial and Executive powers? The feelings of every American forbid it. Are we to consult the Volumes of the Political writers of Europe? Or shall we not rather look into the pages of our Constitution and Statute Book and conclude that if we find the power not given there, it is not held.

In these, we shall look in vain for the power in question. If this wide Door is opened for the admission of Constructive posers we shall be involved in endless discussions upon executive claims and the Framers of the Constitution, instead of accurately defining the limits between this and the other branches of Government would leave us at Sea upon a Subject on which of all others, they felt the greatest jealousy and alarm.

1824-002 Court Papers from John Kemper's Slander suit against Owen Thomas and others for slanderous words while the plaintiff was Lt. Col. of the 85th Regiment, 5th Battalion, 2nd Division, Va. Militia. (Cont.)

6. Further testimony by Colonel John Kemper [taken from his testimony at his Court Martial and entered into the Slander suit Court record]

If the Executive can claim title under this general grant, the powers which they derive under it being given by the Constitution are independent of the Legislature. And we shall presently hear that the power of the sword is in its nature Executive. That the Executive, like the King, is the fountain of honour and many other pretensions Equally preposterous. For once [word illegible] afloat and throw your chart ^ the Constitution ^ overboard and you know not wither you will be driven.

I have taken this view of the subject not because I apprehend that the Executive entertain such preposterous pretensions, but to shew to what extravagant lengths we should be carried by the enlarged construction which alone the proceeding of the Executive now under consideration can be justified.

I conclude then that the powers of our State Executive are strictly limited to those which are granted either by the Constitution or by Statute. And I challenge any man to produce a clause either in the one or the other which gives to them an appellate jurisdiction over the Regimental Court of Enquiry.

Neither are the Governor and Council the Commanders in Chief of the Militia because such a Command is not given to them either by the Constitution or by Statute. The Constitution declares that the Governor & council may embody the Militia and when embodied, the Governor alone is Commander in Chief; Consequently when not embodied, he is not the Commander and the Govern & Council are not the Commanders at any time and let it be recollected that it is disobedience of a resolve of this body of which I am accused.

To Military men I need not urge the absurdity of vesting the Chief command in a plurality of hands and making the Governor alone the commander in War & tramelling [sic] him with the council in time of peace.

The Constitution & Acts of Assembly give to the Executive certain specified powers: these and these only they may lawfully exercise. And the Chief Command of the Militia or the Control over the Courts of Enquiry are not amongst the number. On the Contrary, we find a distinction drawn between the Regimental Courts of Enquiry and Courts Martial from the decision of the latter and Appeal [word illegible] to the Executive; Not so from those of the former. And when we reflect that these Courts are both constituted by the same Act, the inference is irresistible that the Legislature did not mean to give an Appeal to the Executive from the decisions of the Courts of Enquiry.

Yet the Executive in the case before us have exercised the Authority of an Appellate Court and that, too, without the formality of an appeal. If I am right in the view which I have taken and the Executive cannot lawfully exercise any authority which is not given by the Constitution or by Statute, and that nothing can be found either in that instrument or the Statute Book which authorises them to Control the decisions of the courts of Enquiry, it follows that the resolution of the Governor and Council for disobedience of which I am arrested was an usurpation and it was not only Lawful but meritorious to resist it. The more exalted the man or body of men by whom an Act of Tyranny is committed, the more it is the duty of the Citizen who is the object of it to resist.

If the resolution of the Executive was unwarranted, it is a matter of no importance as it regards this branch of the subject, whether the Court of Enquiry exceeded its authority or not. If its Order was unwarranted Capt Hunton & his Troop were not bound to obey it.

1824-002 Court Papers from John Kemper's Slander suit against Owen Thomas and others for slanderous words while the plaintiff was Lt. Col. of the 85th Regiment, 5th Battalion, 2nd Division, Va. Militia. (Cont.)

6. Further testimony by Colonel John Kemper [taken from his testimony at his Court Martial and entered into the Slander suit court record]

But Mr President, I maintain that the Court of Enquiry acted strictly within its lawful limits.

It will be found that the Act of 1792 authorises the Commanders of Companies to fix the time and place of Company Musters and that under the Term Companies Cavalry are included. And that the Musters of Cavalry and Artillery and of the rest of the Militia are provided for in the same Section. See N Vo^l Revised Code, page 403.Sect: 17.

The same act requires Notice of Company Musters.

The Act of 1795 speaks of the Musters of Artillery and Cavalry in one section (to wit, the 15th and of the rest of the Militia in the one following: vide N Vo^l 468.9. the Section requiring the Musters of Artillery & Cavalry is silent to the person by whom the private or Company musters shall be appointed. That which speaks of the musters of the rest of the Militia continues that power to the Commanding Officers of Companies and requires Notice of Company Musters.

It is to be observed that the 14th Section which authorises the raising of Companies of Grenadiers or light Infantry, cavalry & Artillery declares that the Companies of Grenadiers or light Infantry shall perform the same routine of duty and be subject to the same rules regulations and Orders as the rest of the Militia but omits to apply that provision to the Artillery & Cavalry. Vid 1 Rev. Code 468 Sec: 14, and repeals the Act of 1792 in Sect. 48. But could it be contended that the Legislature intended to place the musters of Cavalry and Artillery on a different footing from the rest of the Militia.

That the Commanding Officers of those Companies should not appoint their Musters, and that they should not perform the same routine of duty and be subject to the same Rules, regulations and Orders as the rest of the Militia? Certainly not. Because the whole Act shou'd be taken together, and it is not to be presumed because they speak of the Cavalry & Artillery in a separate Section that they meant to make a difference between them and the rest of the Militia in that respect.

In 1804 the Legislature again [took] up the subject of the Militia and reenact the provisions of the former Laws with some variation. They reenact the Section of the Act of 1795, which provides for the Musters of Cavalry and Artillery verbatim. And they reenact the 16th Section of the same Act with this important change: that instead of the Company Muster being appointed by the Commanding Officers thereof, they transfer that power to the Regimental Courts of Enquiry & for that reason dispense with Notice of Company Musters.

Now if it can be fairly argued that the Act of 1795, by providing for the Company Musters of Cavalry and Artillery in a separate Section and remaining silent as to the person by whom the time and place of the Musters shou'd by appointed ought not to be so construed as to place the Musters of that portion of the Militia on a different footing from the rest, surely it may be argue with increased force that the Act of 1804, in reenacting that Section, did not intend to make a difference when it supplies the omission of the former Act and expressly declares that the Cavalry and Artillery shall perform the same routine of duty and be subject to the same Rules, regulations and orders as the rest of the Militia.

1824-002 Court Papers from John Kemper's Slander suit against Owen Thomas and others for slanderous words while the plaintiff was Lt. Col. of the 85th Regiment, 5th Battalion, 2nd Division, Va. Militia. (Cont.)

6. Further testimony by Colonel John Kemper [taken from his testimony at his Court Martial and entered into the slander suit court record]

Uniformity of regulations where attainable, is desirable upon all subjects upon more than in relation to Military affairs. The act shou'd be taken together as forming one system and such construction shou'd be placed upon it, as will make it consistent and not absurd and contradictory. If the Courts of enquiry have not the power to appoint the private Musters of the Cavalry and Artillery to whom does that power belong?

The adjutant General tells us that Captain Huntons Troop is to select its own parade Ground, that is, that this question is to be decided by the Members of the Troop. How I pray? By a concurrent vote of the whole Troop or by a majority of voices? If by a majority of voices, is a Majority of the whole number necessary to a decision? And if not, what proportion shall form a Quorum to proceed to this business? Shall the votes of the Officers have greater weight than those of the private Men? Or shou'd the captain be overruled by the Sargent [sic] and Corporal? Who is to preside at the deliberations, for although the Captain commands when on parade, yet as this is a previous question in the decision of which a private has as much weight and is a[s] deeply concerned as the Captain, he may with great propriety contend for the Chair.

Has the Captain a right to appoint the Muster? The Act of 1792, which gave it to him, is repealed. But he may do it because he Commands the Company. If so, then the Major may make the appointment because he Commands the Captain. And the Colonel, because he Commands the Major. Let us conclude rather, as the Law is silent on the subject of the private Musters of Artillery and Cavalry, as the 16th Section authorizes the Courts of enquiry to appoint the Musters of the rest of the Militia and the 14th Section of the same act declares that the Cavalry and Artillery shall be subject to the 'same Rules, Regulations and orders as the rest of the Militia,' that the Courts of Enquiry have the power to appoint he Musters of the Cavalry & Artillery, also why should they occupy a higher station than the rest of the Militia.

The Adjutant General tells us that as more is expected from them they are justly entitled to more privileges. Let me tell that officer that when the Tug of War shall come if he expects more from his Gentlemen Volunteers than from the ordinary Militia, his expectations will be wo[e]fully disappointed. And I believe I am not singular in the opinion that they are the worst description of Troops.

The equality claimed by the Soldier with his officer and the idea of exclusive privileges inculcated by the Adjutant General utterly unfit them for that discipline and subordination, without which an Army is an Armed Mob.

But if they are entitled to exclusive privileges because they are Volunteers why should not the Volunteer companies of Light Infantry be equally entitled. I believe the Adjutant General himself acknowledges that they are included in the term 'light Companies'. The notion of bestowing exclusive honours and privileges on a Select portion of the Troops may be well calculated for the Meridian of Constantinople or Varis.

The Phrase would sound well in the ears of a Janasary or a Member of the Legion of Honour but in America, we are flattered with a belief that all [are] equal and that 'No Man or set of Men are entitled to exclusive or separate emoluments or privileges from the Community but in consideration of public services' and I have yet to learn that Captain Hunton has extraordinary claims on that Score.

1824-002 Court Papers from John Kemper's Slander suit against Owen Thomas and others for slanderous words while the plaintiff was Lt. Col. of the 85th Regiment, 5th Battalion, 2nd Division, Va. Militia. (Cont.)

6. Further testimony by Colonel John Kemper [taken from his testimony at his Court Martial and entered into the slander suit court record]

I persuade myself that I have shewn to the Court that the Executive Erred both in the Assumption of Authority to control the decisions of the Courts of enquiry and in the Construction which they place on the Act of 1804. For the Court of enquiry did not exceed its authority in appointing the private Musters of Captain Hunton's Troop and consequently I was bound, ^ not ^ to yield obedience to the Executive.

But admit for argument's sake that the reverse of all this is true, that the Court was wrong and the Executive right, and of course I should have obeyed the Executive & not the Court.

I was placed in a delemma [sic]. I was compelled to decide an intricate question of Law, one on which the Executive Council was divided. If I obeyed the mandate of the Executive, I disobeyed the order of the Court. It remained for me, after giving the subject all the consideration which it merited, to decide according to the dictates of my own understanding.

That I did decide according to my firm and settled convictions, I give this Court the most solemn assurances and upon an attentive review of the subject, I found no reason to change my opinion when called on to speak or act on this subject. It is in Evidence to the Court that I uniformly referred to the Act of Assembly and endeavoured and I believe not ineffectually to convince some of the Members of the Troop that their duty required obedience to the order of the Court of enquiry. I refer to the Testimony of Mr. Norris. But if I erred, I have yet to learn that an Error in Judgment in selecting between two contending authorities which involved the decision of an intricate question of Law is imputable as a crime.

I have heretofore been taught that criminality consists in intention. If Sir, I am aright in the view which I have attempted to give of the powers of the Executive and the Courts of Enquiry, it behooves my Adversary to pause before he declares his willingness to establish such a doctrine.

Passing by the second specification under his charge as a matter not worth (if true) the serious consideration of the Court in as much as an unexecuted intention has never yet been held to be a crime and if I had arrested them without being influenced by a malicious motive, I had a right to do so, I come to the charge of contempt of my superior in command, contained in the third specification.

If I used the expressions attributed to me, it is proof that they were used in reference to the letter of the Adjutant General. But, Sir, is in the State of irritation in which I then was, expressions of passion escaped me when speaking of the proceedings of the Executive, they were not without palliation or excused as a short statement of facts will prove.

The Executive, upon an ex parte representation contained in a Memorial of the Officers of Captain Hunton's Troop a right of which they have refused me, pronounced sentence of Condemnation upon the Court of Enquiry in which I presided without condescending to notify me of the complaint or afford me an opportunity to vindicate myself & thus conveyed an unqualified censure of my Conduct.

Ignorant that a complaint [the sentence stops here, the though not completed, and the testimony resumes on another page]

1824-002 Court Papers from John Kemper's Slander suit against Owen Thomas and others for slanderous words while the plaintiff was Lt. Col. of the 85th Regiment, 5th Battalion, 2nd Division, Va. Militia. (Cont.)

6. **Further testimony by Colonel John Kemper** [taken from his testimony at his Court Martial and entered into the slander suit court record]

Mr President, it has been well observed that an Officer accused of any Offence connected with his profession could not be tried before a tribunal where justice ^ both ^ to the Public & the accused is more likely to be obtained than a Court composed of his brother Officers. From this profession they are best Qualified to judge of such Offences, from the pride of fame and high sense of honour which animates the bosom of every Genuine Soldier.

that there is no danger ^ that ^ tenderness for the accused will induced them to permit the Roll to be disgraced by ^ containing the named of ^ a dishonoured man, hence the purity of the Army and the safety of the Commonwealth. Whilst on the other hand, the rights of the accused are equally secure. They are indeed his peers. By their decisions, they establish precedents, which will apply to themselves under similar circumstances and therefor have every inducement to observe the sacred Maxim: "As yte would that Man should do to you, do ye also to them. Likewise.'

If other Consideration were wanting to inspire the Confidence which I feel, they would be found in the Dignity, Impartiality and Intelligence manifested by the Court through out the progress of this Trial. And Sir, I should not do justice to my own feelings if I quitted this subject, without acknowledging my Obligations to the Gentleman who prosecutes for the Commonwealth for the Candour and Liberality with which he has discharged his duties.

Mr President I Have done, I set down with this Consoling reflection, that whatever the Decision the Court may be on the Question which now remains, it cannot taint my Honour.

(signed) Jn° Kemper Lt Col°, 85th Regt Va Ma

---

7. **The summation by the Captain Eppa Hunton, the Prosecutor in the Court Martial** [taken from the Court Martial papers and entered into the slander suit court record]

Mr President & Gentlemen of the Court,

You have nearly closed your deliberations on the matter in controversy between the Commonwealth and Col. Kemper, and I assure you Gentlemen that it has pained me sorely to stand here in the situation of prosecutor. I have always had an aversion to controversies of any Kind and have been so fortunate as to avoid until the present transaction, a dispute of either personal or public. The [word illegible] of our County may be searched in vain for proof to the contrary. Consequently I have not had the aid of experience ^ or Litigation ^ to place before you the matter in a way to do Justice to it as well as my self.

I must here, however, confess that the other side was not so formidable as I expected, when taken on military subjects, and to use and apply the expression of an address circulated yesterday by Mr Scott, although indifferently qualified, was the best of the two. This feeling of regret was increased after the decision of yesterday, inasmuch as I felt considerable solicitude that the world should know that I had not charged without being able to establish the facts, although if established, they were not so arranged, as to lie before you in a military point of view.

1824-002 Court Papers from John Kemper's Slander suit against Owen Thomas and others for slanderous words while the plaintiff was Lt. Col. of the 85th Regiment, 5th Battalion, 2nd Division, Va. Militia. (Cont.)

7. **The summation by Captain Eppa Hunton, the Prosecutor in the Court Marital** [taken from the Court Martial papers and entered into the slander suit court record]

All the specifications and charges except the 3^d charge and its Specifications are dispensed with; consequently I confine myself in the few remarks I am about to make, entirely on that subject. I pass over anything that can said against me: I [word illegible] by the idle wind they disturb me not. Whenever it shall be necessary to investigate my conduct as an officer, I shall be prepared to stand as high as Col. Kemper: indeed it would be only necessary to read a letter of Genl. Taylor addressed to a Gentlemen of this County stating that he had without my consent placed me in nomination as an officer for the sate army then about to be raised, I might too, on this ground, have proved my conduct in the three tours of duty which I served, during the last war.

But the Character of neither of us has much to do in this matter, a man may act well for the first 30 years of his life & badly the balance. I shall proceed under the pure conviction of mind that the 3^d charge and its specifications has been either admitted or sufficiently established, the Court will bear in mind that is not simply a disobedience but it has been proved that there was a resolute determination on the part of Col. Kemper not only to disobey but to thwart and frustrate the proceedings of the Executive on the subject.

This disobedience is not without the Knowledge of the facts, for it expressly declared in the order he has received that this order of the Court of Enquiry was illegal. This order not only declares the illegality of the order but gives the powerful reasons and quotes the very law to prove it. It was then not only disobeying the Adjt. Gen^{ls} orders, but it was going contrary to and destroying the solemn act of the Executive in Council assembled.

As to the insult, which is said to be offered to Col. Kemper in the order, I deny it and appeal to the Leter for proof. As to the legality of the proceedings of the Executive and the Order of the Adjutant Genl, this Court is better informed and more able to construe and understand the Law than I am. They no doubt will examine the oath of Office the Executive must take before they enter on their duties and apply it to the execution of their duties in the present case, and there will appear a perfect consistency. You will discover that every person has the right to appeal from the decision of any Court Martial, when he conceives himself aggrieved, to the Executive. See M[ilitia] L[aw] page 59, Section 17.

I conceive that the Executive of our State according to my information on Militia Law is to all Military Tribunals what the high Court of Appeals is to all civil Tribunals. Such a Tribunal must be [word illegible] and of no effect if their authority does not extend to such cases as the one before you and it would be in vain for them to act at all unless they are obeyed.

I am bold to declare that no Militia Law can be produced in this State which authorizes the Court of Enquiry to fix the petty muster grounds of the Cavalry or Artillery. I say further that Cavalry & artillery neither in service nor out of service was ever properly known by the name of light company's. The militia Law draws the distinction. See page 9, 10, 11. See 14-15 & 16. Here I think it is fair to conclude that the order of the court of Enquiry was illegal, that the troop had a right to appeal, that the Executive had not only a right to hear & redress us, but they are bound by their duty to do it: that they have a right to interfere or explain, that interference or explanation is to all to whom it may ^ be ^ addressed binding; that going contrary to it in the present case was disobedience, not simply but of the highest degree: that the order is not insulting in [word illegible] Slightest degree and if it had been so, and the [word illegible] entirely illegal, nothing in a military point of view could justify such contempt towards them.

1824-002 Court Papers from John Kemper's Slander suit against Owen Thomas and others for slanderous words while the plaintiff was Lt. Col. of the 85th Regiment, 5th Battalion, 2nd Division, Va. Militia. (Cont.)

7. **The summation by Captain Eppa Hunton, the Prosecutor in the Court Marital** [taken from the Court Martial papers and entered into the slander suit court record]

Before such an enlightened Court, it is vain and fruitless to attempt to justify such conduct by saying that Col. Kemper had two orders, one from the Executive & one form the Court Martial. I deny that the Court martial ever gave such an order to Col. Kemper. The order is directed to me and as it regards Col. Kemper, he is not responsible for the compliance of it. I am bound for my disobedience to that order if it cane be called disobedience at all, and have [word illegible] my authority, and I doubt not, but that the Court of Enquiry are perfectly satisfied to suffer me to embrace the sanction of the Executive. I ask what precedent could be brought forward by Col. Kemper for his order.

The Court of enquiry made the order in my presence and spread it on their Journals and where was the necessity and obligation of Col. Kemper to give the new and unprecedented order of 26th of Feby last. Then he had but one order and by that, he should have been governed. As to my fractious or provoking and not being any excuse I deny it, and appeal to the world for justification. There are men now in hearing who know I wished this matter settled in peace. That until lately, I expressed my self favourably of Col. Kemper & since then not against the Court of Enquiry; so far from ever saying anything against the Court I would at any time until this matter assumed so determined a shape, have submitted the dispute again before them and ^ have abided ^ by their decision.

Your decision, Gentlemen of the Court, is perhaps the most important that ever was determined by a Court Martial in our State, and I have [the] pleasure in testifying my pleasure & approbation in the discharge of your duties thus far, and have as much confidence that the final result will be ^ materialistic ^ of an enlightened, firm and impartial court: it will be a precedent of the most important that ever was determined by a Court Martial in our [word illegible]. It will be a decision on points of Law, interesting to every one who regards his rights, and has respect for the sacred and fundamental privilege which is made the duty ^ of the Executive to secure us in the enjoyment of ^ Executive Authority or in this particular instance ^ prostrate ^ it before the fist of those who may choose to assail it in a similar way. You will support me in the enjoyment of my undeniable rights or you throw me and my Troop on the mercy of Col. Kemper who has no mercy in store for either.

8. **Exceptions (in the Slander Suit papers)**
Kemper v. Thomas &c.

The Plaintiff gave evidence to shew that the Defendant [next two lines of text are scratched out] after the … ^suppose[d]^ libellous papers had been withdrawn from the archives of the executive, and shewn in the County, said the following words in said paper.

To wit, (here insert them) were not intended by the subscribers, Rather to the justices of the County Court, but to the Plaintiff and others.

Whereupon the counsel for the Def[dts] moved the Court to instruct the jury that the … testimony was inadmissible and ought not to be considered by them. But the Court instructed the jury that no evidence [next two words illegible] the said paper could be admitted to shew its offensive or libellous meaning; but that as the declaration in this case, and the manner [word illegible] respecting this matter, and as the Contents of the said paper ^ an ^ it was competent to the Plaintiff to prove by testimony, then do that; he was the party alluded to by the said part of the contents thereof.

1824-002 Court Papers from John Kemper's Slander suit against Owen Thomas and others for slanderous words while the plaintiff was Lt. Col. of the 85th Regiment, 5th Battalion, 2nd Division, Va. Militia.
(Cont.)

8. **Exceptions (in the Slander Suit papers)**

To which [space left blank] opinions and instruction, the ... Defendants counsel objected excepts and pray that there [sic] exceptions may be signed, Sealed and made a part of the record in this case Which is done accordingly.
 (Signed) R.W. White

9. **The Jury's decision**
According to the jacket of the suit papers, the slander suit began in 1821. By April 21, 1824, four parties in the suit, Alexander Edmonds, Robert Green, Joseph Blackwell and Wm. Edmonds Jr., had died. The jury was sworn in on April 21st and deliberated for three days. On April 23, 1824 Amos Johnson declared, "We of the Jury find the Defendants not Guilty as in the Declaration Charged."

1793-002-1821-006 Historical Signature Folders
[AUTHOR'S NOTE: This folder contains records with signatures of well-known Virginians. Most of these records are either discharges, warrants, or pension notifications signed by Virginia's governors. **The date and index number refer to the year of the drawer in which the records were found, not the date of the actual record.**]

1. **1793-002 Benjamin Taylor's Pension Warrant**

I do, with the advice of Council, hereby certify, that **Benjamin Taylor late private in the Illinois Regiment and disabled in an Engagement with the Indians in the year 1781**, is put on the list of Pensioners with an allowance of fifteen pounds yearly commencing the first Day of January One thousand seven hundred and ninety three, pursuant to an Act of Assembly passed at the last Session for "allowing pensions to certain persons." Given under my hand as Governor of the Commonwealth of Virginia at Richmond this 26th Day of March 1793.
Sam: Coleman
 (Signed) **Henry Lee**

At a Court held for Fauquier County the 22d Day of April 1793
 This pension Warrant was presented to the Court and ordered to be recorded.
  Teste
   (Signed) F. Brooke C.C.

2. **1793-003 John Wheeler Pension Warrant. Recorded Decr 1793.**

I do with the advice of Council hereby certify that pursuant to an Act of Assembly passed the 30th of November 1791, **John Wheeler, who served as a Soldier in the Virginia Line during the late War and in the course thereof received several Wounds, is put on the list of Pensioners** with an allowance of eight pounds yearly commencing the first Day of January One thousand Seven hundred and Ninety two.
 Given under my hand as Governor of the Commonwealth of Virginia at Richmond this 11th Day of October 1793.
Sam Coleman
 (Signed) **Henry Lee**

1793-002-1821-006 Historical Signature Folders

3. **1796-003 Militia Commissions**
   [To] Francis Brook Esquire, Clerk of Fauquier, at the Court House
      Fauquier, April 26th 1796
    Dear Sir
     Enclosed is a List of Officers to whom I administered the oath and gave Commissions, and you observe by the 7th Section of the Militia law passed Last Septr that when the oath is taken before a single Magistrate, he is required to certify it to the next Court, which from the hurry, I omitted yesterday and not being able to attend to Day from an immediate call to James Rives, I must by the favour of you to present it to Court and have it recorded with perfect respect.
     I am Yr friend & servt.,
      (Signed) **Robt. Randolph**

   A List of Officers who were sworn and received their Commissions.
   Septr 11th 1796
    Lieutenants
     James White No 15
     Benjamin Tillis No 16
     Saunders Morris No 17
    Ensigns
     Taliaferro Shumate No 17
     Thos Brooks No 18
     Stephen Robinson No 19
     William Dulin No 14
     Edwin Porter No 16

   A List of Officers to whom I administered the Oath and gave Commissions

Captains	William Bradford	1	Battalion	85 Regt
do.	George Eastham	2	Battalion	85 Regt
Ensigns	Ben Tillis	2	Battalion	85 Regt
do.	James White	1	Battalion	85 Regt

    (Signed) **Robt Randolph**

4. **1809-007 Judah Levi's Pension Warrant**
    I do with the advice of the Council, hereby certify that **Judah Levi, aged about 28 years, late a Private in a detachment of the Virginia line, under the command of Colo Buford, Was disabled in the Service of the United States by Several wounds on the head and face and a wound by a bayonet through the left thigh;** & whose pay was at the rate of L24 per annum,

   And that he is continued on the Pension list, with an allowance of Fifteen pounds per annum from the first Day of January One thousand Seven hundred and Eighty Six.

   Given under my hand as Governor of the Commonwealth of Virginia, At Richmond, this #0th Day of January 1789~
    T Meriwether
     (Signed) **Beverley Randolph**

1793-002-1821-006 Historical Signature Folders

5. **1809-008 Joseph Gardner's Pension Warrant**
    I do with the advice of the Council hereby certify that **Joseph Gardner, aged about 35 years, late a private in the first Virginia Regiment** and whose pay was at the rate of L24 per annum, **was disabled in the Service of this Commonwealth, by a wound on his left arm;** and that he is allowed the Sum of Ten pounds yearly, to commence from the first Day of January One thousand Seven hundred and Eighty Six.

    Given under my hand as Governor of the Commonwealth of Virginia, at Richmond, this 27th Day of October 1788.
    T Meriwether
            (Signed)   **Edm: Randolph**

6. **1809-009 Elizabeth Cunningham's Pension Warrant (widow of John Cunningham)**
    On Jacket of papers: "28th of April 1789 one years allowance ordered to be paid on the within.
    I do, with the advice of the Council, hereby Certify that **Elizabeth Cunningham, widow of John Cunningham deced, who was a Private in the 3^d Virginia Regiment and died in the Service of the United States** Is allowed the Sum of Ten pounds yearly, to commence from the first Day of January One thousand Seven hundred and Eighty Eight.

    Given under my hand as Governor of the Commonwealth of Virginia, at Richmond, this 9th Day of June 1788.
    T Meriwether
            (Signed)   **Edm: Randolph**

7. **1814-001 Wm. Hillary's Appointment as 1st Lieutenant of Artillery**
    No.
          The Commonwealth of Virginia
          To **William Hillary**   Greeting
    KNOW YOU, that from the special trust and confidence in you fidelity, courage, activity and good conduct, our Governor, with the advice of the Council of State, and in pursuance of the act, intituled "An act to amend and reduce into one the several acts of the General Assembly for regulating the Militia of this Commonwealth," doth appoint your the said **William Hillary, First Lieutenant** of a Company of **Artillery,** in the Second Regiment, and Second Division of the said Militia, to rank as such agreeably to the number and date hereof.

    In testimony whereof, these our letters are sealed with the Seal of the Commonwealth and made patent.
    Witness, James Barbour our said Governor, at **Richmond, this 27th Day of July 1814.**
    (Seal)   (Signed)   **J.S. Barbour**
    REGISTERED:
    J W Pleasants

1793-002-1821-006 Historical Signature Folder

8. **1821-001** John Rector's Military Commission as 1st Lieutenant in 44th Regiment.
[On the Jacket is "Fauquier C[ty] to wit
   The within mentioned John Rector appear'd before the Subscriber, one of the Justices of the peace for the said Cty and made oath that he has accepted of the commission of Lieutenant, Given under my hand this 27th of May 1821.
   (Signed)   **Charles L. Carter**

28th May 1821 Ordered to be entered among the Records of this Court

   No.
           The Commonwealth of Virginia
   To **John Rector**   Greeting
      Know you, that from the special trust and confidence in you fidelity, courage, activity and good conduct, our Governor, on the recommendation of the Court of **Fauquier** county, and in pursuance of the act, entitled "An act to amend and reduce into one the several acts of the General Assembly for regulating the Militia of this Commonwealth," doth appoint your the said **John Rector, Lieutenant** in the **forty fourth** Regiment, **fifth** Brigade and **Second Division** of the said Militia, to rank as such agreeably to the number and date hereof.
      In testimony whereof, these our letters are sealed with the Seal of the Commonwealth and made patent.
   Witness, James P. Preston our said Governor, at **Richmond,** this 7th **Day of August 1819.**
   (Seal)   (Signed)   **James P. Preston**
   REGISTERED:
   J W Pleasants

9. **1821-006**   Warner Sullivan's Commission as Ensign, 44th Regiment
   On Jacket of papers:
   Fauquier County to wit
      Warner Sullivan personally appeared before me a Justice of the peace for the county aforesaid & qualified to the within Commission by taking the several oaths required by Law to be taken by Militia officers. Given under ,my hand the 30th Day of May 1821.
         (Signed)   William Bell
   Sullivan, Warner   Commission
   31st may 1821 Ordered to be entered among the Records of this Court.

   No.   The Commonwealth of Virginia
       To **Warner Sullivan**   *GREETING*
   KNOW YOU, that from the special trust and confidence in you fidelity, courage, activity and good conduct, our Governor, on the recommendation of the Court of **Fauquier** county and in pursuance of the act, entitled "An act to amend and reduce into one the several acts of the General Assembly for regulating the Militia of this Commonwealth," doth appoint your the said **Warner Sullivan Ensign** in the **forty fourth Regiment, fifth Brigade** and **Second Division** of the said Militia, to rank as such agreeably to the number and date hereof.
      In testimony whereof, these our letters are sealed with the Seal of the Commonwealth and made patent.
   Witness, Thomas M. Randolph our said Governor, at **Richmond,** this **20th Day of July 1820.**
   (Seal)   (Signed)   **Th° M. Randolph**
            Registered J. W. Pleasants

1825-001 Resolution respecting Colonel Robert Randolph's Death

At a meeting of the ^ members & ^ Officers of the Court and Members of the Bar of Fauquier County, at the court House, on Monday the 26th September 1825, it being Court Day, the following resolution was unanimously adopted.

Resolved that this meeting being deeply impressed with a sense of the private and public virtues of Col. Robert Randolph, an officer of the Revolution and presiding Justice of Fauquier County, as a Testimony of their sorrow for his death, wear crape on the left arm for thirty days.

Thus end the records dating from 1759-1825 in the first box of Military Records from the Fauquier County Court's Clerk's Loose Papers.

ABBREVIATIONS IN INDEX

ABBREVIATION	FOR
&c.	and others
+ als.	and others
Battn.	Battalion
Capt.	Captain
Cav.	Cavalry
Como.	Commonwealth (of Virginia)
Corp.	Corporal
Ct.	Court
dau.	daughter
deft.	defendant
Ens.	Ensign
Gen., Genl.	General
gr. dau.	grand daughter
gr. son	grand son
Jr.	Junior
Lt. Col.	Lieutenant Colonel
Lt., Lieut.	Lieutenant
PA.	Pennsylvania
pltf.	plaintiff
Prvt.	Private
PSC	Public Service Claim
Qtrmstr	Quartermaster
Rev. War	Revolutionary War
Rgt.	Regiment
Sgt.	Sergeant
Sgt. Maj.	Sergeant Major
Sr.	Senior
v.	versus
Va.	Virginia

Surname Given Name	page(s)
ADAMS	
Peter	41
Peter (Rev War Col.)	43, 71
Samuel (Qtrmstr, 36th Rgt.)	29
ALCOTT	
---- Major (Rev War)	61
ALIOTT [Alcott?]	
---- Major (Rev War)	41
ALLISON	
David (Rev. War Prvt., 1782)	3
ALLENSWORTH	
James (1775 Soldier,)	1
ANDERSON	
Daniel (son of Joseph)	73
Elijah (Prvt., 1782 Rev War Soldier)	3
Jenny (dau. of Joseph)	73
John (Rev War Prvt., 1782)	4
Joseph (Rev War Soldier, 11th Va. Rgt.)	73-74
Joseph (son of Joseph)	73
Milly (dau. of Joseph)	73
Spencer (Rev War Soldier, 3rd Va. Rgt.)	44-45
Susan (wife of Spencer)	45
Thomas (son of Joseph)	73
Wm. (son of Joseph)	73
ARAM	
Enoch	20
ARMSTRONG	
George (Prvt., 1782 Rev War Soldier)	3
ARUNDEL	
---- Capt. (Rev War.)	63
ASAMS	
Thomas (Prvt., 1782 Rev War Soldier)	3
ASH	
George (Prvt., 1782 Rev War Soldier)	3
ASHBY	
John (Rev. War Capt.)	7, 66
Nathl. (Rev. War Lt., 3rd Va. Rgt.)	7
Nathl. (1797 Militia Officer)	13
Nimrod (1797 Militia Officer)	13
Saml. (1802 Militia Capt.)	17

Surname Given Name	page(s)
ASHTON	
Lawrence (1807 Sheriff)	22
ATHEY	
John (1789 Order to Clerk of Court)	24
ATIHESON	
John (1775 Soldier)	1
Samll. (1775 Soldier)	1
ATWELL	
Charles (Rev War Capt of Artillery)	41, 61.
Charles B. (Affidavit of Service)	41-42
AUSTIN	
George (Rev. War Prvt., 1782)	5
John (1775 Soldier)	1
BAILEY	
Carr (Rev. War Prvt., 1782)	5
Wright (Rev. War Prvt., 1782)	5
BAKER	
Elijah (1816 Mounted Rifleman, 85th Rgt., Va. Militia)	30
Moses (1816 Mounted Rifleman, 85th Rgt., Va. Militia)	30
Samuel (witness, Col. Kemper's Court Martial)	90
BALL	
---- Captain's Mill (in 1805 Regimental Order for Court Martial Bounds)	19
---- Captain (1793 Militia Return)	9
Burgess (Rev. War Capt, later Rev. War. Col.)	39, 65
David (Rev War Soldier, 3rd Va. Rgt.)	38, 42, 45-46
George L. (1807 oath as Ensign, 85th Rgt., Va. Militia)	23
John (Rev. War Captain)	3, 4
William (1793 List of Guards)	9
BARBEE (See also Barby)	
---- Captain (1793 Militia Return)	9
BARBOUR	
---- Captain (Rev. War.)	49
J. S. (Governor of Va.)	112
BARBY (See also Barbee)	
Benjamin (Rev. War Prvt., 1782)	4

Index for Military Records from Fauquier County Virginia Clerk's Loose Papers 1759-1825

Surname Given Name	page(s)
BARKER	
William (1802 Captain)	17
BARTON	
Elijah (Rev. War Prvt., 1782)	5
Elisha (Rev. War Prvt., 1782)	5
BEALE	
Charles (1816 Mounted Rifleman, 85th Rgt., Va. Militia)	30
BEDOLPH	
Mary (1800 Rev. War Pensioner List #2)	16
BELL	
James (son of John)	61
John (Rev War waggoner, Soldier for Artillery)	41, 61
Landy (son of John)	61
Mary (dau. of John)	61
Mary Ann (dau. of John)	61
Moses (son of John)	61
BISHOP	
William (Rev. War Prvt., 1782)	3
BLACKABY	
Wm. (1813 Assault on George Pursley; In Como. v. Blackaby)	29
BLACKWELL	
---- Col. (in 1805 Regimental Order for Court Martial Bounds)	19
Christopher (son of Joseph)	67
John (General)	25, 26, 42
John (Rev War Capt.)	38, 39, 45
Joseph (Rev War Capt., 3rd, 6th, 10th Va. Rgt.)	66-67
Joseph (Rev War Col.)	38
Joseph (Militia officer in Col. Kemper's Court Martial papers)	92
Joseph (Defendant in Kemper v. Thomas &c. Slander Suit)	94-95; 98
Death noted	109
Mary (Brent; wife of Joseph Blackwell)	67
Mary (dau. of Joseph + Mary)	67
Samuel (appraised 1781 saddle)	25
Sarah (dau. of Joseph + Mary)	67
Thomas (Rev War Officer)	12
William (Rev War Capt.)	51
William (1816 Mounted Rifleman, 85th Rgt., Va. Militia)	30

Surname Given Name	page(s)
BLOXOM	
Comfort (1800 Rev War Pensioner, List #2)	16
BLUEFORD (See also Buford)	
---- (Rev. War Col.)	38
BONAIS	
---- (Rev. War Lt. Col.)	11
BOOKER	
Sarah (1799 Rev. War Pensioner List #1)	15
Sarah (1803 Rev. War Pensioner List)	18
BOONER	
Beverley (in 1807 Townsend Dade Court Martial papers)	20
BOSNE	
Henry (Rev War Prvt., 1775)	4
BOTTS	
Seth (in 1807 Townsend Dade Court Martial Papers)	20
BOUSH	
Mary (1800 Rev. War Pensioner, List #2)	16
BOWER	
William (Capt., in 1824 Col. John Kemper Court Martial Papers)	82, 84, 92
(as defendant in Kemper v. Thomas &c. Slander suit)	94-95; 98
BOWMER	
William (1802 Militia Officer removed from County)	17
BOYD	
Daniel (Rev. War Soldier on Cont. Est.) (Pension Declaration)	69-71
BRADFORD	
Wm. (1796 Capt. in Co., 1st Battn, 85th Rgt.)	13
(oath as Militia Officer)	110
BRADSTON	
William (1803 Rev. War Pensioner)	18
BRADY	
Hezekiah (appraised 1761 gun in French & Indian War for Minor Winn)	25
Joseph (in 1807 Townsend Dade Court Martial papers)	20

116

Surname Given Name	page(s)
BRAMBLETT	
Reuben (Rev. War Prvt., 1782)	5
BRAY	
Timothy (War of 1812, Artillery) (1821 Petition to Congress for increase in Pension)	75-76
BRENT	
---- Mrs. (mother-in-law of Joseph Blackwell) (in Joseph Blackwell's 1820 Pension Declaration)	67
Robert (witness, Col. John Kemper's Court Martial Trial papers)	90
BROADUS	
Thomas (Col.) (in 1807 Townshend Dade Court Martial papers)	21
BRONAUGH	
John (Major) (in 1805 Regimental Order for Court Martial Bounds)	19
BROOKE	
Francis (Clerk of Fauquier County Court) (1793 Letter)	8
Thomas (Ensign) (1796 Militia Recommendation, 85th Rgt.)	13
Thomas (Capt.) (in 1807 Townshend Dade Court Martial papers)	21
BROOKS	
Mary (1800 Rev. War Pensioner, List #2)	16
BROWN	
John (Rev. War Prvt., 1782)	3
John (in John Kemper's Court Martial papers)	92
John (defendant in Kemper v. Thomas &c. Slander suit)	94-95; 98
Joseph (1816 Mounted Rifleman)	30
Marmaduke (1781 Public Service Claim)	25
Marmaduke (Rev. War Prvt., 1782)	4, 5
Martin (Rev. War Prvt., 1782)	5
Thomas (Capt. 1816 Mounted Rifleman)	30, 31
Thomas (witness, John Kemper's Court Martial papers)	90, 92
Thomas (defendant, Kemper v. Thomas &c. Slander suit)	94-95; 98
Thomas Jr. (1816 Mounted Rifleman)	30

Surname Given Name	page(s)
BRUCE	
William (Rev War Capt. in John Horrell's Pension papers)	43, 71
BRYAN	
William (in 1796 Bond)	12
BUCKNER	
----- (1796 Capt, 1st Battn, 85th Rgt.)	13
Thornton	21, 23
Thornton (in 1807 Townshend Dade Court Martial papers)	21
Thornton (Witness, John Kemper's Court Martial papers)	88, 90
BUFORD	
---- (Rev. War Colonel)	69
BULLETT	
Permeanis (Rev. War Lt., 1782)	5
BURDETT	
Joseph (Rev War Prvt., 1782)	3
BURGOINE (See also Burgoyne)	
John (British Rev. War General)	57
BURK (See also Burke)	
Court Martial papers (Rev War Prvt., 1782)	3
BURKE (See also Burk)	
Elizabeth (1800 Rev. War Pensioner, List # 2)	16
BURN	
Jane (1800 Rev. War Pensioner, List # 2)	16
BUTTLER	
William (Rev. War Colonel)	57
CALDWELL	
Joseph (recommended as Lt., 1818, Militia, Capt. Ball's Co.)	40
CALVERT	
Landy	61
CAMPBELL	
Collen (in 1807 Townshend Dade's Court Martial papers)	20

Surname Given Name	page(s)
CAMPBELL (Cont.)	
Hugh R. (Judge Advocate, in Townshend Dade's Court Martial papers)	21, 22
CAMRON	
Catharine (1799 Rev. War Pensioner, List #1)	15
CANNOY	
Luke (in 1807 Townshend Dade's Court Martial papers)	20
CARDAM	
George (Rev War Prvt., 1782)	5
CARNEY	
George (in 1807 Townshend Dade's Court Martial papers)	20
CARR	
Elizabeth (1799 Rev. War Pensioner, List # 1)	15
Samuel (Major) (in John Kemper's Court Martial papers)	80, 82, 86, 89
CARRINGTON	
---- (Rev. War Col.)	59
CARTER	
---- (Rev. War Colonel)	41, 61
Judith (1800 Rev. War Pensioner, List # 2)	16
Martin E. (1st Lt., recommended 1816 in Capt. Eppa Hunton's Cav. Troop)	31
Martin E. (in John Kemper's Court Martial papers)	87, 90, 91, 92
Martin E. (defendant in Kemper v. Thomas &c. Slander suit)	94-95; 98
CATLETT	
Thomas (Rev. War Ensign)	56
CAVE	
James (1816 Roll of Mounted Riflemen)	30
John (1816 Roll of Mounted Riflemen)	30
CHAMPE & Co.	
John Champe & Co. (Treasury Account)	1
CHAPMAN	
John (Rev. War Capt.)	68
Sidnay F. (1st Lt., 2nd Battn., 85th Rgt. Mounted Rifleman)	30, 31
Sidney F. (in John Kemper's Court Martial papers)	90

Surname Given Name	page(s)
CHEW	
---- (Resigned as Cornet, Capt. Carter's Co., 1819)	43
CHILD	
Alexander (1816 Mounted Rifleman)	30
CHILDS	
Stephen (Rev. War Prvt., 1782)	5
CHILTON	
---- (Capt., 1796 1st Battn., 85th Rgt.)	13
Charles (Rev. War Capt.)	55
John (Rev. War Capt.)	50
John (1793 Guard List)	9
Joseph	20, 25
Samuel (witness, John Kemper's Court Martial papers)	90
Thomas (1797 Militia Officer)	13
Thomas (1802, 1807 Col., 44th Rgt.)	17, 22
CHINN	
Charles (Affidavit in John Horrell's Pension Declaration)	44
CHRISTIE	
Charles (1793 Guard List)	9
CHURCHWELL	
Richard (1793 Guard List)	9
CLARK	
Eve (1800 Rev. War Pensioner, List # 2)	16
CLARKSON	
William (1797 Militia Officer)	13
CLEMENTS	
Charles (Rev. War Pensioner, 1803)	18
COFFEE	
John (1793 Guard List)	9
COLBERT	
---- (Rev. War Capt.)	58
COLE	
Richard (in 1807 Townshend Dade's Court Martial papers)	20
COLLINS	
Charles (1799 Rev War Pensioner, List # 1)	15

Surname	Given Name	page(s)
COMBS		
	--- Major (in John Kemper's Court Martial papers)	92
	Burr (Lt., Va. Militia, 1822 Oath as Officer)	76
	James (witness, John Kemper's Court Martial papers)	90
	John (1816 Roll of Mounted Riflemen)	30
	Robert (Appraised 1761 gun for French + Indian War for Minor Winn)	25
	Seth (Major, witness in John Kemper's Court Martial papers)	81, 82, 83, 90
CONNER		
	Stephen (Soldier, Rev. War, Col. Byrd's Rgt.)	23
CONWAY/CONWEY		
	George (Rev. War Prvt., 1782)	5
	John (1796, 2nd Battn., 85th Rgt., Removed from County)	13
	Peter (Lt., 1788 Militia)	7
COOK/COOKE		
	John E. (Dr.'s Affidavit for Tim Bray)	76
	Mary (1803 Rev. War Pensioner)	18
	Ozias (Rev. War Prvt., 1782)	3
COOPER		
	John (1816 Roll of Mounted Riflemen)	30
CORBIN		
	Benjamin (1816 Roll of Mounted Riflemen)	30
CORDER		
	Benjamin (Rev. War Prvt., 1782)	4
CORNWALLIS		
	Lord (British General)	39, 57, 63, 65
CORUM		
	Richard (Rev. War Prvt., 1782)	4
COURTNEY		
	William (1800, Rev. War Pensioner, List #2)	16
	(1803, Rev. War Pensioner)	18
COX		
	Charles (1816 Roll of Mounted Riflemen)	30
	John (1816 Roll of Mounted Riflemen)	30
	William (1816 Roll of Mounted Riflemen)	30
CRIMM		
	Zachariah (1816 Roll of Mounted Riflemen)	30

Surname	Given Name	page(s)
CROCKETT		
	Joseph (Rev. War Colonel)	68
CROSBY		
	William (Rev. War Prvt., 1782)	4
CRUMP		
	Travis (Ensign, 1788 Militia)	7
CULLINS		
	John (1800 Rev. War Pensioner, List # 2)	16
	(1803 Rev. War Pensioner)	18
CUMMINGS		
	John (1816 Roll of Mounted Riflemen)	30
CUNNINGHAM		
	Elizabeth (widow of John, Petition for Pension)	7
	(1799 Rev. War Pensioner, List # 1)	15
	(1803 Rev. War Pensioner)	18
	(1788 Pension Warrant)	111
	John (Rev. War Soldier, 3rd Va. Rgt., killed in service)	7
DABNEY		
	---- (Rev. War. Colonel)	39
DADE		
	Townsend (Major, 1807 Court Martial)	20-22
DAM		
	Philip (in Townsend Dades' Court Martial papers)	22
DARNALL		
	Joseph (Rev. War Prvt., 1782)	4
DAVIS		
	Ann (1799 Rev. War Pensioner, List # 2)	15
	(1803 Rev. War Pensioner)	18
	James (1775 Soldier)	1
DAY		
	Charles (1816 Roll of Mounted Riflemen)	30
	William (1793 Guard List)	9
DEARING		
	---- Captain (1793 Militia Return)	9
DEARMONT		
	William (1788 Ensign, Va. Militia)	7

Surname Given Name		page(s)
DE BELL		
---- Captain	(in 1795 John Ville Rev War Service papers)	11
DIGGES		
Edward Jr.	(witness, John Kemper's Court Martial papers)	90
Ned	(1793 Guard List)	9
William H.	(witness, John Kemper's Court Martial papers)	90
DIGGS		
--- Major	(in John Kemper's Court Martial Papers)	92
DILLARD		
Mary	(1800 Rev. War Pensioner, List # 2)	16
	(1803 Rev. War Pensioner)	18
DIXON		
George	(Rev. War Prvt., 1782)	4
DOBSON		
Mary	(1799 Rev. War Pensioner, List # 1)	15
DOLTON		
Mary	(1800 Rev. War Pensioner, List # 2)	16
DONIPHAN		
---- Captain	(1793 Militia Return)	9
Joseph	(Rev. War Quarter Master Sgt., 1782)	5
DOUGLAS		
Hugh	(Colonel, in Townshend Dade's Court Martial papers)	21
DRONE		
Eleanor	(dau. of William)	48
Henry	(son of William)	48
Richard	(son of William)	48
Thomas	(son of William)	48
William	(Rev. War Soldier; 1820 Rev. War Pension Declaration)	47-48
DUFF		
George	(as Ensign, 1803 Militia Recommendation)	18
DULIN		
William	(as Ensign, 1796 Militia Commission)	110

Surname Given Name		page(s)
DULIN (Cont.)		
William	(as Ensign, 1796 Militia Recommendation)	13
William	(Captain, War of 1812)	35
William	(Witness in John Kemper's Court Martial Papers)	90
DUNCAN		
Charles	(witness, 1815 Camp Equipment)	29
EASTHAM		
George	(1796 oath as Captain)	110
John L.	(In John Kemper's Court Martial Papers)	92
	(Defendant in Kemper v. Thomas &c. Slander Suit)	94-95; 98
EDMONDS		
Alexander	(1816 Recommendation as Cornet, Capt. Eppa Hunton's Cav. Troop)	31
	(In John Kemper's Court Martial Papers)	92
	(Defendant in Kemper v. Thomas &c. Slander Suit)	94-95; 98
	(Death noted)	109
E	(Rev War Prvt., 1782)	3
Elias	(Rev. War Captain of Artillery)	50
	(Rev. War Lt. Colonel)	63
Elias	(witness, John Kemper's Court Martial Papers)	90
George	(1797 Militia Officer)	13
John	(1797 Militia Officer)	13
John	(Captain, 1802 Regimental Account)	17
John Jr.	(In John Kemper's Court Martial Papers)	92
	(Defendant in Kemper v. Thomas &c. Slander Suit)	94-95; 98
William	(1797 Militia Officer)	13
William Jr.		14
William Jr.	(In John Kemper's Court Martial Papers)	92
	(Defendant in Kemper v. Thomas &c. Slander Suit)	94-95; 98
	(Death noted)	109
EDMUNDS		
John	(1788 Ensign, Va. Militia)	7
Sarah	(1799 Rev. War Pensioner, List # 1)	15
	(1800 Rev. War Pensioner, List # 2)	16
EDRINGTON		
Charles	(1816 Roll of Mounted Riflemen)	30
EDWARDS		
Benjamin Jr.	(1816 Roll of Mounted Riflemen)	30

Surname Given Name	page(s)
EDWARDS (Cont.)	
Benjamin Jr. (1816 Roll of Mounted Riflemen)	30
Lency (Rev. War Prvt., 1782)	5
Mary (1800 Rev. War Pensioner, List # 2)	16
ELGIN	
Charles (Major; in John Kemper's Court Martial papers)	80, 82, 86, 89
ELLISS	
James (Rev. War Prvt., 1782)	4
Nathan (Rev. War Prvt., 1782)	4
ELLOTT	
John (Rev. War Prvt., 1782)	5
EMBREY (See also Embry)	
George (1816 Roll of Mounted Riflemen)	30
EMBRY	
Abijah (1816 Roll of Mounted Riflemen)	30
Daniel (1816 Roll of Mounted Riflemen)	30
ENGLISH	
James (Defendant in Thompson v. English Slander Suit)	35-36
(Ensign, Capt. Ball's Co., 85th Rgt.)	43
(Affidavit in Gideon Johnston's Pension Declaration)	64-65
ENNIS	
Elijah (1816 Roll of Mounted Riflemen)	30
EUSTACE	
---- (Captain, 1793 Militia Return)	9
Hancock (Ensign, 1788 Militia List)	7
(Resigned, 1796)	13
William Jr. (Capt., 1788 Militia List)	7
EWELL	
Thomas (Rev War Captain)	38
FALLIS	
---- (Captain, 1796)	13
FANNING	
---- (Capt., War of 1812)	77
FANTLEROY (See also Fauntleroy)	
Henry (Rev. War Capt.)	39
FARROW	
Nimrod (Affidavit)	57

Surname Given Name	page(s)
FAUNTLEROY (See also Fantleroy)	
Henry (Rev. War Capt.)	65
FEEBECKER	
---- (Rev. War Colonel)	51
FENN	
Thomas (1800 Rev. War Pensioner, List # 2)	16
FERGUSON	
Robert (1800 Rev. War Pensioner, List # 2)	16
FICKLIN	
Charles (1816 Roll of Mounted Riflemen)	30, 31
FISHER	
Frederick (1800 Rev. War Pensioner, List # 2)	16
FITZHUGH	
Dudley (Recommended as Lt., Capt. Nash's Co., 1818; refused to serve)	40
W. D. (in John Kemper's Court Marital papers)	92
William D. (defendant in Kemper v. Thomas &c. Slander suit)	94-95; 98
FLETCHER	
James (Rev. War Prvt., 1782)	4
FLOWER	
Joseph (Adjutant)	11
FLOWRIE	
---- (Capt.; 1793 Militia Return)	9
FOOTE	
William (Capt., 1788 Militia List)	7
FOSTER	
Frederick (Rev. War Pensioner, 1803)	18
Nat (1793 List of the Guard)	9
FOUSHER	
William (1793 List of the Guard)	9
FOX	
Mathias (1816 Roll of Mounted Riflemen)	30
FRANKLIN	
Elizabeth (Wife of John Franklin, Rev. War Pension Declarant)	68
John (Rev. War Soldier, 3rd Va. Rgt. of Dragoons)	67-68

Surname	Given Name	page(s)
FREEMAN		
Edward	(Rev. War Prvt., 1782)	5
John	(son of Sally Freeman)	73
Sally	(In Joseph Anderson's 1820 Pension Declaration)	73
FURGUSSON		
Robert	(Rev. War Pensioner, 1803)	18
GAFNEY		
James	(Rev. War Prvt., 1782)	4
GAMBLE		
Margaret	(1800 Rev. War Pensioner, List # 2)	16
GARDNER		
Joseph	(Rev. War Prvt., 1st Va. Rgt.)	111
GARNER		
Charles	(Rev. War Soldier, petition for Tax Relief)	6
Joseph	(Pension Warrant, delivery order)	24
GATES		
----	(Rev. War Officer)	50
GIBSON		
----	(Major; in 1805 Regimental order for Court Martial Bounds)	19
----	(Rev. War Col.)	38
John	(Rev. War Prvt., 1782)	4
Jonathan	(as Ensign, 1796 Militia Recommendation)	13
Thomas	(Rev. War Corporal, 1782)	5
Thomas	(Captain, 1788 Militia List)	7
	(Captain, 1793 Militia Return)	9
William E.	(1816 Roll of Mounted Riflemen)	30
GILLISON		
John	(Major, in Townshend Dade Court Martial papers)	21
	(1807 oath as Militia Officer)	23
GLASCOCK		
----	(Captain, 1793 Militia Return)	9
Benjamin	(Lieut., 1788 Militia List)	7
Peter	(in 1802 Regimental Account)	17
GODDARD		
Joseph	(Enoch Smith's 1783 Rev. War Discharge delivered to him)	24
GOOCH		
C. W.	(Adj. Gen., John Kemper's Court Martial)	78-79; 84

Surname	Given Name	page(s)
GORDION (See also Gordon)		
Albion	(Rev. War Pensioner, 1803)	18
GORDON		
Albion	(1800 Rev. War Pensioner, List # 2)	16
Samuel	(hired as substitute in War of 1812)	32-33
GOULDING		
William	(Rev. War Pensioner, 1803)	18
William T.	(1800 Rev. War Pensioner, List # 2)	16
GRASTY		
George	(Capt.; in John Kemper's Court Martial papers)	80, 82, 86, 89
GREEN		
----	(Rev. War General)	39, 56
Andrew	(1800 Rev. War Pensioner, List # 2)	16
	(1820 Pension Declaration)	68-69
John	(Rev. War. Col.)	62, 66
	(Rev. War Lieut. of Artillery)	59
Jonathan	(Rev. War Prvt., 1782)	5
Robert	(Affidavit)	56
	(In John Kemper's Court Martial Papers)	92
	(Defendant in Kemper v. Thomas &c. Slander suit)	94-95; 98
	(Death noted)	109
Thomas	(killed at Brandywine; Certificate of Service)	6
GREGORY		
Hannah	(1799 Rev. War Pensioner, List # 1)	15
GRIFFITHS		
Evan	(Appraiser of 1761 gun of Minor Winn's for French & Indian War)	25
GRIGSBY		
Baylis	(Affidavit)	41
Nathaniel	(1797 Militia Officer)	13
	(Affidavit)	41
Taliaferro	(Rev. War Prvt., 1782)	5
GROOM		
John	(1800 Rev. War Pensioner, List # 2)	16
GROTIN		
Margaret	(1800 Rev. War Pensioner, List # 2)	16
GROVES		
Lucy	(dau. of Thomas + Milly Groves; in Thomas Groves 1820 Pension Declaration)	55
Milly	(Wife of Thomas Groves, 1820 Rev. War Pension Declarant)	55
Thomas	(Rev. War Soldier, 11th Va. Rgt.)	37-38; 55-56
Thomas	(Drummer, 1804 Regimental Account)	19

Surname Given Name	page(s)
GUNNION	
William (as Ensign, 1802 Militia Recommendation)	17
HADDUX	
Nimrod (Rev. War Prvt., 1782)	4
HAINES (See also Hanes)	
Samuel (Rev. War Lt. Col.)	62
HALE	
Henry D. (Lt., 5th Brigade, 44th Rgt.; 1816 Oath as Militia Officer)	31
HAMPTON	
John (Cornet; resigned 1816)	31
(Ensign, 1818 Militia Recommendation)	40
(Witness, John Kemper's Court Martial Suit Papers)	85, 90, 92
(Defendant in Kemper v. Thomas &c. Slander suit)	94-95; 98
Thomas R. (Lt., 44th Rgt., 1822 Oath for Militia Officer)	78
HANES (See also Haines)	
Samuel (Rev. War Capt.)	56
HARDING	
Philip (1816 Roll of Mounted Riflemen)	30
HARGROVE	
Ann (1799 Rev. War Pensioner, List # 1)	15
(Rev. War Pensioner, 1803)	18
HARRISON	
---- (Rev. War Col.)	59
Charles (Rev. War Col.)	63
John Peyton (Capt.; 1788 Militia List)	7
HATHAWAY	
Francis (Ensign, 1805 Oath as Militia Officer)	19
John (Rev. War Lieut., 1782)	4
HAWES	
Thomas (Rev. War Col.)	73
HAYS	
John (In Townshend Dade's Court Martial Papers)	20
HEALE	
Joe (Resigned from Company, 1st Battn., 44th Rgt., 1796)	13

Surname Given Name	page(s)
HEATH	
William (Rev. War Col.)	38, 44, 45, 49
HEFLING	
William (Roll of 1816 Mounted Riflemen)	30
HENSON	
Robert (in 1805 Regimental Order for Court Martial Bounds)	19
HERALD (See also Horrell)	
John (1820 Pension Declaration)	44
HERNDON	
John (as Lieut., 1811 Oath as Militia Officer)	26
(as Major, 1820 Oath as Militia Officer)	69
(as Col., 1821 Oath as Militia Officer)	76
HICKERSON	
Hosea (Roll of 1816 Mounted Riflemen)	30
Hyram (Roll of 1816 Mounted Riflemen)	30
HICKS	
Kimble (In 1775 List of Arms)	1
HIGHLAND	
Furguson (1799 Rev. War Pensioner, List # 1)	15
HILLARY	
William (1st Lieut., Artillery Company, 1814)	111
HILLION	
Selby (1799 Rev. War Pensioner, List # 2)	15
HITT	
Harmon (service in Militia)	8
HODGES	
Joseph (1803 Rev. War Pensioner)	18
HOGAN	
John (Lieut., 1788 Militia List)	7
HOGSHIRE	
Ann (1800 Rev. War Pensioner, List # 2)	16
HOLMES (See also Homes, Hoomes)	
Peter (1st Lieut., in 1815 Camp Equipment Receipt)	29
HOMES (See also Holmes, Hoomes)	
George (in 1775 List of Arms)	1

Surname	Given Name	page(s)
HOOE		
Rice	(Capt., in John Kemper's Court Martial papers)	81, 90
HOOMES (See also Holmes; Homes)		
Benjamin	(1800 Rev. War Pensioner, List # 2)	16
HORRELL (See also Herald)		
Hugh	(son of John Horrell, 1820 Rev. War Pension Declarant)	72
Isaac	(son of John Horrell, 1820 Rev. War Pension Declarant)	72
John	(Rev. War Soldier, 1st Md. Line, 1820 Pension Declaration)	43-44
	(Rev. War Soldier, 1st Md. Line, 1821 Pension Declaration)	71-72
John	(son of John Horrell, 1820 Rev. War Pension Declarant)	72
Matthew	(son of John Horrell, 1820 Rev. War Pension Declarant)	72
Nancy	(dau. of John Horrell, 1820 and 1821 Rev. War Pension Declarant)	43, 72
Patsy	(dau. of John Horrell, 1820 Rev. War Pension Declarant)	72
Peter	(son of John Horrell, 1820 Rev. War Pension Declarant)	43
Will	(son of John Horrell, 1821 Rev. War Pension Declarant)	72
HORTON		
John	(Rev. War Prvt., 1782)	4
HOWELL		
Jemima	(1799 Rev. War Pensioner, List # 1)	15
	(1803 Rev. War Pensioner)	18
HUDSON		
Ann	(wife of Rust, Hudson, 1820 Rev. War Pension Declarant)	57
Rust	(Rev. War Soldier, 2nd Va. Rgt., 1820 Pension Declaration)	56-57
Ursa	(grand dau. of Rust Hudson, 1820 Rev. War Pension Declarant)	57
HUGHLETT		
William	(Rev. War Soldier, 2nd Va. Rgt., 1820 Pension Declaration)	62
HUMSTON		
Edward	(Heir at Law of Rev. War Sgt. Nathaniel Quarles, 1808)	23
Susanna	(Wife of Edward Humston; Heir at Law of Rev. War Sgt. Nathaniel Quarles, 1808)	23

Surname	Given Name	page(s)
HUNTON		
Charles	(in John Kemper's Court Martial papers)	92
	(Defendant in Kemper v. Thomas &c. Slander suit Papers)	94-95; 98
Eppa	(Capt., 1816 Recommendation as Militia Officer)	31
	(Capt.; in John Kemper's Court Martial papers)	78, 79, 80, 81, 83, 84, 92
	(Defendant in Kemper v. Thomas &c. Slander suit Papers)	94-95; 98; 106-108
J. B.	(1st Lieut., 1816)	31
Silas B.	(Resignation as 1st Lieut., 1816)	31
Thomas	(Capt. of Cavalry; 1799 Commission and Oath)	14
	(Justice of Peace; signed William R. Smith's 1806 Militia Officer oath)	20
	(in John Kemper's Court Martial papers)	92
	(Defendant in Kemper v. Thomas &c. Slander suit)	94-95; 98
HYLAND		
Ferguson	(1803 Rev. War Pensioner)	18
INGRAM		
Thomas	(witness, in John Kemper's Court Martial Papers)	90
JACKMAN		
Joseph	(1793 List of the Guard)	9
JAMES		
-----	(Capt., 1793 Militia Return)	9
David	(Adjutant + witness in John Kemper's Court Martial papers)	85
John	(Capt., 1788 Militia List)	7
Thomas	(Ensign; 1802 Oath as Militia Officer)	18
JENKINS		
Anne	(widow of Joshua Jenkins, a Rev. War Soldier killed in war; Pension Declaration)	7
Joshua	(Rev. War Sgt., Capt. Chilton's Company, 3rd Va. Rgt.; died in service)	7, 23
Thomas	(1809 Heir at Law of Joshua Jenkins)	23
JENNINGS		
-----	(Capt., 1793 Militia Return)	9
A./Augustine	(1803 Militia Recommendation)	18
	(1805 Regimental Order for Court Martial Bounds)	19
Carola G. A.	(1818 election as Officer, Capt. Hunton's Cavalry Company)	37
Gustavus	(Captain, 1788 Militia List)	7
Thomas B.	(witness, 1815 Camp Equipment Receipt)	29

Surname	Given Name		page(s)
JENNINGS (Cont.)			
Thomas O.	(witness in John Kemper's Court Martial papers)		90
William	(Capt., 1793 Militia Return)		9
JETT			
Anthony	(Rev. War Prvt., 1782)		4
JOHNSON (See also Johnston)			
Amos	(Jury foreman in Kemper v. Thomas &c. Slander suit)		109
Marshall	(Rev. War Prvt., 1782)		4
Welford	(Capt., 1802 Regimental Account)		17
Yellis	(in 1805 Regimental Order for Court Martial Bounds)		19
JOHNSTON (See also Johnson)			
Gideon	(Rev. War Capt. of Artillery; 1820 Rev. War Pension Declaration)		62-65
William	(son of Gideon Johnston, Rev. War Capt.)		63
JONES			
John W.	(Rev. War Prvt., 1782)		5
Joseph	(Fife Major, 1804 Regimental Account)		19
Ruben	(Rev. War Prvt., 1782)		5
Thomas	(Capt., in John Kemper's Court Martial papers)		80, 82, 86, 89
William	(Rev. War Sgt., 1782)		5
William Jr.	(1816 Roll of Mounted Riflemen)		30
KEITH			
James	(1816 Roll of Mounted Riflemen)		30
KELLY			
Alexander	(Affidavit, Daniel Boyd's 1820 Pension Declaration)		70
John P.	(witness in John Kemper's Court Martial papers)		90
KEMPER			
Armstead	(resignation as Lieut., 1818)		40
Charles	(Rev. War Prvt., 1782)		3
George	(1793 List of the Guard)		9
	(1796 promotion in 1st Battn., 85th Rgt.)		13
	(Witness, in John Kemper's Court Martial papers)		90
James	(Rev. War Prvt., 1782)		3
John	(Rev. War Sgt., 1782)		4
John	(Lieut. Colonel, Colonel, Court Martial papers)		79-93
	(1812 War Service mentioned; in Court Martial papers)		79-93

Surname	Given Name	page(s)
KEMPER (Cont.)		
John	(Pltf., Kemper v. Thomas &c. Slander suit)	94-109
	(Testimony, Kemper v. Thomas &c. Slander suit)	99-108
Reuben	(1793 List of the Guard)	9
Stephen	(1793 List of the Guard)	9
Tilman	(Rev. War Corporal, 1782)	4
KENDAL		
John	(1816 Roll of Mounted Riflemen)	30
KERNES (See also Kerns)		
Mary	(widow of Jeremiah Kernes, War of 1812 Service; War of 1812 Pension papers)	27-28
KERNS (See also Kernes)		
Jeremiah	(Prvt., Capt. Jennings Company, Va. Militia, War of 1812; See Pension papers of Mary Kernes)	27-28
KIBBLE		
James	(1793 List of the Guard)	9
KINCAID		
John	(Lieut., 1813 Illegal enlistment by; in Jones v. Kincaid Ended Cause)	28
	(Lieut. of Artillery, War of 1812)	75
John W.	(Lieut., War of 1812)	77
KING		
Daniel	(1816 Roll of Mounted Riflemen)	30
Richard	(Rev. War Prvt., 1782)	4
KIRKPATRICK		
Samuel	(1800 Rev. War Pensioner, List # 2)	16
LAKIN		
Benjamin V.	(Provost Marshall, Townshend Dade Court Martial papers)	21-22
LAWS		
John	(Rev. War Soldier, 11th Va. Rgt.; 1820 Rev. War Pension Declaration)	51-53
John Horton	(son of John Laws, Rev. War Soldier)	51
Margaret	(wife of John Laws, Rev. War Soldier)	51
Sally	(daughter of John Laws, Rev. War Soldier)	51
Samuel	(son of John Laws, Rev. War Soldier)	51
LAYTON		
-----	(Capt., 1793 Militia Return)	9
Robert	(Capt., 1788 Militia Return)	7

Surname	Given Name	page(s)
LEE		
Henry	(Governor, 1793 Letter from Clerk of Fauquier County Court)	8
	(Signature, Benjamin Taylor's 1793 Rev. War Pension Warrant)	109
	(Signature, John Wheeler's 1793 Rev. War Pension Warrant)	110
Henry	(Rev. War Colonel, Legion of Light Dragoons)	47
Phillip	(Rev. War Capt.)	44
LEMAN		
John	(1799 Rev. War Pensioner, List # 1)	15
LEONARD		
Robert	(1800 Rev. War Pensioner, List # 2)	16
	(1803 Rev. War Pensioner)	18
LEVI (See also Levy)		
Judah	(Rev. War Prvt, on Continental Establishment; 1789 Pension Warrant)	110
LEVY (See also Levi)		
Judah	(Rev. War Prvt., Pension Allowance)	6
	(1789 order to deliver Rev. War Pension)	24
LEWIS		
C.	(Rev. War Prvt., 1782)	5
Edward	(1799 Rev. War Pensioner, List # 1)	15
Stephen	(Rev. War Cornet, Cavalry Troop)	47
LIGHTFOOT		
P.	(Aid de Camp, John Kemper's Court Martial papers)	79
LINCOLN		
-----	(Rev. War General)	55
LONG		
Gabriel	(Rev. War Capt.)	57
LOVELL		
Elizabeth	(1800 Rev. War Pensioner, List # 2)	16
LOWE		
-----	(Rev. War Capt.)	54
LOWRY		
William	(Lieut., 1788 Militia List)	7
LUCKETT		
Richard	(1816 Roll of Mounted Riflemen)	30

Surname	Given Name	page(s)
LUTRELL		
John	(Rev. War Prvt., 1782)	3
Joshua	(Rev. War Prvt., 1782)	3
Robert	(Rev. War Prvt., 1782)	4
LYNN		
Auther	(Rev. War Lieut.)	49
William	(Rev. War Prvt., 1782)	3
LYNOR		
Nancy	(daughter of Philip Lynor, Rev. War Soldier, 3rd Va. Rgt.)	50
Peggy	(daughter of Philip Lynor, Rev. War Soldier, 3rd Va. Rgt.)	50
Phillip	(Rev. War Soldier, 3rd Va. Rgt.; 1820 Rev. War Pension Declaration)	50
Polly	(daughter of Philip Lynor, Rev. War Soldier, 3rd Va. Rgt.)	50
Thomas	(son of Philip Lynor, Rev. War Soldier, 3rd Va. Rgt.; a millwright)	50
LYON		
Mary	(1799 Rev. War Pensioner, List # 1)	15
LYONS		
James	(Rev. War Soldier, 3rd Va. Rgt.; 1820 Rev. War Pension Declaration)	53-54
James	(son of James Lyons, Rev. War Soldier, 3rd Va. Rgt.)	54
John	(son of James Lyons, Rev. War Soldier, 3rd Va. Rgt.)	54
Nancy	(daughter of James Lyons, Rev. War Soldier, 3rd Va. Rgt.)	54
MALLORY		
Phillip	(Grantor in 1806 Sale of Military Lands)	20
	(Rev. War Captain)	23
MANN		
Elizabeth	(1800 Rev. War Pensioner, List # 2)	16
MARGARAM/MARGARAN		
Henry	(Rev. War Conductor of Artillery)	41, 61
MARLOW		
John	(1802 Militia Recommendation)	17
MARR		
Daniel	(Captain, 2nd Battn., 85th Rgt.; 1803 Militia Recommendation)	18
	(Captain; Affidavit)	37-38
John	(1818 Militia Recommendation)	40

Surname Given Name	page(s)
MARSHALL	
James (1816 Roll of Mounted Riflemen)	30
John (1799 Rev. War Pensioner, List # 1)	15
(1800 Rev. War Pensioner, List # 2)	16
(Rev. War Capt., now Chief Justice)	51
Thomas (Captain, 1775)	1
(Late Rev. War Colonel, 3rd Va. Rgt.)	23, 44, 63
MARTIN	
George (1802 Militia Recommendation as Ensign)	17
George Sr. (1803 Militia Recommendation)	18
Reuben (1789 order concerning Public Service Claim delivery)	24
William (hired substitute for War of 1812)	34-35
MASON	
A. T. (President of Court Martial Proceedings, John Kemper's Court Martial papers)	79, 80, 86, 88, 89, 91
Armistead T. (See A.T.)	
Thomas (Brigadier General and President of Townshend Dade Court Martial Proceedings)	20, 21, 22
MAY	
Joseph (Treasury Account)	1
MAYES	
James (1803 Rev. War Pensioner)	18
Joseph (1800 Rev. War Pensioner, List # 2)	16
McAMITH	
James (1800 Rev. War Pensioner, List # 2)	16
McBRIDE	
William (Rev War Sgt., 1782)	4
McCARTY	
Mary (1800 Rev. War Pensioner, List # 2)	16
(1803 Rev. War Pensioner)	18
McCLANAHAM	
David (Rev. War Prvt., 1782)	4
William (Rev War Soldier on Continental establishment)	69-70
McCLINTICH/McCLINTICK	
Alice (1799 Rev. War Pensioner, List # 1)	15
(1803 Rev. War Pensioner)	18

Surname Given Name	page(s)
McCONCKIE (See also McConkie)	
Robert N. (1816 Roll of Mounted Riflemen)	30
McCONKIE (See also McConkie)	
Alexander (1816 Roll of Mounted Riflemen)	30
McFARLANE	
Alexander (1800 Rev. War Pensioner, List # 2)	16
McGOVERN	
Eleanor (1800 Rev. War Pensioner, List # 2)	16
McGUIRE	
William (1800 Rev. War Pensioner, List # 2)	16
McKENNY	
John (1800 Rev. War Pensioner, List # 2)	16
McKNIGHT	
Benjamin (Rev. War Soldier; 1820 Rev. War Pension Declaration)	57-58
McNISH	
William (Affidavit, Gideon Johnston's 1820 Rev. War Pension Declaration)	64-65
McRAE	
John (in Townshend Dade's Court Martial papers)	20
MEADE	
Richard K. (Rev. War Captain)	63
MERCER	
----- (Rev. War Brigadier General)	57
(Rev. War Colonel)	50, 53
John Francis (Rev. War Captain)	49
METCALF (See also Metcalfe)	
William (Rev. War ensign, 1782)	4
William (Rev. War Sgt., 1782)	4
METCALFE (See also Metcalf)	
William (Clerk of Court Martial, 1802 Regimental Account)	17
MILLAN	
A Braham (1818 Recommendation as Ensign)	40
MOORE	
Thomas L. (witness, John Kemper's Court Martial papers)	90

Surname	Given Name	page(s)
MOREHEAD		
Armistead	(Lieutenant, 1788 Militia List)	7
John Jr.	(Ensign, 1788 Militia List)	7
MORGAN		
Daniel	(Rev. War Colonel)	51, 57
	(Rev. War General)	38, 39
John	(Rev. War Sgt., died in service)	6
Joseph	(in John Kemper's Court Martial papers)	92
	(defendant, Kemper v. Thomas + als. Slander suit)	94-95; 98
MORRIS		
Sanders	(1796 Militia Recommendation as Lieutenant)	13, 110
MORRISON		
John	(1793 List of the Guard)	9
MOSS		
Nathaniel	(Soldier, 1775)	1
MOXLEY		
Mrs.	(in 1805 Regimental Order for Court Martial Bounds)	19
MULLIKEN		
William	(Rev. War Corporal, 1782)	4
William	(Rev. War Sgt., 1782)	4
MURPHEY		
John	(Rev. War Prvt., 1782)	5
MUSGROVE		
William	(1800 Rev. War Pensioner, List # 2)	16
NASH		
Eppa	(witness, John Kemper's Court Martial papers)	90
NEALE		
James	(1805 Oath as Lieutenant)	19
NELLSON (See also Nelson)		
John	(1793 List of the Guard)	9
NELSON (See also Nellson)		
Joseph	(Rev. War Ensign, 1782)	4
NORISS (See also Norris)		
James	(Rev. War Soldier, 1782)	3
NORRIS (See also Noriss)		
John	(Rev. War Ensign, 1782)	4
Robert	(resignation as Cornet, 1818)	37
	(witness, John Kemper's Court Martial papers)	87
NORTHENT		
Richard	(Rev. War Prvt., 1782)	3
OBANION (See also Obannion, Obannon)		
Joseph	(Captain, 1788 Militia List)	7
OBANNION (See also Obanion, Obannon)		
Samuel	(Lieut., 1788 Militia List)	7
OBANNON (See also Obanion, Obannion)		
Joham	(Capt., 1802 Regimental Account)	17
John	(Capt., in Townshend Dade Court Martial papers)	21
William	(Capt., 36th Rgt., 1815 Camp Equipment Receipt)	29
ODEN		
William	(1793 List of the Guard)	9
OLIVER		
Cornileas	(1816 Roll of Mounted Riflemen)	30
Hezekiah	(1816 Roll of Mounted Riflemen)	30
Thomas	(1816 Roll of Mounted Riflemen)	30
ONEALE		
Farthing	(Rev. War Capt. of Cavalry)	47
OREER		
John	(Ensign, 1788 Militia List)	7
OVERSTREET		
Leander	(1800 Rev. War Pensioner, List # 2)	16
OWENS		
Charles	(Rev. War Soldier, Va. Line)	69
Joshua	(Clerk, 1807 Court Martial Muster Fines)	22
PARKER		
Alexander	(Rev. War Capt.)	37
Marshall	(1816 Roll of Mounted Riflemen)	30
Martin	(Rev. War Prvt., 1782)	4
PAYNE		
George H.	(as Lieut., Election of Militia)	43
James	(in John Kemper's Court Martial papers)	92
	(defendant in Kemper v. Thomas &c. Slander Suit)	94-95; 98
William Sr.	(named in 1789 suit for debt)	8

Surname	Given Name	page(s)
PEAK		
	George (Rev. War Prvt., 1782)	5
PEARLE		
	---- (Captain, 1793 Militia Return)	9
PEYTON		
	Bernard (Adjutant General, John Kemper's Court Martial papers)	92, 93
	Henry (Capt., 1802 Regimental Account)	17
PICKETT		
	James (defendant in Kemper v. Thomas &c. Slander suit)	94-95; 98
	Martin (Joseph Garner's 1789 Pension delivered to him)	24
	(Judah Levi's 1789 Pension delivered to him)	24
	William (Rev. War Prvt., 1782)	3
PICKETT & COMPANY		
	Martin (Reuben Martin's 1789 Public Service Claim delivered to him)	24
POLLARD		
	Patrick H. (1816 Roll of Mounted Riflemen)	30
POPE		
	Henry L. Y. (Affidavit for Gideon Johnston's 1820 Rev. War Pension Declaration)	64-65
PORTER		
	Edwin (as Ensign, 1796 Militia Commission)	110
	(1796 Militia Recommendation)	13
POSEY		
	---- (Rev. War Major)	55
POSSEY		
	Thomas (Rev. War Col.)	39
POWELL		
	Francis (daughter of John Powell, Rev. War Soldier, 1st Va. State Rgt.)	39
	John (Rev. War Soldier, 1st Va. State Rgt., 1818 Rev. War Pension Declaration)	38-39
	Kitty (grand daughter of John Powell, Rev. War Soldier, 1st Va. State Rgt.)	39
	Robert (son of John Powell, Rev. War Soldier, 1st Va. State Rgt.)	39
PRESTON		
	James P. (Governor of Va., signed John Rector's 1821 Military Commission)	113
PRICE		
	Keys (Rev. War Prvt., 1782)	5
PURCELL		
	George (Soldier, War of 1812; 1822 War of 1812 Pension Declaration)	77-78
PURSLEY		
	George (Soldier, U.S. Army; assaulted by Wm. Blackaby in Como. v. Blackaby)	29
QUARLES		
	Nathaniel (Rev. War Sgt.; Heirs, 1808)	23
RAMEY		
	Jacob (Soldier, Fauquier County Militia, 1775)	1
RAMSAY		
	Mary (1800 Rev. War Pensioner, List # 2)	16
RANDOLPH		
	Beverly (Governor of Va.; signed Judah Levi's Pension Warrant)	111
	Edmund (Governor of Va.; signed Joseph Gardner's 1788 Rev. War Pension Warrant)	111
	(Governor of Va.; signed Elizabeth Cunningham's 1788 Rev. War Pension Warrant)	111
	R. (1802 Oath as Ensign)	18
	Robert (Rev. War officer)	54
	(1796 Militia Commission)	110
	(Col., 85th Rgt., 1801 Regimental Account)	17
	(1804 Regimental Account)	19
	(In John Kemper's Court Martial papers)	90
	(Memorial by Fauquier Court and Bar at his death)	113
	Thomas (Governor of Va.; in John Kemper's Court Martial papers)	92
	Thomas M. (Governor of Va.; signed Warner Sullivan's 1821 Military Commission)	113
RANSDELL		
	Chilton (in 1804 Regimental Account)	19
	Edward (Soldier, Fauquier County Militia, 1775)	1
	Thomas (Rev. War Capt.)	51
	Thomas (Military Bounty Land Warrant #167 for land in Kentucky)	14-15
	Wharton (Soldier, Fauquier County Militia, 1775)	1
	William O. (1816 Roll of Mounted Riflemen)	30
RANSE		
	Lewis (1800 Rev. War Pensioner, List # 2)	16

Surname	Given Name	page(s)
RAWLINGS		
Susannah	(1800, Rev. War Pensioner, List # 2)	17
RECTOR		
John	(as 1st Lieut., 44th Rgt.; 1821 Military Commission)	112
RENNOE (See also Renoe)		
John	(1793 List of the Guard)	9
RENOE (See also Rennoe)		
George	(in Townshend Dade's Court Martial papers)	20, 22
RICHARDS		
Jacob	(1793 List of the Guard)	9
RIDDLE		
Richard	(1799 Rev. War Pensioner, List # 1)	15
RIGG		
Betsy	(1800 Rev. War Pensioner, List # 2)	17
RILEY		
George	(Rev. War Prvt., 1782)	4
RITCHIE		
----	(War of 1812 Capt.)	77
RIXEY		
----	(Capt., 1793 Militia Return)	9
ROACH		
Gerard	(son of John Roach, Rev. War Soldier, 1st Va. Rgt.)	60
John	(Rev. War Soldier, 1st Va Rgt.; 1783 Discharge request)	23
	(Rev. War Soldier, 1st Va. Rgt.; 1820 Rev. War Pension Declaration)	59-60
Letty	(daughter of John Roach, Rev. War Soldier, 1st Va. Rgt.)	60
Patty	(wife of John Roach, Rev. War Soldier, 1st Va. Rgt.)	60
Polly	(daughter of John Roach, Rev. War Soldier, 1st Va. Rgt.)	60
ROBERTSON (See also Robinson)		
Lucy	(1800 Rev. War Pensioner, List # 2)	17
ROBINSON (See also Robertson)		
James	(1800 Rev. War Pensioner, List # 2)	16
Stephen	(Ensign, 1796 Militia Commission)	13, 110
ROCHAMBEAU		
----	(Rev. War Brigadier General)	41, 61
ROCKINGHAM		
Mary	(Treasury Account for her slave)	1
RODOLPH		
John	(Rev. War Capt. of Cavalry)	47
ROEBUCK		
Mary	(1800 Rev. War Pensioner, List # 2)	17
ROGERS		
----	(Capt., 1793 Militia Return)	9
Reuben	(Rev. War Prvt., 1782)	5
ROLLINS		
----	(Colonel)	57
ROOKARD		
Hiram	(as Lieut., 1821 Oath as Militia Officer)	74
ROSE		
Patty	(1799 Rev. War Pensioner, List # 1)	15
William A.	(witness, John Kemper's Court Martial papers)	90
ROWLAND		
Susannah	(1800 Rev. War Pensioner, List # 2)	17
ROY		
Richard	(in Townshend Dade's Court Martial papers)	22
Wiley	(1796-1797 in 1st Battn., 85th Rgt.)	13
RUBLE		
Jesse	(1800 Rev. War Pensioner, List # 2)	17
RUSSELL		
Joseph	(Rev. War Prvt., 1782)	5
SANFORD		
Meridith	(Heir at Law of Mary Kerns; Mary Kern's War of 1812 Pension papers)	28
SANGSTER		
Elizabeth	(widow of Thomas Sangster, War of 1812 Captain; 1812 Pension papers)	28
SAUNDERS		
James	(Judge Advocate, John Kemper's Court Martial papers)	80, 82, 86, 89, 90, 91
Nathaniel H.	(1816 Roll of Mounted Riflemen)	30
SCANTLING		
Fielding	(Rev. War Prvt., 1782)	3
SCOGGIN		
William	(Rev. War Prvt., 1782)	4

Surname Given Name	page(s)

SCOGGIN (Cont.)
William (Rev. War Sgt., 1782)   4

SCOTT
----- (Rev. War General)   46, 49
Charles (witness, John Kemper's Court Martial papers)   90
Levi (in Townshend Dade's Court Martial papers)   20

SCRURRY (See also Scurry)
John (1803 Rev. War Pensioner)   18

SCURRY (See also Scrurry)
John (1799 Rev. War Pensioner, List # 1)   15

SHACKELFORD
James (Rev. War Prvt., 1782)   4

SHACKLETT
Edward (Rev. War Soldier; discharge request)   23
Hezekiah (in 1783 order for Thomas White's Rev. War discharge)   24

SHARP
James (Rev. War Prvt., 1782)   4

SHEPHERD (See also Shepperd)
Ann (1799 Rev. War Pensioner, List # 1)   15
     (1803 Rev. War Pensioner)   18
John (1803 Rev. War Pensioner)   18
William (1800 Rev. War Pensioner, List # 2)   17
     (1803 Rev. War Pensioner)   18

SHEPPERD (See also Shepherd)
Abraham (Rev. War Capt.)   57

SHUMATE
John (Rev. War Major)   25
Taliaferro (as Ensign, 1796 Militia Commission)   110

SINCLAIR (See also StClair)
Robert (Lieut., 1788 Militia List)   7

SINGER
George (Rev. War Prvt., 1782)   4

SINGLETON
William (Ensign, 1788 Militia List)   7

SKINKER
William (Affidavit for Joseph Anderson's 1821 Rev. War Pension Declaration)   74
W.L.L. (in John Kemper's Court Martial papers)   92

SLAUGHTER
Stanton (Capt., Townshend Dade Court Martial papers)   21
     (Lt. Col.; in John Kemper's Court Martial papers)   80, 82, 86, 89

SMALLWOOD
---- (Rev. War General)   43, 71

SMITH
----- (Capt., 1793 Militia Return)   9
Enoch (in 1783 order for Rev. War discharge)   24
Enoch (Lieut., 1798 Militia Commission)   14
James (Provost Marshall, 1804 Regimental Account)   19
James (1816 Roll of Mounted Riflemen)   30
James Arrow (Rev. War Soldier; 1820 Rev. War Pension Declaration)   46-47
John (Rev. War Soldier, 2nd PA. Rgt., 1820 Pension Declaration)   58-59
John (drafted, Foot service, War of 1812)   36
John (in John Kemper's Court Martial papers)   90
John P. (in John Kemper's Court Martial papers)   92
     (Defendant in Kemper v. Thomas &c. Slander suit papers)   94-95; 98
Johnston (Deposition-- John Ville's Discharge)   11
Joseph (son of John Smith, Rev. War Soldier, 2nd PA. Rgt.)   59
Joseph (in Townshend Dade's Court Martial papers)   20
Joseph D. (in John Kemper's Court Martial papers)   90
Leanner (wife of John Smith, Rev. War Soldier, 2nd PA. Rgt.)   59
Levina (wife of James Arrow Smith, Rev. War Soldier)   47
Marshall (in John Kemper's Court Martial papers)   90
Mary (daughter of John Smith, Rev. War Soldier, 2nd PA. Rgt.)   59
Sally (daughter of John Smith, Rev. War Soldier, 2nd PA. Rgt.)   59
Thomas (Capt., 1793 Militia Return)   9
Thompson (in John Kemper's Court Martial papers)   90
William (son of John Smith, Rev. War Soldier, 2nd PA. Rgt.)   59
William (Rev. War Sgt., 1782)   5
William (1800 Rev. War Pensioner, List # 2)   17
William B. (Affidavit for William Drone's 1820 Rev. War Pension Declaration)   48
William R. (Capt. of Cavalry, 2nd Rgt.; 1806 Oath)   20
     (Capt.; Col.; in John Kemper's Court Martial papers)   86, 91, 93

SNALE
Elizabeth (Rev. War Pensioner, List # 2)   15

SPARKS
---- (Rev. War Capt. of Artificers)   58

Surname Given Name	page(s)
SPILLER	
Phillip (Rev. War Prvt., 1782)	5
SPINDLE	
Thomas (Major, in Townshend Dade's Court Martial papers)	21
SPOTSWOOD	
William (Rev. War Col.)	58
STACEY	
Sarah (1800 Rev. War Pensioner, List # 2)	17
STAMPS	
John (Rev. War Prvt., 1782)	5
STARK	
Lin (Capt., 1788 Militia List)	7
ST CLAIR (See also Sinclair)	
Fielding (Adjutant, 1804 Regimental Account)	19
STEPHENS (See also Stevens)	
Bryant (1816 Roll of Mounted Riflemen)	30
James C. (3rd Lieut., Roll of Mounted Riflemen)	30, 31
STEVENS (See also Stephens)	
Edward (Rev. War Col.)	66
Richard (Rev. War Capt.)	73
STEWARD (See also Stewart, Stuart)	
William (Rev. War Prvt., 1782)	3
STEWART (See also Stewart, Stuart)	
---- (Ens., 1818 Recommendation as Lieut.)	40
Allen (Affidavit for John Roach's 1820 Rev. War Pension Declaration)	60
Thomas (Affidavit for John Roach's 1820 Rev. War Pension Declaration)	60
STONE	
Francis (1816 Roll of Mounted Riflemen)	30
Nimrod (Rev. War Prvt., 1782)	5
STRIBLING	
William (Rev. War Soldier; 1820 Rev. War Pension Declaration)	49
STROTHER	
Jeremiah (Affidavit for Timothy Bray's 1821 Petition for Increase in Pension)	75
STUART (See also Steward, Stewart)	
Alexander (1803 Rev. War Pensioner)	18

Surname Given Name	page(s)
STUART (Cont.)	
William (1797 Militia Officer List)	13
SUDDITH (See also Suddoth)	
Francis (1793 List of the Guard)	9
SUDDOTH (See also Suddith)	
John (Rev. War Prvt., 1782)	4
Lewis (as substitute for Wm. Martin in War of 1812, pltf. in Suddoth v. Martin Breach of Covenant Suit)	34-35
(War of 1812 Prvt., Capt. Wm. Dulin's Co.; Discharge)	35
Toaneis (Rev. War Sgt., 1782)	4
Owen (Major, in Townshend Dade's Court Martial papers)	21
Warner (as Ensign, 1821 Militia Commission)	112
SUTTLE	
Edward (Rev. War Prvt., 1782)	5
John (Soldier, Fauquier County Militia, 1775)	1
SWARTZ	
-----(Adjutant)	11
TANNER	
Dorothy (1803 Rev. War Pensioner)	18
TARTE	
Alexander (in 1795 suit for debt)	10
TARLTON	
Banastre (British Col. in Rev. War)	69
TAYLOR	
Benjamin (Rev. War Prvt., Illinois Rgt.; 1793 Pension Warrant)	10
Nimrod (Rev. War Prvt., 1782)	3
Richard (1800 Rev. War Pensioner, List # 2)	17
TEAGLE	
Joseph (1816 Roll of Mounted Riflemen)	30
THARP	
Thomas (1816 Roll of Mounted Riflemen)	30
THATCHER	
Hannah (1800 Rev. War Pensioner, List # 2)	17
(1803 Rev. War Pensioner)	18
THAYER	
Albert (son of Wm. Thayer, Rev. War Sgt. Major, 5th Va. Rgt.)	40, 66

Surname Given Name	page(s)
THAYER (Cont.)	
Betty/Betsy (daughter of Wm. Thayer, Rev. War Sgt. Major, 5th Va. Rgt.)	40, 66
Francis (son of Wm. Thayer, Rev. War Sgt. Major, 5th Va. Rgt.)	40, 66
Hiram (son of Wm. Thayer, Rev. War Sgt. Major, 5th Va. Rgt.)	40, 66
Taliaferro (son of Wm. Thayer, Rev. War Sgt. Major, 5th Va. Rgt.)	40, 66
William (Rev. War Sgt. Major, 3rd Va. + 5th Va. Rgt.;1818 Rev. War Pension Declaration)	40
(Rev. War Sgt. Major, 5th Va. Rgt.; 1820 Rev. War Pension Declaration)	65-66
THOMAS	
[Illegible first name] (Rev. War Prvt., 1782)	5
Owen (in John Kemper's Court Martial Suit papers)	92
(Defendant in Kemper v. Thomas &c. Slander suit papers)	94-95; 98
THOMPSON	
Elizabeth (wife of Wm. Thompson; daughter Gideon Johnston, Rev. War Capt.)	63
John (1800 Rev. War Pensioner, List # 2)	17
William (War of 1812 Soldier; in 1817 Thompson v. English Slander Slander suit papers)	35-36
William (husband of Elizabeth (Johnston) a daughter of Capt. Gideon Johnston, a Rev. War officer)	63, 64-65
William (Dr.; Affidavit for Joseph Anderson's 1821 Rev. War Pension Declaration)	74
William (witness, John Kemper's Court Martial suit papers)	90
TILLIS	
Ben (Ensign; 1796 Oath as Militia Officer)	110
(Lieut., 1796 Oath as Militia Officer)	110
TIMBERLAKE	
---- (Capt., 1793 Militia Return)	9
TOOMEY	
Elisabeth/Elizabeth (1799 Rev. War Pensioner, List # 1)	15
(1803 Rev. War Pensioner)	18
TRIPLETT	
William (Rev. War Capt.; 1781 Requisition of saddle from Marmaduke Brown)	25
(Rev. War Capt., 1782)	5

Surname Given Name	page(s)
TUCKER	
William (1799 Rev. War Pensioner, List # 1)	15
(1803 Rev. War Pensioner)	18
TURNER	
Hezekiah (Capt. of Co. of Fauquier County Militia 1775)	1
Samuel (Lieut., 1788 Militia List)	7
TYLER	
William (Col., in Townshend Dade's Court Martial Suit papers)	21
URTON	
William (Affidavit for John Horrell's 1821 Rev. War Pension Declaration)	72
UTTERBACK	
Armistead (Cornet, Capt. Carter's Co.; 1819 Election of Militia Officers)	43
(witness, John Kemper's Court Martial Suit papers)	90
French (Affidavit for Wm. Drone's 1820 Rev. War Pension Declaration)	48
VILLE (alias WILLS)	
John (Rev. War Prvt., Fusiliers, 1st Partisan Legion; Service + Discharge papers filed 1795)	11
(In 1795 Suit for Debt)	10
WADSWORTH	
---- (Rev. War Col.)	41, 61
WALDEN	
John (as 2nd Lieut., 1816 Recommendation for Capt. Eppa Hunton's Cavalry Troop)	31
(Lieut.; in John Kemper's Court Martial Suit papers)	87
WALLACE	
---- (Rev. War Officer)	49
Gustavus Brown (Rev. War Capt.)	53
James M. W. (Dr.; Affidavit for George Purcell's War of 1812 Pension Declaration)	77
Robert (In John Kemper's Court Martial Suit Papers)	91
WARD	
Thomas (1764 Militia Claim)	1

Surname	Given Name	page(s)
WARNER		
Samuel	(substitute for Samuel Gordon in War of 1812; Pltf. in Warner v. Gordon Breach of Contract Suit papers)	32-33
WASHINGTON		
William	(Rev. War Capt.)	46
WATSON		
Zephaniah	(1816 Roll of Mounted Riflemen)	30
WAYNE		
Anthony	(Rev. War Gen.)	65
WEAVER		
-----	(Capt., 1793 Militia Return)	9
WEDON (See also Weedon)		
George	(in Townshend Dade's Court Martial Suit papers)	20
WEEDON (See also Wedon)		
----	(Brig. Gen., Letter to Commanding Officer, Fauquier County Militia, 1781)	2
----	(Rev. War Colonel)	50
George	(Rev. War Colonel)	53
Richard	(In Townshend Dade's Court Martial Papers)	22
WEST		
Benjamin	(1816 Roll of Mounted Riflemen)	30
Charles	(Ensign, 1788 Militia List)	7
George	(Rev. War Colonel)	69
N. S.	(1816 Roll of Mounted Riflemen)	30
William W.	(1816 Roll of Mounted Riflemen)	30
WHEELER		
John	(Rev. War Soldier, Va. Line; 1793 Pension Warrant)	10
	(1795 Pension Allowance)	11
WHITE		
James	(as Lieut., 1796 Militia Commission)	13, 110
John	(Witness, in John Kemper's Court Martial papers)	87, 90
Josiah	(Major; in Townshend Dade's Court Martial papers)	21
Robert	(1800 Rev. War Pensioner, List # 2)	17
Thomas	(Rev. War Soldier, Va. State Rgt.; 1783 Order for Discharge)	24
Thomas	(Capt., in Townshend Dade's Court Martial papers)	21

Surname	Given Name	page(s)
WHITT		
Mary	(1800 Rev. War Pensioner, List # 2)	17
WICKLEFF		
Charles	(Rev. War Prvt., 1782)	5
David	(1816 Roll of Mounted Riflemen)	30
WILKERSON		
Sarah	(1800 Rev. War Pensioner, List # 2)	17
WILLIAMS		
James	(Major Gen., Townshend Dade's Court Martial papers)	20, 21
	(Major Gen., John Kemper's Court Martial papers)	79
John	(Rev. War Prvt., 1782)	3
John	(in Townshend Dade's Court Martial papers)	20
Jonas	(1813 Illegal enlistment of Jonas cited in Jones v. Kincaid suit papers)	28
Jonas Sr.	(1813 Illegal enlistment of his son Jonas cited in Jones v. Kincaid suit papers)	28
Simon	(Soldier, Fauquier County Militia, 1775)	1
WILLIS		
John	(Rev. War Col.)	46
WILLS (alias VILLE)		
John	(Rev. War Prvt., Fusiliers, 1st Partisan Legion: Service + Discharge papers filed 1795)	11
WILLS		
John	(In Townshend Dade's Court Martial Papers)	20
WILSON		
Nathaniel	(Soldier, Fauquier County Militia, 1775)	1
Willis	(1803 Rev. War Pensioner)	18
WINDHAM		
Mary	(1799 Rev. War Pensioner, List # 1)	15
	(1803 Rev. War Pensioner)	18
WINN		
----	(Capt., 1793 Militia Return)	9
James	(signed 1761 receipt for gun for French + Indian war use)	25
Minor	(Received 1761 receipt for gun appropriated for French + Indian War)	25
	(1797 List of Militia Officers)	13
WITHERS		
----	(Capt., 1793 Militia Return)	9
Enoch	(in 1805 Regimental Order for Court Martial Bounds)	19

Surname	Given Name	page(s)

WITHERS (Cont.)
- John (Rev. War Prvt., 1782) — 3
- Robert W. (witness, John Kemper's Court Martial papers) — 88, 90
- Thomas T. (Dr.; Affidavit for Timothy Bray's 1821 Petition for Increase in War of 1812 Pension) — 76
- Thomas T. (Dr.; Affidavit for George Purcell's War of 1812 Pension Declaration) — 77
  (witness, John Kemper's Court Martial papers) — 90
- William (Rev. War Prvt., 1782) — 3

WOOD
- James (Governor of Va.; signed Enoch Smith's 1798 Militia Commission) — 14

WOODSIDE
- William (1780 Public Service Claim for 5 waggons and teams) — 6

WRIGHT
- James (Rev. War Capt., signed Sgt. John Morgan's 1783 Certificate of Service) — 6
- Mary (1799 Rev. War Pensioner, List # 1) — 15

YOUNG
- John (Ensign, 1788 Militia List) — 7
- William (Ensign, 1788 Militia List) — 7

ABOUT THE AUTHOR

JOAN W. PETERS is a professional genealogist, certified as a genealogical record specialist, local historian, and author of *Fauquier County, Virginia, Clerks Loose Papers: A Guide to the Records* which won the 2002 National Genealogical Society's award for writing excellence in sources and methodology. She served as the preservation archivist for the Fauquier County Circuit Court between 1993-2000, preserving the court's loose papers and Chancery records, under the support of three grants from the Library of Virginia. Her areas of special interest are to be found in transcribing local records in Fauquier, Stafford, and Prince William Counties, Virginia, for use by the research public, Revolutionary War research, and research of Virginia's 18th and 19th century free African-Americans, as well as problem-solving genealogical puzzles for clients, and researching and platting titles of historic properties.